the calendar of loss

the calendar of loss

Race, Sexuality, and Mourning in
the Early Era of AIDS

DAGMAWI WOUBSHET

Johns Hopkins University Press
Baltimore

This book was brought to publication with the generous assistance of the Hull Memorial Publication Fund of Cornell University.

Johns Hopkins University Press
2715 North Charles Street
Baltimore, Maryland 21218-4363
www.press.jhu.edu

Library of Congress Cataloging Data can be found on the last printed page of this book, which is an extension of this copyright page.

A catalog record for this book is available from the British Library.

Special discounts are available for bulk purchases of this book.
For more information, please contact Special Sales at 410-516-6936 or
specialsales@press.jhu.edu.

Johns Hopkins University Press uses environmentally friendly book materials, including recycled text paper that is composed of at least 30 percent post-consumer waste, whenever possible.

For
Rafael Mason, my soul mate,
&
Woubshet Workalemahu and Workeye Abebe, my parents,
for their unbounded love, tenderness, and wisdom

Contents

Preface

For the living, there is no constituency as formative as the dead—a fact I learned growing up in 1980s Ethiopia, where loss governed time and temperament. I remember those mornings when a death announcement would break the day like an alarm clock. Once the curfew expired at dawn, someone from the neighborhood *edir* would take to the streets, blowing a horn and calling out the deceased's name, alerting neighbors to the death that had occurred overnight.[1] That same day—the first day—the *edir* would pitch a tent in front of the bereaved home, and for three full days the tent and the house would brim with mourners and keening. The expression of unchecked feeling would begin to subside slowly by the seventh day, and then continue to ease by the fortieth day, and the eightieth, and then by the first year and the seventh year—the wake days through which Ethiopians measure time. In the world of my childhood, it was a given that the dead determined how the living kept time, that the boundary between private and public grief was blurry, and that mourners were uninhibited in showing their grief—moaning, shouting, sobbing, keening, and heaving their bodies.

Death in the Ethiopia of the 1980s was not merely a natural fact of life, however, nor was mourning dictated exclusively by the cultural rites and the calendar of loss. Our lives were also seized by the Derg's reign of mass death. I am part of a generation of Ethiopians called *ye Derg lej*, the Derg's children, born after the 1974 revolution that toppled Emperor Haile Selassie and put in power Colonel Mengistu Haile Mariam and the Derg's communist regime. During the short interval of Derg rule from 1974 to 1991, more than a million Ethiopians died as a direct result of the junta's policies of terror, violence, war, and tyranny. As children of the revolution, we were exposed to mass violence, roundups and killings, corpses in city gutters, and survivors denied the remains of their beloveds who had been shot to death—unless, to redeem the body, the mourners paid for the cost of the bullets the government had used in the execution.

Between sunrise and the midnight curfew, we honed a sense of loss in keeping with Ethiopia's elaborate tradition of mourning—what the sound of a brass horn signified at daybreak, what the sight of raised tents signaled, what the call-and-response of keening entailed, how grief was embodied and embroidered, how the timeline of loss was calculated. And inevitably, we also developed a heightened political sense of loss—how the state used death as a political instrument, how it disposed of its disprized citizens, how it exercised authority over the living and the dead, how it exacerbated grief by denying or delaying the bereaved from carrying out the work of mourning that was their birthright.

The disprized dead I grew up with, who constituted Ethiopia's macabre landscape in the 1980s, were the casualties of terror, war, famine, and repression. The AIDS dead, the subjects of this book, had yet to figure into Ethiopian consciousness in the '80s, even though at the time they had begun to fill graveyards and to fuel political movements in my future home, the United States. AIDS did not become a public matter and crisis in Ethiopia until the mid-1990s, after Derg rule had collapsed. In the first decade of the epidemic's history, AIDS was not a domestic Ethiopian issue; because of the extreme censorship under the Derg, it was not an issue at all: for the duration of the decade, we were kept unaware of the new epidemic raging elsewhere in the world.

I was thirteen when I moved to the United States in 1989, but unlike the thirteen-year-olds who grew up in this country, who had at least an inchoate sense of the raging epidemic, I had absolutely no knowledge of AIDS. I vaguely recall first learning about it in a health education class in high school and later, in college, eventually picking up on what it commonly signified in America: a gay disease. My perception of AIDS changed, however, when I came out at twenty-two and began to read the writings of the generation of gay men who had immediately preceded me. I sought out their work to find the vocabulary with which to voice my own unarticulated feelings, stories to corroborate my own queer longings, truths to free me from the deep sense of shame and fear that dogged my late teens. What I read did all of that and more. It was liberating to read works by Melvin Dixon, Essex Hemphill, Paul Monette, and a host of other gay writers whose self-ownership was decisive in my sexual coming of age. But with its focus on AIDS and the deaths of a generation of gay men, this body of writing was also devastating, and it became formative in ways that I didn't anticipate. I realized that many of my immediate gay forebears were gone, cut down prematurely by a catastrophe that was allowed to rage. And each poem I read, each memoir, each testimony tallied death with a deep sense of pathos and politics that gripped me like the losses of my childhood.

In the late 1990s, at the same time I was discovering the mass deaths of my queer forebears, my childhood friends—indeed, a generation of Ethiopian men and women my age—began to die in droves of AIDS-related illnesses. From my neighborhood alone, Nebyu (who lived two houses to the right of us and had the height of the sky), Eske (who lived across the street and had color like the highland sun), and Ephrem (four houses to the left, whose sweet talk disarmed my world), young men with whom I shared the deepest boyhood friendship, love, and longing, died back-to-back within a year. And while working on this book over the past decade, I lost many more friends and family members whose deaths, like other AIDS deaths in Ethiopia, were swathed in shame and silence.

However much this is a scholarly study of the early years of AIDS, my sense of mourning is colored by these formative experiences of loss, which traverse boundaries and identities. Although I did not know them in the flesh, I have lived closely with the dead who populate this book, and I am shored up by their fierce courage, vision, and tenderness. Disprized in their own time, they continue to be disavowed in ours. This book is a modest effort to speak again their mourning and to reanimate lives that demand remembering.

Acknowledgments

This book has been a long time in the making and would not have been possible without the generosity of the many people I thank here. It started out as a dissertation in the History of American Civilization Program at Harvard. My advisors, Marc Shell, John Stauffer, and Cornel West, all gave me invaluable support, affirmation, and criticism. I am grateful to them for allowing me to trust my own instincts and for showing me what it means to be a generous teacher and an interdisciplinary thinker. I had the great fortune of having as my cohorts in graduate school Salamishah Tillet, Suleiman Osman, and Hua Hsu, brilliant friends who continue to inspire me. I am especially thankful to my dear friend Salamishah for being a rare interlocutor: always helping me to refine my arguments and always reminding me of the virtues of our vocation both in and outside of academia.

The many talks and events organized by the W. E. B. Du Bois Institute were formative in my graduate education. I would like to thank Henry Louis Gates Jr., Evelyn Higginbotham, and especially my aunt Eleni Gebre Amlak, who under the auspices of the Du Bois Institute started the African AIDS Initiative International, one of the first organizations to speak out on HIV/AIDS in Ethiopia. My gratitude also goes to Lidet Tilahun, who directed the African Hip Hop Research Project and livened up Cambridge with the best dinner parties. I thank her for her precious friendship, wise counsel, and care and for welcoming me into her family in New England then and in Addis Ababa now.

I also thank the following people, who made my time at Harvard remarkable: Jamaica Kincaid, Tommie Shelby, James Kloppenberg, Werner Sollors, Biodun Jeyifo, Abiola Irele, Sharmila Sen, Brad Epps, Gwendolyn DuBois Shaw, Tim McCarthy, Mimi Tilahun, Danel Tilahun, Fasil Amdetsion, Abebaw Belachew, Lyndon Gill, Jordan Tilahun, Workeneh and Bedelu, Regine Jean-Charles, Matt Briones, Martha Nadell, Melaku Muluneh, Imani Perry, George Blaustein, and Dale Gadsden.

Much of this book was revised at Cornell over several years with the extraordinary support of many friends and colleagues. Lyrae Van Clief-Stefanon is why I call Ithaca home. Rae, thanks for everything, including your brilliant close readings of several chapters. Margo Crawford's friendship, feedback, and encouragement have been immeasurable. Salah Hassan, Shelley Wong, Ken McClane, and Eric Cheyfitz are friends who double as mentors, and I owe them a great deal of thanks. I am indebted to other friends and colleagues who read the full manuscript and gave me extensive feedback, especially Jeremy Braddock, Mary Pat Brady, Paul Sawyer, and Sarah Warner. Others who gave me useful advice on shorter and longer pieces of the book include Duane Corpis, Carole Boyce Davies, Rayna Kalas, Andy Galloway, Roger Gilbert, Kate McCullough, A. T. Miller, and Shirley Samuels. Special thanks to Mary Pat, Roger, and Ken for their unwavering commitment, including organizing for me a very useful manuscript workshop. And for their encouragement, I thank Liz Anker, Laura Brown, Iftikhar Dadi, Ramez Elias, Shelley Feldman, Cheryl Finley, Molly Hite, Ishion Hutchinson, Fouad Makki, Barry Maxwell, Natalie Melas, Viranjini Munasinghe, Tim Murray, Mukoma Wa Ngugi, Michael Ralph, Carina Ray, Jen Tennant, Elizabeth Tshele, and Nicole Waligora-Davis.

I have received continued support from Cornell's Society for the Humanities, including research grants to travel to Ethiopia during summers and the opportunity to participate twice in DeBary Interdisciplinary Mellon Writing Groups. The first one, "Centering Africa" (2008–2009), included Johanna Crane, Dan Magaziner, Judith Byfield, Jeremy Foster, Sandra Greene, and Stacey Langwick. The second one, "Queer Temporality and Risk" (2012–2013), included Lucinda Ramberg, Masha Raskolnikov, Camille Robcis, Lynne Stahl, and Sara Warner. Both were very productive groups, and I thank all the participants for their valuable suggestions. I had the pleasure of presenting parts of this book at Cornell for the Rabinor Lecture in American Studies, the Institute of Comparative Modernities, and the Visual Studies Program. It was also a pleasure to be invited to present at the Center for Lesbian and Gay Studies at the City University of New York, the Cogut Center for the Humanities at Brown University, the 2013 *Callaloo* Conference at Oxford University, the College of Arts and Sciences at the University of Virginia, and the Alle School of Fine Arts at Addis Ababa University. I owe special thanks to Meaza Biru of Sheger 102.1 FM in Ethiopia for inviting me to do a month-long radio series in Amharic, "The Art of Death and Dying," which drew heavily from materials in this book.

A significant portion of the manuscript was written in Addis Ababa. I am grateful to the Institute of Ethiopian Studies at Addis Ababa University for inviting me to be a fellow during the 2010–2011 academic year, and I am particularly indebted to Elizabeth Wolde Giorgis and Andreas Eshete. Alongside the resources of the institute, Elizabeth opened up her home and her world of friends and helped me find my mooring. Els'ye, thank you for everything, including the best house parties. I am inspired by all the work you do to fortify the arts and humanities in Ethiopia. Andreas's generosity has been beyond measure, and I have come to treasure his friendship and brilliant mind. Also thanks to Bekele Mekonnen, Behailu Bezabih, Salem Mekuria, Zeneberwork Tadesse, Bahrnegash Bellete, Haddis Tadesse, Tekalign Wolde-Mariam, Thomas and Astu, Hailu Habtu, Bede Mekonnen, Binyam Sisay Mendisu, Tewodros Gebre, Semeneh Ayalew, Netsanet Woldesenbet, Simeneh Betreyohannes, Aida Ashenafi, Aida Muluneh, Hiruy Arefe-Aine, Sammy Abdella, Adey Abera, Eyassu Woldesenbet, Mekde, the late Yonas Admasu, and especially Abebaw Belachew—for your encouragement and generosity, for indulging me with the riches of Addis.

I very much appreciate the advice and help of librarians and archivists at the Schomburg Center for Research in Black Culture and at the Manuscripts and Archives Division of the New York Public Library, particularly Stephen Fullwood, who gave me choice suggestions on different black queer archives. I thank Brenda Marston for helping me facilitate an undergraduate seminar on AIDS literature and art using the rich archive of the Human Sexuality Collection at Cornell. The students in that seminar—including Andrew Boryga, Anna-Lisa Castle, Evelyn Soto, and Nevena John Pilipovic-Wengler—were remarkable and helped me to sharpen my arguments and close readings.

I was tremendously fortunate to have Sharon Holland and Robert Reid-Pharr workshop this manuscript, and to have Marlon Ross as the scholar the press engaged to do the reader's report. All three gave me invaluable feedback, and the book is much better because of their suggestions. The book has benefited significantly also from the editorial acumen of Sheri Englund, who helped me to revise the manuscript at a critical juncture.

Charles Rowell has been an extraordinary mentor and friend, and I cannot thank him enough for his tireless support and encouragement and for bringing me into the fantastic world of *Callaloo*. It is a privilege to have my book appear in this new series, for which he serves as the general editor. Eric Gottesman has been a true comrade, and I thank him for entrusting me with the work of *Sudden Flowers*. For their unfailing support, I also thank Eli Kent, Sara Lewis, and Thomas Glave.

At Johns Hopkins University Press, Suzanne Flinchbaugh has been an enthusiastic supporter of this book and Catherine Goldstead and Mary Lou Kenney great stewards during the process of its publication. Also, thanks to Merryl Sloane for her very thoughtful and thorough edits and to Leonard Rosenbaum for the superb index.

What follows in these pages is a reflection of the love and labor of my family. I am forever grateful to everyone who doted on me while I worked on this book: Ahadu, Tesfu, Gashe Bili, Azu, Dea, Etemye, Akye, Beku, Eleni, Medye, Fanye, Yadel, Carmel, Rekik, Bethel, Belain, Beza, Beruk, and my late uncle Sirak. My aunts Enonina, Adi, and Etyle Altayu deserve special praise for nourishing me with the most divine *doro wot*, *kitfo*, and *tej* each time I visited Washington, DC. Above all, my immeasurable gratitude to my partner, Rafael, and my parents, Woubshet and Workeye, to whom I dedicate this book. The best parts of these pages came in conversation with Rafael, and indeed the book would have been inconceivable without his brilliant suggestions and his unwavering commitment and care over the last fifteen years. I thank him for the miracle of his love, for helping me to be the man I am. My parents raised me with boundless tenderness and love, and what merit this book has is also a reflection of that foundation. They continue to inspire me with their wisdom and grace. እጅግጣና ጤና ይስጥልኝ

the calendar of loss

introduction

Looking for the Dead
Disprized Mourners and the Work of Compounding Loss

As police and pallbearers fought, the casket carrying the body of Tim Bailey tipped and nearly struck the asphalt. In that flash moment, over the chaos, one of the mourners began to shout, "You've dropped the dead." He wailed it again, "You've dropped the dead!" And again, "You've dropped the dead!"—each cry piercing the embattled funeral procession.[1]

Anticipating his own 1993 death, Bailey, a gay AIDS activist and member of ACT UP/New York and its affinity group the Marys, had committed his remains in the service of an activist funeral, willing his body to have a political afterlife. At first, Bailey told his friends and fellow AIDS activists that "he wanted his body thrown over the White House gates. Because he was enraged by the government's lethargy—outright inhumanity—in confronting the AIDS crisis."[2] While they shared his commitment to making his corpse a subject of both mourning and politics, Bailey's friends couldn't bear to discard their beloved's remains. "We told him we couldn't throw his body over the gates. Not because we didn't share his fury. But because we loved him too much to treat his mortal remains that way."[3] In his final days, Bailey instructed them, "All right. Do something formal and aesthetic in front of the White House. I won't be there anyway. It'll be for you."[4]

The Marys, in concert with other ACT UP activists, carried out Bailey's wish, staging an extraordinary event of mourning and militancy. It was the Marys who had introduced the open-casket funeral into ACT UP's repertoire of direct actions as an act concretizing and consecrating those who died of AIDS. Open caskets forced the public to see the dead it disavowed, while honoring those disprized dead with public rites and recognition. Just months before Bailey's funeral, the Marys had carried out their first political funeral for one of their members, Mark Lowe Fisher, in the streets of New York City. Now they were in the nation's capital with the body of another member and friend who had died—as the epitaph on the processional banner stated—"of AIDS complications: government neglect, greed, and indifference."

Bailey's political funeral was held on July 1, 1993, three days after his death. Early that day, members of the Marys picked up the body from a funeral home in New Jersey and drove the van/hearse to Washington, DC, arriving on the Capitol grounds shortly after mid-day. They were greeted by scores of activists who had driven down on two chartered buses from New York to honor Bailey's last wishes to "do something formal and aesthetic": an open-casket procession of his body from the Capitol to the White House.[5] When the van with Bailey's casket arrived in Washington, it was met not only by activist-mourners, however, but also by armed undercover and uniformed police, whose goal was to keep the corpse of a person with AIDS from appearing in public. It didn't matter that Bailey's survivors, including his executor and his brother, had come armed with the deceased's will and other legal permits, not to mention a group of insurgent mourners determined to carry out his last wishes. While the procession could go on, the police insisted, the body could not be displayed openly.

Surrounded by mourners and police, Bailey's body became the subject of a siege. At first, the police tried to stymie the public display of the body by drawing out the occasion, calling in more officials to vet the survivors' documents and a coroner to verify the body as dead. "This siege went on from something like one o'clock in the afternoon to six o'clock at night,"[6] and erupted at the end when the mourners resolved to take the body out, insisting to the police: "This is a non-violent political funeral procession for Tim Bailey. This is not a demonstration. This is a funeral procession. We are going to proceed with this coffin to the White House as a funeral procession."[7] And, again, with palpable rage: "What the hell are you afraid of? That maybe ordinary citizens will see what our government is doing? Is that what you are afraid of? That people may get to see exactly what this government does? We have a dead body here. We have a corpse. Why the hell do we have to hide a corpse?"[8]

"Don't pull it out. Do not pull it out," an officer ordered the pallbearers. "Place it back." As the body came out, the police confronted the rows of activists, who had formed a human chain to shield the casket and pallbearers. With wanton violence, the police began their attack, tearing up the group, grabbing one activist by the nape, putting another in a choke hold, tackling others to the ground. "No violence. No violence. No violence," the activists called out in unison, fighting to maintain their grip and barrier.[9]

The casket tilted precariously as the police forced their way toward it, and it almost came crashing down as they began ramming the pallbearers and casket into the van. In that moment, one mourner began to keen, "You've dropped the dead!"—the sound and substance of his anguish as haunting and material as the tumbling coffin.

Somehow the pallbearers managed to land the body safely inside the hearse. The violence against the dead and the living soon subsided, and the funeral came to a close. The van was escorted off the Capitol grounds, then out of town, by patrol cars that followed it all the way to Baltimore, an hour away. Bailey's closest friends then drove on with the body to New Jersey and returned it to the funeral home. The corpse they had retrieved in the morning was returned hours later reembodied with a remarkable posthumous life and political agency.

With its striking emotional, political, and aesthetic significance, as well as its unique timeline of loss, this extraordinary work of mourning exemplifies other works of early AIDS grief considered in this book. *The Calendar of Loss* revisits the early years of the AIDS pandemic, from 1981, when the first cases were reported, to 1996, when effective antiretroviral therapy was introduced. Looking back, it focuses particularly on the efforts of early AIDS mourners, like Bailey, who grieved their own impending death alongside the deaths of many others. The formal and political character of their grief confounds and traverses the limits of mourning in ways that demand careful study.

Works of early AIDS mourning, including both published writings and other forms of speech, such as political funerals, are steeped in what I call a "poetics of compounding loss." These narratives of mourning do not recount, respond to, and reflect upon singular events of mourning, but instead explicitly underscore—and are in some ways almost deliriously obsessed with and full of rage over—the serial and repetitive nature of the losses they confront. These mourners deal with the deaths of lovers and friends one after another in rapid succession and in devastatingly contracted spans of time. This is such a central element of the collective trauma of queer life in the 1980s and '90s that a trope of inventory taking surfaces time and again as a haunting leitmotif in this body of mourning. The theme appears in various forms: lists of the dead, series of names, estimates of body counts, and phrases such as "one by one" and "beyond counting." The inventory taking signifies for these queer mourners both the devastation in their own lives (lover after lover, friend after friend) and the collective devastation in the lives of countless others like them. But compounding loss connotes not merely an overwhelming quantity or scale. In addition, the negative aspects—the pain, the confounded psyche, the exhausted body and soul—of each loss are compounded by the memory and experience of the losses just before. The time, consolation, and closure that allow the bereaved to "move on" are, for these mourners, painfully aborted. This is precisely why Melvin Dixon, one of the exemplary figures of AIDS poetry, chooses not to write a series of elegies to each lost beloved, but instead writes the single poem "And These Are Just a Few . . ." as a commemoration of all of his lost lovers and close friends. Stanza by stanza, the loss compounds.

The serial losses these writers confront provide the context for yet another trope: the chilling reflexivity of the subject's mourning. With each passing lover, with the mounting numbers of the dead, the bereaved is provided with yet more evidence of the certain fatality of the virus also at work inside him. He mourns not only past deaths, but also impending ones, including his own. The "poetics of compounding loss" is thus a phrase meant to capture the most salient formal characteristics of this body of literature: the leitmotif of inventory taking; the reconceptualization of relentless serial losses not as cumulative, but as compounding; and the notion that this compounded loss is heightened by reflexivity, with the subject's loss both object and subject, past and prospective, memory and immediate threat.

Despite the complexity and dexterity of these literary texts, the tableau of AIDS mourning during this period would be incomplete without the inclusion of other genres beyond creative writing. Obituaries, protest paraphernalia and protest speech, and funerals were all part of what happened and should be brought into the analysis. Funerals, whether public or private, were rife with conflict and often included explosive and artful political acts of speech and defiance. As Bailey's funeral illustrates, the key motifs included the breaking of silence, fury over government inaction, and ultimately a vociferous refusal by those mourners living with and dying of AIDS to quietly accept their condition as what I call "disprized" mourners—the bereaved who are denied the rites, honor, and dignity of public mourning, and whose losses are instead shrouded in silence, shame, and disgrace. And yet these mourners turned to their sorrow as a necessary vehicle of survival. Silence = Death, the clarion call of early AIDS activism, put open, truthful mourning at the center of their protest, insisting that lives could be saved through the very speech acts precipitated by death. In carefully choreographed acts of mourning and provocation, for instance, ACT UP dumped crematory ashes on the lawn of the White House and staged open-casket funerals in the streets of New York City and Washington, DC. These acts of speech and embodiment—full of wit and biting political commentary, and often dramatically and artfully choreographed—are central to the archive of early AIDS loss. They show the insurgent uses of mourning for the ostracized and also illuminate the rich interplay between the aesthetics and politics of grief.

The unique formal and extraformal dimensions of this body of mourning have significant implications for the way we theorize loss. The mourning I address in this book departs from the paradigmatic psychoanalytic theory of loss, Sigmund Freud's "Mourning and Melancholia." The chief reason the mourning-versus-melancholia paradigm falls short is because it fails to envisage the exceedingly perilous life these subjects inhabit: a life where death is not a singular lost object, but instead is ever present, and where the mourner is also dying. The entire concept of transference is meaningfully altered here, shaped by a preoccupation with a lost object that is not only external, but also the self. A more appropriate theoretical lens for this body of work is the paradigm of loss that underwrites African American mourning, most poignantly captured in slave songs and spirituals. The paradigm of black mourning accommodates the work of early AIDS mourners in important ways, especially in the insistence that death is ever present, that death is somehow always impending, and that survivors can confront all this death in the face of shame and stigma in eloquent ways that also often imply a fierce political sensibility and a longing for justice.

Coming out of the intersection of African Diaspora and queer studies, *The Calendar of Loss* also expands to include another class of mourners devastated by this catastrophe: I end the study with a comparative look at AIDS orphans mourning in Africa. I draw on the work of Sudden Flowers, the first AIDS art collective in Ethiopia, which is mainly composed of children between the ages of nine and seventeen who have lost their parents to AIDS. Through a range of forms—text, photography, performance, public installation, and film—the collective has produced a remarkable body of art to counter the silence and stigma of AIDS in Ethiopia. A comparative look at the work of Sudden Flowers shows how these disparaged children—bereft of parents and shunned by the world around them—articulate a formal sense of compounding loss and other feelings of disprized grief. In their self-willed representations, these children picture themselves not merely as objects of adults' gaze and sentiment, but as subjects who employ grief to enfranchise themselves. Indeed, these children speak of their own disparaged lives as AIDS orphans, and of a world ravaged by this pandemic, in ways that hauntingly echo the sorrow of queer communities across the Atlantic. In their respective countries, in the early years of the epidemic and amid a violent public sphere, both classes of AIDS mourners embodied AIDS openly and fearlessly, manifesting and mourning their beloved dead whom their compatriots refused to see and grieve. Along with this fierce agency, these children's mourning also shares a poetics of loss that is distinctly queer, iterating a grammar of death that is unfixed and issuing a calendar of loss for a precarious future.

Arraying side by side the sorrow of orphans from Africa and that of queer communities from America opens up innovative ways of thinking together the shared grief of the disparate constituencies profoundly impacted by this catastrophe. Informed by a black queer critical practice, *The Calendar of Loss* also eschews a model of AIDS scholarship that isolates people of color in a separate chapter, away from and contingent on the experiences of white gay men, or gestures to them parenthetically, as if an afterthought. Drawing on a diverse set of characters and archives, this book reconstructs the early era of AIDS differently, elucidating together my central claims about the formal properties of compounding loss, the political uses of disprized grief, and the theoretical insights of black sorrow.

A POETICS OF COMPOUNDING LOSS

"And These Are Just a Few . . ."—like many of the other poems in Melvin Dixon's posthumous book, *Love's Instruments*—provides a vivid example of a poetics of extraordinary devastation.[10] Dixon begins this death-inventory poem with a dedication and a question:

> This poem is for the epidemic dead and the living.
> Remember them?

In subsequent stanzas he lists, names, and draws small portraits of the AIDS dead dear to him. In stanzas 4 and 5, for example, he writes:

> This poem is for Joseph, remember Joe? Whose longing
> For the language of black men loving black men
> became our lore.

> This poem is for Samuel, remember Sam? Who taught
> those who could
> Barely read until the skin around his mouth peeled off
> in pages.

After recalling twelve friends, Dixon approaches death more closely in the penultimate stanza as he mourns the death of his lover, Richard, and even closer in the last verse as he hails his own imminent death:

> This poem is for Richard, remember Rich? Poised
> with puns

For the quick meter of his mind, for the constancy of
our embrace.

This poem is for the epidemic living and the dead.
Remember them, remember me.

In the first line of the poem, "the epidemic dead" precede the living, but in
the last stanza the order shifts and the initial stress is now on "the epidemic
living"—the chiasmus, the rhetorical figure of inversion, blurring the difference
between the two. Even more poignantly, the poem's initial, rhetorical question
("Remember them?") by the end turns into a chilling, posthumous imperative
("Remember them, remember me"), as Dixon includes himself in the poem's
roster of the dead. Dixon's posthumous voice and chiasmus, both of which blur
the divide between the living and the dead, are not used merely for figurative effect, but to underscore the poet's literal proximity to death.

Dixon's poem is recollective (it remembers past deaths) and prospective
(it hails imminent deaths, including his own). In addition to synchronizing
a unique timeline of loss, the poem also takes a tally of the dead, and each loss
builds on the loss that precedes it. Although the number of deaths in Dixon's
poem is thirteen, the total loss is greater than that figure, since each death con-
tains within it and builds upon the preceding loss. After reading about the death
in stanza 2, the third death feels even more devastating, and the fourth even
more, and the fifth, and sixth, and seventh, and so on, as Dixon chooses not
to write separate poems for each death, but one poem for the series of deaths
that saturate his life. The seriality of the poem underscores the relentlessness
of death, that there is no reprieve from mourning the deaths that surround
him. The poet does not have time to get over his loss, to overcome any of these
losses, since before he has a chance to do so he is confronted with yet another
death, and another, and another, and another. Furthermore, as we surmise
from Dixon's proleptic final words, "remember me," and also from the title of
the poem (a death toll beginning in medias res and extended further with an el-
lipsis), the accounting of loss exceeds the actual deaths tallied in the poem. We
hear, too, in Dixon's evocative use of anaphora—the serial repetition of "This
poem is for" and "remember"—the aggregating losses being recorded, invento-
ried, and accounted for. The anaphora "This poem" is materialized additionally
in each stanza, as the dead become a collection of "language," "lore," "peeled off
pages," "puns," and "meter," each loss manifested as a text within a larger text
of loss.

In Essex Hemphill's epic poem "Heavy Breathing," the poet is aboard the X2 bus traversing Washington, DC.[11] Gazing out, Hemphill offers not only a panorama of an American city in the '80s under siege—by government neglect, racism, violence, crack, and AIDS—but also an introspective, foreboding sense of his own upcoming death. Midway through the poem, he encapsulates his life in these short lyric lines:

> I know I don't live *here* anymore
> but I remain in this body
> to witness

These are words expressed at the threshold of death, which places the poet in another world (he stresses, "I don't live *here* anymore"), and they conjure up a macabre image of his body as a living remains ("I remain in this body"). In addition to hailing his own death, Hemphill's poem also articulates an inventory of loss that exceeds any finite measurement:

> The toll beyond counting,
> the shimmering carcasses
> all smell the same,
> No matter which way
> the wind blows
> I lose a god
> or a friend.

Hemphill is a witness to his own death as well as to the mounting deaths around him, which are innumerable, beyond counting, beyond a determinate figure.

The inventory of ever-mounting loss is not limited to poetry. There are ample illustrations of it in prose and in other creative responses to AIDS, including film and dance. Larry Kramer's "1,112 and Counting," for example, is one of the earliest public responses to AIDS, an article with which Kramer sought to rouse his readers into action by calling attention to the alarming and, as the title suggests, compounding rate of AIDS deaths. Kramer's temporal characterization of loss is not unlike Dixon's and Hemphill's. Notice how he ends his impassioned article, how he tallies and times the losses:

> Here is a list of 21 dead men I knew:
> Nick Rock
> Rick Wellikoff
> Jack Nau

Shelly

Donald Krintzman

Jerry Green

Michael Maletta

Paul Graham

Toby

Harry Blumenthal

Stephen Sperry

Brian O'Hara

Barry

David

Jeffery Croland

Z.

David Jackson

Tony Rappa

Robert Christian

Ron Doud

And one more, who will be dead by the time these words appear in print. If we don't act immediately, then we face our approaching doom.[12]

Kramer wrote this essay in 1983 with a sense of fear and with foresight about the growing epidemic, which is the reason he intertwines a political call to action with a personal inventory of the dead he knew. Like the calculation of loss in the essay's title—1,112 (the estimated number of AIDS deaths in the United States in March 1983) *and counting*—Kramer's personal tally at the end of the piece also employs a figure of loss that confounds a fixed number. Like Dixon's and Hemphill's embodiment of both past and pending death, Kramer corporealizes the compounding series of AIDS deaths with the figure of the "one more" ticking death at the end of his list, a death he also introduces at the beginning of his tally proleptically in the past tense—"Here is a list of 21 dead men I knew"— an arithmetic of loss based on both past and prospective deaths.

These authors address the unique timeline of their loss through the very temporal process of writing. As Kramer does in his essay—"And one more, who will be dead by the time these words appear in print"—others also rely on writing as an immediate calendar on which to mark both past and upcoming losses. As Paul Monette says in the opening lines of *Borrowed Time: An AIDS Memoir*: "I don't know if I will live to finish this. . . . Maybe it's just I've watched too many sicken in a month and die by Christmas."[13] Monette's writing calendar is interwoven with a calendar of loss. As he writes, he is also measuring his mortality: he's witnessed "too many sicken in a month and die by Christmas" and knows that he too may not live long enough to see his writing/life through. Monette reiterates this point in the preface to *Love Alone: Eighteen Elegies for Rog* that amid this catastrophe, the calendar of mourning and the calendar of writing are ineluctably bound: "These elegies were written during the five months after [Roger, Monette's lover] died, one right after the other, with hardly a half day's pause between. Writing them quite literally kept me alive."[14]

The entangled calendar of mourning and creative labor is just as noticeable in Marlon Riggs's film *Black Is . . . Black Ain't* and Bill T. Jones's choreography *Still/Here*.[15] *Black Is . . . Black Ain't* was wrought at the precipice of death, directed by Riggs from his hospital bed and released posthumously. In the film's overture, Riggs says: "AIDS forces you—because of the likelihood that you could die [*he snaps!*] at this moment—AIDS forces you to deal with that." It is from this literal threshold of death that Riggs begins to explore what black is, and what black ain't—from markers of identity like color, gender, and sexuality to black art and cultural forms like music, performance, and cuisine—and he does so cinematically through montage, suturing interviews, personal and archival films, bits of his own dreamscapes, poetry readings by Hemphill, and dances by Jones. While the documentary leaps across different forms, times, and places, it returns periodically to the present tense of the film, which is set in Riggs's hospital room. And each successive time the film returns to its present time and place, to the hospital room, it shows Riggs's waning health, putting in stark relief the filmmaker's prospective death, the anticipated time from which he grieves and films.

As Riggs's film visualizes pending death, *Still/Here* embodies it in movement. The dance piece *Still/Here* is informed by the death of Jones's lover and creative partner, Arnie Zane, and by Jones's own life as an HIV-positive man. Between 1982, the year they founded the Bill T. Jones/Arnie Zane Dance Company, and Zane's death of AIDS complications in 1988, the two choreographed and collaborated on dances that brought new life to the duet form, working out on the stage their different physicalities, styles, and identities—one of them six feet one inch, the other five feet four; one with an acute sense of articulation, the emphatic, and the spiritual, the other stressing structure, image, and seriality; one the son of African American sharecroppers from the South who settled in upstate New York, the other the son of a Lithuanian Jew and an Italian Catholic who immigrated to New York City. Characterized by high-energy contact, quick movement, and serialized gestures, their early duets were forms of rebellion, says Jones, "cloaked in seductive form"—two lovers, two artists, "trying to be honest about how [they] were different."[16]

As the first major piece that Jones choreographed after Zane's death, *Still/Here* loudly echoes his lover's absence and the loss of their personal and creative partnership. It also embodies Jones's own HIV-positive status and, at the time he was working on the dance in the early '90s, the real possibility of his own death, an identity he shared with the new collaborators he chose to conceptualize the work. Jones drew together the dance's repertoire from "survival workshops" that he conducted with people dealing with AIDS, cancer, multiple sclerosis, and other terminal illnesses in several U.S. cities. During these workshops, Jones had the participants express in movement and words their looming deaths and what it felt like to be still/here. From their words, movements, and feelings, Jones created a dance that both bore out and transformed the participants' elemental affects, sounds, and gestures of life at the threshold of death. As Jones noted in an interview, *Still/Here* was his effort to make a "beautiful dance, an interesting, vital, and challenging dance [that] will say everything [he] learned from survivors." It was a dance, he added, informed by the reality of impending death: "I really don't want to leave. I am only forty-two years old. But, this is the time when you make the poems. That's all there really is. The making of the poems. Now."[17]

The creative texts of early AIDS mourning are too numerous to name here. I have noted just a handful of examples above, and have focused only briefly on a set of formal qualities that delineates them as a group. I consider these formal qualities in depth in subsequent chapters, but I hope it is possible to glean from these brief examples alone the unusual timeline and grammar of loss that distinguish this corpus of mourning. Their double-tensed orientation toward loss is unconventional, if not counterintuitive, jarring against a normative grammar of loss, which, strictly speaking, should be expressed in the past tense. Loss's grammar is usually directed toward past events and passed-away people and the effect of these past losses on our present lives and psyches. This retrospective sense of loss is clear in early AIDS mourning, which emphasizes that which is already past, gone, absent. What is particularly striking, however, is that this body of mourning also shows that loss can have another direction, that loss can refer not just to elapsed time, but also to the soon-to-be-lost future. Redirecting loss to signify that which is still outstanding, still living, still here demands a reorientation of loss's grammar, which is precisely what early AIDS mourning achieves: its grammar of loss is at once behind and ahead of time, giving formal structure to both past and impending deaths. It's important that we examine closely the calendar of loss that underwrites early AIDS mourning, for it has a direct bearing on how these mourners reconstituted "high" genres of literary mourning, like the elegy, and popular ones, like the obituary, as well as common rites of death, like the funeral.

THE POLITICS OF DISPRIZED GRIEF:
MOURNING = SURVIVAL

Any study of early AIDS art must acknowledge the repressive context under which this art took shape, a context that willfully suppressed queer mourning and the extraordinary devastation that prompted it. The art and politics of early AIDS mourning are intertwined partly because, regardless of form, publicly mourning the ostracized is always a political undertaking, and partly because it was through these creative acts of mourning—"acts of intervention," to borrow David Román's phrase[18]—that AIDS mourners consecrated new queer connections and counterpublics in the 1980s and early '90s. Indeed, I call the bereaved who populate this book disprized mourners, on the one hand, to signify the political and cultural context that devalued the AIDS dead and curtailed for their queer survivors the rites and recognitions that follow death; and, on the other, to characterize the prerogatives of disparaged grief as a radical basis of group ties and survival—as an immediate political act to enfranchise the dead and stymie this catastrophe, and as a fundamental ethical act to inhume the dead and consign them to posterity. By the phrase "disprized mourners," therefore, I mean to signal the status of AIDS deaths in the public sphere (the disparagement of the AIDS dead and their queer survivors) and at the same time the extraordinary agency that the vilified corpses and their bereaved found in the political/ethical act of mourning.

In "Mourning and Militancy," Douglas Crimp offers an incisive characterization of early AIDS mourning and its prerogatives: "The violence we encounter is relentless, the violence of silence and omission almost as impossible to endure as the violence of unleashed hatred and outright murder. Because this violence also desecrates the memories of our dead, we rise in anger to vindicate them. For many of us, mourning *becomes* militancy."[19] Crimp's words accurately capture the violent conditions under which early AIDS grief occurred, and under these conditions of violence why that grief took on political character. For socially ostracized groups, mourning is neither solely a private undertaking nor an apolitical feeling, but instead is a collective enterprise (says Crimp, "we," "our dead," "many of us") and a radical way of asserting group agency. The prerogatives of mourning that Crimp delineates in his essay—as an affect and practice that is productive, collective, political, and necessary—radiate from the texts and rites of early AIDS mourners. And perhaps no other statement captures them more succinctly than Silence = Death, the public outcry of AIDS activists in the late '80s and early '90s. At the time, what was so brilliant about Silence = Death was that it issued a statement whose truth value was precisely in its declaration. Looking back now what I also find striking about this iconic sign is the other equation embedded in it: Mourning = Survival. There is an implicit conditional grammar in Silence = Death, which anticipates mourning as one counter-response to silence: if silence equals death, we are led to ask, then what equals life, what equals survival? One popular counterpoint among AIDS activists was Action = Life, which stressed the necessity of action and activism as countervailing forces to silence and omission. Although never articulated as such at the time, I would like to propose Mourning = Survival as another resounding counterpoint and as an instructive way of thinking about the imperatives of grief that underwrite Silence = Death and early AIDS mourning more broadly: namely, the political imperative to break the public silence around the mass deaths of gay men and, concurrently, the ethical imperative to inter the dead with certain due burial rites/rights.

Of the different forms of early AIDS mourning, political funerals put these imperatives into sharpest relief. What is so evocative and provocative about the AIDS funeral was the way it reanimated the body of the dead to concretize deaths the public refused to see. As Simon Watney points out, "It is *death* that has been consistently ruled out of the picture and it is death to which the political funeral draws attention."[20] By making the body the linchpin of a political demonstration, AIDS funerals materialized what a hateful public refused to see, and used that material evidence to indict the nation for its collusion in the countless AIDS deaths—embodied in the publicly displayed corpse. Furthermore, as Debra Levine argues in her superb essay "How to Do Things with Dead Bodies," the AIDS funeral realized the "corpse's presence to perform itself as [a] mode of political speech," enabling the dispossessed body to take on a remarkable "political afterlife," indeed extending the life of the corpse beyond the life of the deceased.[21]

The idea of an AIDS political funeral was conjured up initially by David Wojnarowicz. In a clairvoyant passage that inspired ACT UP to incorporate funerals into its repertoire of political actions, Wojnarowicz writes: "I imagine what it would be like if friends had a demonstration each time a lover or a friend or a stranger died of AIDS. I imagine what it would be like if, each time a lover, friend or stranger died of this disease, their friends, lovers or neighbors would take the dead body and drive with it in a car a hundred miles an hour to Washington, DC, and blast through the gates of the White House and come to a screeching halt before the entrance and dump their lifeless form on the front steps."[22] Although members of ACT UP did not blast through the gates of the White House, they conducted their first political funeral by throwing the cremated ashes of their beloved dead onto the grounds of America's politically sacred house.[23] "The signal virtue of an AIDS funeral on the lawn of the White House," Watney writes, "was that it fused the irreducible fact of the death of the individuals on a vast scale to the political circumstances that have contributed so much to the growing mortality rates."[24]

A political funeral at the White House stands out for its high symbolism, for turning the seat of government into a graveyard, but other AIDS funerals were just as remarkable in transforming a quotidian mourning rite into a significant political ritual. Wojnarowicz's own funeral was carried out in the streets of the East Village in New York City and publicly identified his death from AIDS as a political event. Along with the casket and the caravan of mourners, a series of placards made the event clearly legible to passersby—like the large banner at the front of the procession, which had inscribed on it the epitaph:

DAVID WOJNAROWICZ
1954–1992
DIED OF AIDS
DUE TO
GOVERNMENT NEGLECT

As the epitaph sums up, Wojnarowicz's—and, by extension, others'—death was born out of government policies. This was a central message of all AIDS political funerals: "not to impose politics onto death," as Watney says, but to make "plain the extent to which AIDS deaths have been political all along."[25]

AIDS funerals were not limited to the ones organized by ACT UP, of course. There were also scores of more private funerals that became political when friends rose up and interrupted the service to demand recognition of the deceased's sexuality, the cause of death, and the deceased's queer survivors, facts that were often suppressed by the family. When Assotto Saint disrupted the funeral of his friend and fellow poet Donald Woods and confronted the family for trying to hide Woods's sexuality and death from AIDS, he was enacting, albeit in a more private setting, the same imperatives of mourning, of reanimating the queer dead, that AIDS political funerals carried out in the streets. I consider Saint's fearless act more closely in chapter 2, where I read it in conjunction with the brilliant short story Thomas Glave's "The Final Inning." As Glave says, his story "was inspired, in part, by the death of a black gay poet named Donald Woods, who was very out in his personal and political life. I heard from a friend, the late Assotto Saint, another black gay poet who died of the disease. Assotto said that he felt so stricken during the service that he got up and began to shout at Donald's family about their hypocritical silence."[26] In the same way that political funerals contravened the nation's interdiction on queer/AIDS public mourning, Saint's act breached the family's regulating silence, enacting instead an unpoliced mourning that could express Woods's queer life and his illness and death from AIDS.

Melvin Dixon recounts a similar incident that occurred at the funeral of his friend Gregory, one of the thirteen men he elegizes in the poem "And These Are Just a Few . . . ":

> Then there is the chilling threat of erasure. Gregory, a friend and former student of mine, died last fall. . . . His siblings refused to be named in one very prominent obituary, and Greg's gayness and death from AIDS were not to be mentioned at the memorial service. Fortunately, few of us heeded the family's prohibition. While his family and society may have wanted to dispose of Greg even after his death, some of us tried to reclaim him and love him again and only then release him.[27]

To ensure survival, Dixon stresses the urgency of breaking the interdiction on queer/AIDS mourning as a necessary way of enfranchising the dead and mitigating "the chilling threat of erasure." Looking back, I am struck by the number of people who were vulnerable to similar erasures in their obituaries, funerals, and other obsequies. Even someone as prominent as Essex Hemphill, whose work epitomizes the renaissance of black gay art in the 1980s and early '90s, was interred by a family bent on burying the truths of his life and death. Charles Nero recalls: "Shortly after his own death, efforts began to erase who Essex was and who he had been. At his funeral his mother testified that one month before he passed Essex had given his life over to Christ. The minister preached a sermon warning against the dangers of alternative lifestyles. These attempts from family and church to deny that Essex was a gay man who had died of a disease intricately linked to homosexuality should not surprise us."[28]

It is precisely this kind of posthumous disposal of queer life that AIDS political funerals and fearless interventions at private funerals directly challenged and contravened. By deregulating the subjects of public grief, in effect, AIDS funerals (and early AIDS mourning more broadly) remade the public sphere.

As Judith Butler reminds us, "the public sphere is constituted in part by what can appear, and the regulation of the sphere of appearance is one way to establish what will count as reality, and what will not. It is also a way of establishing whose lives can be marked as lives, and whose deaths will count as deaths."[29] By carrying out funerals in the streets, or by reclaiming the dead at private burials, queer mourners deregulated "the sphere of appearance" and made the AIDS dead visible, tangible, real. And in doing so, they helped to engender counterpublics and counterarchives in which queer deaths counted as deaths and queer lives were remarkable as lives.

To mourn deaths that are publicly marked ungrievable, as disprized mourners do, takes enormous political will and imagination; it also takes commitment to an ethics of burying. Here is one last example of an AIDS funeral, like Bailey's, that shows directly the links between compounding loss and the imperatives of disparaged grief. In his impassioned will, "Bury Me Furiously," Mark Lowe Fisher gives direct instructions on what is to be done with his remains:

> I have decided that when I die I want my fellow AIDS activists to execute my wishes for my political funeral.
>
> I suspect—I know—my funeral will shock people when it happens. We Americans are terrified of death. Death takes place behind closed doors and is removed from reality, from the living. I want to show the reality of my death, to display my body in public; I want the public to bear witness. We are not just spiraling statistics; we are people who have lives, who have purpose, who have lovers, friends and families. And we are dying of a disease maintained by a degree of criminal neglect so enormous that it amounts to genocide.
>
> I want my death to be as strong a statement as my life continues to be. I want my own funeral to be fierce and defiant, to make the public statement that my death from AIDS is a form of political assassination.
>
> We are taking this action out of love and rage.[30]

Fisher's last words are moving in their life-sustaining properties.[31] Anticipating his own death, like Bailey, Fisher wills his body to have a posthumous life, to be used as an instrument of militant mourning. He first identifies the aims of the political funeral: to display AIDS deaths unrecognized in public and to expose the government's direct responsibility in perpetuating those deaths, including his own. Then, Fisher imagines his death and funeral as statements that will continue to reflect his life. He will be remembered not only for the life he led, but also for the manner in which his death will be carried out—furiously—and for the way his corpse lived.

Like Fisher, other early AIDS mourners conceived of expressing their grief as a bulwark against the future threat of erasure. In the absence of a public accounting of AIDS deaths, funerals and other forms of mourning were decisive in interring the dead with the truth due to them and not with the lies that normative mourning rites sought to reinforce. And some, like Fisher, were proactive: setting the conditions of their burial, ensuring that their queer lives and queer deaths were properly accounted for. Although his family sought to inter him following heteronormative scripts, Hemphill's own mourning was a different testimony. "Influenced/by phrases like 'Silence = death,'" Hemphill understood mourning's power in the early era of AIDS to archive for posterity queer lives, which would be otherwise effaced by the normative records of state, church, and family. Mourning was a tangible way of leaving behind a trace—that these queer lives and deaths in fact existed. Mourning was a means of surviving oneself, of leaving a record that no normative interment could erase. "Do you think I could walk pleasantly/and well-suited toward annihilation?" Hemphill scoffed in "Heavy Breathing."[32]

BLACK MOURNING AND THE CALENDAR OF LOSS

What theories can we draw on to help us conceptualize these key features of AIDS mourning? Which theories of loss can help us understand more effectively the calendar of loss and the insurgent grief that underwrite this body of work? Here, I step away from the primary materials of this study to consider the heuristic of loss that guides me. Black mourning evinces a particular temporal conception of loss that is very instructive in understanding both the aesthetics and the politics of early AIDS mourning, providing alternatives to the psychoanalytic model dominant in queer studies.

In his signal study of loss, "Mourning and Melancholia," Freud sets up an intrinsic opposition between the "normal mourner," who is able to overcome loss, and the melancholic, who is inconsolable in his grief. Unlike the supposedly "normal mourner," who establishes identification with another object in order to overcome his lost love, the melancholic, whom Freud calls a "pathological mourner," is unable to displace his loss and withdraws inward instead. Since object loss is transformed into ego loss, Freud argues, the melancholic "displays an extraordinary diminution in his self-regard, an impoverishment of his ego on a grand scale," and ultimately such self-diminution results in "an overcoming of the instinct which compels every living thing to cling to life."[33] Other studies have rightly noted the limits of Freud's binary formulation of loss by pointing to his easy pathologizing of nonnormative mourning.[34] But there is another important limitation that makes it difficult to apply this theory of loss to the mourners I consider in this book. Underlying Freud's ideal of mourning in "Mourning and Melancholia"—and in many subsequent studies of loss that follow Freud's lead—is the mourner's presumed future, which is the unstated but necessary condition of overcoming loss. In laying out his blueprint of loss, in short, Freud assumes a priori the survival or future time of any given mourner.

Whereas the mourner's death date is deferred in Freud's essay, it is time-bound in early AIDS mourning. "I have lost the future tense from my vocabulary," says Dixon, underscoring his vantage point as a different kind of mourner, a bereaved whose horizon is a death-bound future.[35] Without prospects of futurity, Dixon and other early AIDS mourners call into question the temporal assumptions of the mourning-versus-melancholia model of grief and, by extension, the binary configuration of loss as either normal or pathological. These are not Freud's "normal mourners," since they are inconsolable in their grief and, moreover, deploy mourning as an instrument of survival; nor are they "pathological mourners," since they achieve cathexis in mourning itself and in its art and activism. However, art and activism, as newly cathected objects, cannot displace loss; on the contrary, they place loss center stage and burden mourning even further with the task of articulating more and more and more deaths. Loss cannot be displaced for these mourners, nor can it be delimited by the normative grammar of mourning, which presumes the future as a condition of consolation.

The opposition between normal and pathological mourning has never been a meaningful one in the formation of African American mourning, however. As Fred Moten states incisively, "the way black mo'nin' improvises through the opposition of mourning and melancholia disrupt[s] the temporal framework that buttresses that opposition."[36] Moten is right to locate the difference between black mourning and the mourning-versus-melancholia paradigm precisely in temporality. There is a striking temporal difference between the two models of loss, since the anticipation of death, as well as its passing, frame the calendar of black mourning. From founding genres like negro spirituals to contemporary forms like hip hop, the canon of black arts and letters sounds a mourning of unremitting loss. In her study of African American mourning, Karla Holloway distinguishes black mourning as that which expresses past and prospective death:

> The anticipation of death and dying figured into the experiences of black folk
> so persistently, given how much more omnipresent death was for them than for

other Americans, that lamentation and mortification both found their way into public and private representations of African America to an astonishing degree. The twentieth century's literature and film, its visual arts and music (from early era spirituals to latter-day rap), and its contemporary street-corner memorials consistently called up a passed-on narrative. Black culture's stories of death and dying were inextricably linked to the ways in which the nation experienced, perceived, and represented African America. Sometimes it was a subtext, but even then the ghostly presence of those narratives reminded us that something about America was, for black folk, disjointed. Instead of death and dying being unusual, untoward events, or despite being inevitably end-of-lifespan events, the cycles of our daily lives were so persistently interrupted by specters of death that we worked this experience into the culture's iconography and included it as an aspect of black cultural sensibility. For black parents and their youngsters, elders and their adult children, the formative years, the waning years, and each day between were haunted by one spiritual's refrain: "soon one morning, death will come a-calling."[37]

Death and dying are not just "unusual, untoward events" or "inevitably end-of-lifespan events," but instead punctuate black life routinely and proleptically. As Holloway notes, the anticipation of death and dying and the expression of that anticipation are formative elements of black culture. Also, as Abdul Jan-Mohamed's insightful study on Richard Wright points out, "the death-bound subject"—"a subject who is formed, from infancy on, by the imminent and ubiquitous threat of death"—is not only the dominant leitmotif of Wright's oeuvre, but also one that permeates African American literature and culture.[38] What underwrites black mourning—what Holloway calls "black death," Moten "black mo'nin'," and JanMohamed the "death-bound subject"—is a nonnormative, temporal relationship to death, which reiterates a death date that is time-bound, as opposed to one deferred to an open-ended future. Given the persistence of death in black life, black culture is imbued with an anticipatory sense of loss, recalibrating the calendar of mourning to record past and prospective losses in a single grammar of loss. Indeed, in the same way that Hortense Spillers has identified a particular, relative grammar with which to understand the formation of African American subjectivity—"theoriz[ing] the hyphen [in African-American] as a 'neither/nor' and a 'both/and'"—we can point to a relative grammar of loss as "both/and" that's also constitutive of an African American "grammar of feeling."[39]

The spirituals best exemplify black mourning's unique calendar of loss and its attendant feelings. That the formative African American creative genre is also predominantly a genre of mourning underscores the grave circumstances under which black life has existed in the United States. The spirituals, as Frederick Douglass observed, amplified "the death-dealing character of slavery."[40] And in "The Sorrow Songs," W. E. B. Du Bois called the spirituals "the rhythmic cry of the slave," identifying that sound, that cry, as a common denominator of spirituals and as a basis of black life.[41] "The music is distinctly sorrowful," Du Bois noted—the very reason he called them sorrow songs.[42] In addition to identifying the constitutive sound of black lyrics (mourning), Du Bois also categorized the spirituals into "ten master songs," including songs of exile, of trouble, of suffering, of fugitivity, of hopeful strife, and so forth. Songs of death and mourning are also among Du Bois's ten master songs. Among a cluster of sorrow songs that amplify compounding death, "Soon One Morning Death Will Come A-Calling," the song Holloway cites, is one keen example, as are "I Feel Like My Time Ain't Long," "I'm Traveling to the Grave," "When I'm Dead Don't Grieve After Me," "Master Is Going to Sell Us Tomorrow," and "Many Thousands Gone." These and other spirituals reveal how slaves were "faced constantly with the imminent threat of death," to borrow Howard Thurman's words.[43] The spirituals bear out, as Thurman observes in his study of the genre, that "[d]eath was a fact, inescapable, persistent."[44] This point is also underlined in James Cone's study of spirituals—that slaves "ritualized in song [the] constant presence of death and the threat of death."[45] By paying close attention to the temporality of loss in this set of songs, rather than simply noting their Christian eschatology, we can glean the nonnormative ways African American slaves conceptualized a death-riddled life and also created a distinct form of lyric/mourning. Thus, I use the spirituals as a conceptual resource from which to draw perspective on nonnormative mourning, and I use that insight, what Du Bois might call "second sight," to view the mourning of other socially outcast groups.

The spirituals and, more broadly, black mourning guide this study in three ways. First, they offer an alternative conceptual paradigm with which to understand early AIDS loss and its concomitant feelings—wherever that mourning resides. The chapter on AIDS elegies includes spirituals as a way of setting up an alternative model of theorizing lyric mourning. I rely on the spirituals to read the elegies of Melvin Dixon, an African American poet, and Paul Monette, a white American poet. Dixon directly references the spirituals to represent AIDS loss, so it is easy to see the intertextual ties between the spirituals and his elegies; Monette does not refer to the spirituals directly or indirectly, and yet his poetics can be conceptualized readily through the spirituals' unique representation of loss. Since the spirituals' grammar of feeling holds the possibility of articulating losses that are both/and, eschewing the generally absolute past tense of death and loss in the English language, we can rely on that grammar to fathom other forms of mourning that are suffused with a series of existing and upcoming deaths.

Second, the spirituals illuminate the work of black gay artists dealing with AIDS, who often appropriated slave songs to express their own perilous lives. No other form casts its influence more significantly in the African American tradition than the spirituals, and certainly no other genre informs subsequent articulations of black mourning more. It is not surprising then that black gay artists often drew from spirituals to make sense of their own immediate catastrophe. When asked why he choreographed *Still/Here*, for instance, Jones responded by invoking two different spirituals: "You know how the old song goes, 'Lord I want to be ready,' this is getting ready"; and "I want to cross over, how else to say it, I want to cross over."[46] In a gripping scene in *Black Is . . . Black Ain't*, despite being bedridden in a hospital room, Riggs sings and sways to "I Shall Not Be Removed." And Dixon translates the spiritual "Many Thousands Gone" into the AIDS elegy "One by One," and he names the essay in which he takes a last look at life after the spiritual "I Will Be Somewhere Listening for My Name."

Third, I turn to the spirituals because they offer insights into the political properties of sorrow: how a disenfranchised group mobilizes mourning as a basis of group ties and insurgent action. In calling early AIDS mourners "disprized mourners," I have appropriated the phrase from Max Cavitch's study of the American elegy, where the chapter on antebellum African American elegists is called "Mourning of the Disprized: African Americans and Elegy from Wheatley to Lincoln." Although Cavitch doesn't discuss the term "disprized," he elaborates in the chapter that "for slaves to publicly mourn at all was boldly to consecrate ties of feeling and of blood that often lay under the heaviest interdictions. . . . despite repressive circumstances, American slaves cultivated and sustained various deathways across generations."[47] There are striking similarities to be found between antebellum African American mourning and early AIDS mourning, including their shared timeline of loss and the ineluctably political character of their grief. The politics of the spirituals have been well noted. Sorrow songs were instrumental in encoding escape, for instance, cyphering the plans of fugitives in songs like "Steal Away to Jesus" and "Hush, Hush, Somebody's Calling My Name." There are countless songs that through biblical tales emplotted the yearning to raze the entire edifice of slavery. "If I Had My Way I'd Tear This Building Down," as James Baldwin put it, wasn't an "innocent church song" about Samson and Delilah, but voiced the insurgent feelings of slaves: "it was lethal," Baldwin said with characteristic economy.[48] And as critics of the spirituals remind us, the sorrow songs were instrumental in forming the affective basis of black life and culture, one of the few self-generated expressions that slaves were able to use to consecrate the ties of feeling, to speak of an unspeakable world, and to concretize freedom and justice.[49] It was through resounding sorrow that slaves found the affective basis of black life and also found one way of surviving and defying a system that deemed them socially dead. For slaves, in short, mourning was a necessary means of survival. Hence, the spirituals offer insight about both the form and politics of mourning; their second sight can guide us to conceptualize more broadly other experiences of disprized grief in our world.

I share the interventionist aims of other studies of loss that depathologize inconsolable mourning and show how, as a structure of feeling, it can be "productive rather than pathological, abundant rather than lacking, social rather than solipsistic, militant rather than reactionary."[50] As the late José Esteban Muñoz astutely notes, inconsolable mourning or melancholia can have productive uses for disprized groups. A nonnormative feeling like melancholia, Muñoz writes, "for blacks, queers, or any queers of color, is not a pathology but an integral part of everyday lives. . . . It is this melancholia that is part of our process of dealing with all the catastrophes that occur in the lives of people of color, lesbians, and gay men. I have proposed a different understanding of melancholia that does not see it as a pathology or as a self-absorbed mood that inhibits activism. Rather, it is a mechanism that helps us (re)construct identity and take our dead with us to the various battles we must wage in their names—and in our names."[51] Muñoz's alternative characterization of melancholia fittingly captures the way in which the disenfranchised often forge a collective identity by sustaining grief and by drawing on that grief to authorize their group ties and actions. In this book, I employ a black mourning heuristic in a similar way to offer a more capacious understanding of mourning, one that takes into account the and/both timeline and grammar of loss, as well as the political uses of grief.

LOOKING FOR THE DEAD NOW

Looking for the dead sounds like an incongruous approach to a catastrophe like AIDS, which is defined in part by its sheer scale; it may seem that it does not require much searching to find the AIDS dead, given their countless numbers. But we live in an era that has effaced from our contemporary life the AIDS past and its many thousands gone. Scholars in queer studies are right to point out that we are living in an age of gay liberalism—a confluence of legal, cultural, and national integration of gays and lesbians into the American mainstream. As Lisa Duggan, David Eng, Jasbir Puar, and others have pointed out, shoring up gay liberalism are some laws that ensure gays and lesbians the rights to normative kinship and citizenship; a mass-mediated, consumer-oriented gay popular culture; and a new face of American nationalism, which draws a sharp contrast to the Arab world in the wake of 9/11 by pointing to the relative "human rights" that gays enjoy in the United States.[52] Gay liberalism has entailed not only an articulation of neoliberal claims to citizenship, however, but also an erasure of the immediate queer past of immense suffering and loss. I would add that another central pillar of gay liberalism is a post-AIDS discourse that emerged in the United States after 1996, following the success of highly active antiretroviral therapy (HAART). HAART transformed AIDS from a terminal illness into something chronic and manageable, and simultaneously launched a new way of speaking publicly about AIDS.[53] This new discourse displaced AIDS both temporally, as a demarcated past against which a new normative gay identity could be forged, and spatially, as an issue that now mattered only in communities of color in the United States or beyond in the global south. This post-AIDS discourse has been indispensable to gay liberalism and its ideals of normalcy, removing the specter of an immediate past of immense devastation from our present moment of gay normalization and triumphalism.

Given gay liberalism's insistent erasure of the past, looking for the AIDS dead *now* becomes a timely intervention. Michel-Rolph Trouillot is keen to remind us that in making history, silence asserts its power at different junctures: "Silences enter the process of historical production at four crucial moments: the moment of fact creation (the making of *sources*); the moment of fact assembly (the making of *archives*); the moment of fact retrieval (the making of *narrative*); and the moment of retrospective significance (the making of *history* in the final instance)."[54] Early AIDS mourners were well aware of these different manifestations of silence, and certainly their amplified rage and mourning were crucial in contesting the normative sources, archives, and narratives that enveloped AIDS in silence at the time. Now, ironically, it's gay liberalism that is helping to silence the history of AIDS, denying it any retrospective significance, since gay normalization demands subduing the immediate past of trauma and its attendant feelings, and projecting instead the present claims of healthy gays with happy feelings whose sole aspiration it seems is to become the standard-bearers of the family and the military. By looking for the dead *now*, therefore, this book aims to challenge gay liberalism's present undertaking to write off the AIDS past, indeed to drop the dead in the service of mainstream inclusion. As Heather Love argues, a "disposition toward the past—embracing loss [and] risking abjection" is one important way of checking the normative enterprise of gay liberalism: "Resisting the call of gay normalization means refusing to write off the most vulnerable, the least presentable, and all the dead."[55] The counter-enterprise of returning to the past and embracing the immediate dead is particularly important for my generation, which sexually came of age in the era of HAART and which has worked to cast aside the AIDS past as one condition of gay normalization. Now we are called to look for our immediate forebears, discover all the losses they endured, and reclaim those losses as a formative part of our own identity.

Because *The Calendar of Loss* approaches the early years of AIDS with hindsight, it differs from the first wave of AIDS scholarship, which emerged concurrently with the creative mourning texts I consider in this book. I have had the luxury of thinking about this body of mourning in the United States historically removed from "the spectacular body count of AIDS."[56] Sarah Schulman is right: "The present does not resemble the past. We went through a mass death experience and then we took a break."[57] This study is also removed from the virulent anti-gay/anti-AIDS discourse that reigned in the 1980s and '90s. Along with AIDS art and activism, early AIDS scholarship bore the burden of demystifying and deconstructing the public representation of AIDS as an *essentially* gay disease. In his introduction to the groundbreaking collection *AIDS: Cultural Analysis / Cultural Activism*, Douglas Crimp characterizes the imperative of critical analysis at the time of the volume's publication in 1988: to "contest the notion that there is an underlying reality of AIDS, upon which are constructed the representations, or the culture, or the politics of AIDS. If we recognize that AIDS exists only in and through these constructions, then hopefully we can also recognize the imperative to know them, analyze them, and wrest control of them."[58] The other essays in his volume share the same critical imperative to deconstruct the very construction of an AIDS discourse, and in doing so to show how medical, political, religious, and popular thinking worked in concert in the same regime of signification. Paula Treichler was correct to call AIDS "an epidemic of signification," since during the early period "no clear line [could] be drawn between the facticity of scientific and nonscientific (mis)conceptions. Ambiguity, homophobia, stereotyping, confusion, doublethink, them-versus-us, blame-the-victim, wishful thinking: none of these popular forms of semantic legerdemain about AIDS [was] absent from biomedical communication."[59] Neither scientific nor popular discourses offered an objective representation of AIDS; they instead worked together to represent AIDS only as spectacle and metaphor.[60] These foundational essays set the tenor and mode of analysis of AIDS scholarship by underscoring the necessity of critique in challenging and upending the dominant scientific and popular thinking toward AIDS.[61]

As a mode of analysis, then, critique was central to the first wave of AIDS scholarship—and necessarily so, given the series of untruths that underwrote AIDS research and representation in the early years. One physician's claim— "We used to hate faggots on an emotional basis. Now we have good reason"[62]— was writ large in the culture and amplified routinely by a cadre of public moralizers like Jerry Falwell, who used apocalyptic language: "AIDS is not just God's punishment for homosexuals; it is God's punishment for the society that tolerates homosexuals."[63] Pat Buchanan opined in 1983 in a syndicated column, "The poor homosexuals—they have declared war upon nature, and now nature is extracting an awful retribution (AIDS)"; and again in 1990, "With 80,000 dead of AIDS, our promiscuous homosexuals appear literally hell-bent on Satanism and suicide."[64] This deeply hateful view, that homosexuality = AIDS = death, was the widely accepted "truth." Scholars in the early years thus found it necessary to deconstruct and delegitimize this "truth" in order to mitigate this discourse's deleterious effects on people living with AIDS and on queer communities more broadly.

This book is indebted to and builds on this foundational work. But because this early body of AIDS scholarship has already perceptively analyzed the discursive uses of AIDS in the early years—as metaphor, spectacle, and signification—*The Calendar of Loss* turns away from that kind of critical work and instead begins to contemplate the forms and uses of grief for early AIDS mourners. Looking back at those years, Gregg Bordowitz recalls that queer men "experienced the representations of our deaths only as spectacle for the general public. There was a real resistance to allowing us to picture the deaths that we experienced, our experience of mortality."[65] This book is a deliberation on how exactly early AIDS mourners pictured their own deaths and experienced their mortality. This shift in emphasis—from a study of AIDS discourse to a study of AIDS mourning—reconstructs the early history of AIDS not from the dominant discourse of AIDS but from the vantage point of the bereaved facing their own mortality.

The Calendar of Loss also builds on subsequent scholarship that has paid close attention to the inextricable link between art and politics in the early era of AIDS.[66] While this book examines the interplay of art and politics, the particular tenor of mourning issued during (and not after) a catastrophe, and the sounds of unresolved grief—and makes the comparative gesture to include different classes of AIDS mourners—it does so by leveraging a different disciplinary perspective. This is the first book-length study of AIDS in the humanities at the intersection of black and queer studies, and I use this important pivot point to reconstruct an interdisciplinary study of not only early AIDS narratives, but also the work of mourning.[67] As Sharon Holland puts it: "The space of death is marked by blackness and is therefore always already queer," a succinct formulation that establishes an intricate connection among blackness, queerness, and loss.[68] I have resolved to elucidate these connections not as discrete categories but as deeply imbricated ones. *The Calendar of Loss* marshals the resources of black and queer studies to put forward an interdisciplinary examination of AIDS loss that neither marginalizes the sorrow of queers of color nor compartmentalizes loss into normal and pathological mourning, mourner and mourned, or even the living and the dead. Rather, this book puts the early era of AIDS in perspective by drawing on a democratic archive of loss that includes a wide cast of mourners and mourning materials and on a heuristic of loss that transgresses binary formulations and elucidates together race, sexuality, and grief.

Mourning defies summation, and the archive of early AIDS mourning is so overwhelming that it thwarts a single study. What I seek to do here is to provide one way of thinking about this early period and the mourning it produced by enmeshing black and queer perspectives. Chapter 1 expands on the claims made in this introduction by concentrating on the elegies of Melvin Dixon and Paul Monette, two exemplary figures of AIDS poetry, reading their work in relation to the spirituals and in contradistinction to the elegy form. Close readings show how these poets formally structure loss as both object and subject, past and proximate, memory and immediate threat, employing an unconventional temporality and grammar, as well as rhetorical devices like apostrophe, metonymy, and prolepsis to hail death, which is both here and imminent. Chapter 2 considers another form of literary mourning, identifying the queer uses of obituaries during the early years of AIDS. Assotto Saint, one of the central figures of the renaissance of black gay art in the 1980s, anchors this chapter, since he used the obituary to record and commemorate the AIDS dead. The chapter also includes a substantive discussion of Thomas Glave's short story "The Final Inning," which illuminates how obsequies attempt to reconcile the rites of the living and the rights of the dead. Chapter 3 examines the visual art of Keith Haring, particularly how Haring employed graffiti and, more broadly, hip hop culture in the making of his distinct visual vernacular and ultimately in imaging AIDS deaths, including his own. Haring in both paintings and journal entries identified his own death-bound life with the police killing of Michael Stewart, an African American graffiti artist, and by way of that identification sought to place his and others' deaths from AIDS in a continuum of black collective death and disenfranchisement. Chapter 4 embraces another class of AIDS mourners devastated by this catastrophe, as I complete this study with a comparative look at AIDS orphans in Africa. Drawing from the archive of the first AIDS art collective in Ethiopia, I examine a series of mourning works generated by bereaved children, particularly the epistles these orphans write to their dead. I argue that their mourning bears a striking resemblance to that of queer communities in the United States, demanding that we think about AIDS mourning and what it means to be queer from the vantage point of previously unthought-of queer places,[69] like Ethiopia, and subject positions, like bereaved children mourning in order to survive. I hope that these chapters open up new perspectives into the early years of the AIDS catastrophe and into the affective, aesthetic, and political properties of sorrow.

I have found that looking for the AIDS dead is an enterprise full of political and ethical meaning. "Bringing back the dead," Holland says, "is the ultimate queer act."[70] Months before he died, Melvin Dixon delivered the keynote address at *OutWrite '92* and reminded his audience: "As for me . . . I may not be well enough or alive next year to attend the lesbian and gay writers conference, but I'll be somewhere listening for my name. I may not be around to celebrate with you the publication of gay literary history. But I'll be somewhere listening for my name. . . . You, then, are charged by the possibility of your good health, by the broadness of your vision, to remember us."[71] In this book, at the very least, I am heeding Dixon's call and the imperatives of the AIDS dead: to remember them.

one

Lyric Mourning
Sorrow Songs and AIDS Elegies

Melvin Dixon and Paul Monette were two of the most distinguished poets of the early era of AIDS, and their elegies are among the finest examples of the pathos and poetics of AIDS mourning. Mourning his partner, Dixon writes, "His illness and death were so much a part of my illness and life that I felt that I too had died," also aptly characterizing his own death-bound life.[1] In *Love's Instruments*, a collection of poems published posthumously, Dixon writes about not only the deaths of his lover and scores of friends, but also his own impending death. In "The Falling Sky," for instance, a poem in memory of his friend and fellow poet Chester Weinerman, the elegiac portrait comprises not one but many losses, including a death-bound lyric subject:

> When at last you knew the sky was falling
> You were too sick to go outside, even when lightning
> Broke the day into pieces shimmering down.
> But in my dream you bolted from the bed,
> You ran to us, screaming "Save me. Save me!"
> And we held you tight, held onto your visible bones.
>
> Now I, too, have started to thin and sweat and cough.
>
> .   .   .   .
>
> Dust already gathers at the grit line of my teeth.
> Ash coats my skin like a uniform with no number.[2]

The portrait of one loss is followed by another, then another, and then by numbers too vast to be distinguished. There is the image of Weinerman "too sick to go outside" and then conjured up again wasting; the speaker of the poem falls ill; and finally, as the simile "a uniform with no number" intimates, there is mass calamity.

Monette's collection of poems *Love Alone: Eighteen Elegies for Rog*—written in the immediate wake of the death of Monette's partner—also exemplifies how loss compounds. In "The Very Same," Monette recalls an exchange with a family member that took place immediately after his beloved's funeral, an exchange that revealed how the time, consolation, and closure that allow other mourners to overcome loss are denied to a poet like him, living with AIDS:

> the wrongest of the wrong things said that day
> as I stepped from the chapel an idiot cousin
> once-removed juggled my shoulder *time to turn*
> *the page* intoned like it's been all so appalling
> we must hasten now to the land of brunch
> there to recover our BMWs our zest for
> winning and half-acre closets sorry I'm
> booked weeks later still fuming with retorts
> BUT THIS *IS* MY PAGE IT CANNOT BE TURNED[3]

The italicized material contrasts the difference between, on the one hand, mourning buttressed by condolences like "time to turn the page," which presume a normative grammar of loss and stipulate the future as a condition of consolation; and, on the other, mourning based on a different grammar and calendar of loss, with the subject's loss both object and subject, past and prospective. With uppercase and italics, with unmistakable rage, Monette articulates that his loss cannot be overcome: "THIS *IS* MY PAGE IT CANNOT BE TURNED." Elegizing another and elegizing oneself are interdependent, which is precisely why many of the poems in *Love Alone* are cast as double anamneses: of Roger's illness and death and the poet's illness and life. "Your Sightless Days" recalls the moment Roger's vision began to wane; "No Goodbyes," his hearing; "Gardenias," his sense of smell—recollections that also rehearse the life of the dying poet.

The way "The Falling Sky" and "The Very Same"—and early AIDS elegies more broadly—reflect on not singular but compounding and reflexive death distinguishes them as a unique type of elegy: one that carries out the genre's binding work of mourning, but also undoes its defining difference between the subject and the object of grief. All elegies can be seen broadly as the "work of mourning"—work, as Peter Sacks writes in *The English Elegy*, "both in the commonly accepted meaning of a product and in the more dynamic sense of the working through of an impulse or experience."[4] Occasioned by the loss of someone or something dear to the poet, the elegy becomes an occasion in itself, enabling the poet to confront that loss by way of words and form. "[E]legies are poems about being left behind," adds Max Cavitch in *The American Elegy*. "They are poems, too, that are themselves left behind, as literary and even material legacies. Their heritage helps constitute the 'work' (both process and artifact) of mourning—a form of psychic labor that is also fundamental to the work of culture."[5] And as works of mourning—as private and public undertakings, personal and collective lamentations, processes and products—elegies are some of the finest examples of how the living grieve for the dead. While early AIDS elegies share these central features of the genre, they are also distinguished by a particular articulation of loss that cannot be generalized. As Dixon's and Monette's poems testify, yes, AIDS elegies are poems about being left behind, but they are also poems about leaving.

In his important study of the English elegy, Sacks draws his schema of loss from Sigmund Freud's "Mourning and Melancholia," insightfully appropriating Freud's phrase "the work of mourning" to think about the elegy as both process and product.[6] But Sacks accepts Freud's opposition of loss between the healthy mourner and the melancholic, a binary frame he uses to read elegies accordingly as either achieving healthy forms of substitution or succumbing to regressive and self-destructive feelings like revenge and melancholia.[7] The limitations of Freud's "Mourning and Melancholia," which I discussed in the introduction— its binary view of mourning and its pathologization of nonnormative feelings —also hold in Sacks's study of the elegy, and we are left wanting for another schema of loss for AIDS elegies: one that accounts for poet-mourners like Dixon and Monette, whose death dates cannot be deferred, but instead are here, time-bound, near and obvious. Their negative feelings, their inconsolable grief, become an instrumental way of fashioning the self and the elegy.

As a subgenre, self-elegy is not particular to AIDS poetry, of course. From Milton's "Lycidas" to Plath's "Lady Lazarus," poets have frequently willed their deaths in lyric form. Nor is inconsolable grief particular to AIDS poetry. As Jahan Ramazani argues in *Poetry of Mourning*, "The modern elegist tends not to achieve but to resist consolation, not to override but to sustain anger, not to heal but to reopen the wounds of loss. . . . Unlike their literary forebears or the 'normal mourner' of psychoanalysis, . . . [modern elegists] refuse such orthodox consolations as the rebirth of the dead in nature, in God, or in poetry itself."[8] Inconsolability, as Ramazani shows, is a dominant affect in the modern elegy, with the self-elegy a recurring subgenre. Although he gestures toward AIDS mourning in a coda, Ramazani's study of modern elegies nonetheless does not take into account the anticipation of the poet's literal death with which AIDS elegies reckon, nor does he look at how that prospective loss rewrites the basic under-

pinnings of the genre. Elegizing the actual proximity of one's own death differs markedly from willing that death only figuratively. AIDS elegists may share
inconsolability with other twentieth-century writers, but theirs comes from
facing their own wasting in addition to others' deaths, sequencing a timetable
of loss for the death-bound poet. "I'm / booked weeks later," says Monette in
"The Very Same," signifying on a datebook in which he has his imminent death
penciled in. Surely, elegizing one's own literal death changes the uses of inconsolability. Ramazani points out that modern poets employ inconsolable mourning mainly for poetic gain—to help them resist the old consolations in nature,
God, and poetry that became suspect in the twentieth century. AIDS elegists
like Dixon and Monette use inconsolable mourning not merely for poetic profit,
however, but literally for survival. As Monette puts it emphatically—"still fuming with retorts / BUT THIS *IS* MY PAGE IT CANNOT BE TURNED"—his survival, his being still here, hinges on continuing to express his rage and retorts on
the lyric page.

Representing the proximity of the poet's death and that death's place on a
calendar of past and prospective losses is central to early AIDS poetics. As Melissa Zeiger observes in *Beyond Consolation*, what distinguishes AIDS elegies
is that the "relations between the living and the dead are changed definitively
by the way speakers in AIDS elegies refuse to deny death by hiding that they are
themselves at risk, are already infected with the HIV virus, or are, as in the case
of Melvin Dixon and others, already dying. As the line between the dead and
the survivors dissolves, so too does the customary elegiac politics of subject
and object."[9] Zeiger's observation aptly captures how early AIDS elegies erased
the governing binary of the genre between the living poet and the lost object of
mourning, and instituted instead a different kind of elegy, in which the entire
work of mourning is definitively altered, now shaped by a lost object that is not
only external to the self, but also includes the self: "BUT THIS *IS* MY PAGE IT
CANNOT BE TURNED."

While the expression of compounding loss may be atypical in elegies, it is a
constitutive feature of spirituals, which is why I suggest reading AIDS elegies
across forms of lyric mourning.[10] The way slave songs formalize loss—how they
calibrate the timeline, chart the grammar, and tune the pathos for serial losses
within a single lyric—can be very instructive in reading other lyrics also forged
amid a mass calamity.[11]

Studies that probe death in the spirituals focus largely on their theology of
loss, illuminating the central role of Christian eschatology in this lyrical tradition. From concretizing death and resurrection to mediating grief and conso-

lation, Christian eschatology is certainly a defining feature of the spirituals.[12] As Lawrence Levine observes, "slave songs are a testament to the way in which Christianity provided slaves with the precedents, heroes and future promise that allowed them to transcend the purely temporal bonds of the Peculiar Institution."[13] In conceptualizing the spirituals, Levine identifies their temporality as being situated in the present but reaching backward to include the past and reaching upward to incorporate the divine. He writes that slaves "extended the boundaries of their restrictive universe backward until it fused with the world of the Old Testament, and upward until it became one with the world beyond. The spirituals are the record of a people who found the status, the harmony, the values, the order they needed to survive by internally creating an expanded universe, by literally willing themselves re-born."[14] While this sacred timeline in the spirituals is undeniable, I want to shift the focus to another temporality of loss delineated in the spirituals: a calendar of death that cannot be summed up by a sacred temporality alone. There are spirituals that cast death not simply backward and upward but also forward in a timeline that brings into view a death-bound lyric subject who stresses death not as transcendence, but as an impending fact here and now. Put another way, while it's true that slaves will themselves to be reborn in spirituals, they also will themselves to die there, rehearsing their imminent deaths and formalizing a prolepsis of mourning in lyric form. How they enact this latter type of loss within the lyric calls for a formal analysis that's not delimited by religious exegesis.[15] Here, I find Howard Thurman's study of the genre to be the most instructive; he is patient in the observation of death in the spirituals without hastening to subsume it all under Christian eschatology. In the spirituals, says Thurman, "the significant revelation is in the fact that death, as an event, is spatial, time encompassed, if not actually time bound, and therefore partakes of the character of the episodic."[16] In considering those spirituals that figure death as something that's time-bound and episodic, we must linger on the rhetorical means by which these lyrics enact or stage a death not yet arrived, which is "to be distinguished from that which may come after death."[17]

There is a class of spirituals that sounds a prolepsis of mourning. "I Feel Like My Time Ain't Long," "I'm Traveling to the Grave," "We're Marching to the Grave," "When I'm Dead Don't Grieve After Me," "Master Is Going to Sell Us Tomorrow," "Many Thousands Gone," and others embody a death-bound (lyric) subject, as Abdul JanMohamed writes, "formed by the imminent and ubiquitous threat of death."[18] Employing figures of speech like metonymy and prolepsis to apprehend a world of more and more losses, this set of songs amplifies an unrelieved sorrow that seems to resist the religious consolations proffered in the lyrics.[19] "Many Thousands Gone" exemplifies this type of spiritual, and I will return to it later when reading Dixon's elegy "One by One." But for now, I consider another haunting example, "Master Is Going to Sell Us Tomorrow," a song that amplifies "the death-dealing character of slavery," to borrow from Frederick Douglass, and that sees slaves as agents "involve[d] [in] an extended act of mourning," to borrow from Paul Gilroy.[20] In this spiritual, the immediate place and time of slavery are figured as the very axis of death, and compounding loss is voiced with unrelenting apostrophe.

Mother, is master going to sell us tomorrow?
Yes, yes, yes!
O, watch and pray

Going to sell us to Georgia?
Yes, yes, yes!
O, watch and pray

Farewell, mother, I must leave you
Yes, yes, yes!
O, watch and pray

Mother don't grieve after me
No, no, no!
O, watch and pray

Mother, I'll meet you in heaven
Yes, my child!
O, watch and pray[21]

This haunting lyric is echoed by Orlando Patterson's characterization of slavery as an institution that condemned slaves to social death, natal alienation, and general dishonor; but this lyric also subverts Patterson's thesis in its clear expression of slave agency.[22] In this mourning call-and-response, death is metonymically figured by the impending sale, which occasions the song and provides furthermore the temporal vantage point from which mother and child bear witness, strategize, instruct and console each other, keep vigilance and faith. Although the spiritual begins interrogatively—the child verifying the time and place of dawning death, the sale tomorrow and the consignment to Georgia—it expresses a retrospective or posthumous mood in the last two verses, a grammar generated in the face of tomorrow's loss and enacted by the lyric's prolepsis of mourning.

Apostrophe and exclamation are the key rhetorical figures in this mourning call. The apostrophe "O" becomes the most repeated sound in the poem, saturating it with moaning that refuses to cease. In the first stanza, for instance, the O is full of both "mother" and the sorrow of "tomorrow"; the O in the second stanza recollects "going" and "Georgia"; and by the fourth stanza, the apostrophe now includes the haunting repetition of "no" that the previous O's anticipated. The shape of the O on the page as well as the form the mouth takes during pronunciation also denote a palpable loss and vulnerability, feelings that are serialized and echoed throughout the lyric. However much the last stanza offers the consolation of reunion in heaven—which in spirituals can signify God's abode as well as the physical geography beyond slavery, above the Mason-Dixon line and west of the Ohio River, where freedom was possible—that consolation is tempered significantly by the repeated O sound, the lyric's alphabet of sorrow. And while, like other spirituals, it "predicts the posthumous reconstitution of familial relationships in a realm beyond the reach of slavery's dissevering power over natal ties," it does so without relinquishing its sound of unrelieved grief, O.[23] In lyric poetry, as Jonathan Culler has observed, "the presuppositions of apostrophe are a force to be reckoned with";[24] in this lyric those forces rest in the death-bound tomorrow that the spiritual is contending with and formalizing in the process. The O, the sound of apostrophe, is a deeply mournful call: we hear that sound sharply tuned in the penultimate stanza, as the apostrophe compounds the poem's exclamation of loss: "No, no, no! / O."[25]

Tomorrow—the sorrow sound echoed throughout the poem, the death-bound day proleptically enacted—occasions this lyric mourning: not in the conventional way we think of tomorrow as the horizon of hope and futurity, but instead as the very day of death. This sense of the future "booked" as the horizon of loss is the critical frame of this chapter, the "second sight" by which I am recasting early AIDS elegies. The spirituals' prolepsis of imminent death provides an alternative form of lyric mourning and a heuristic of loss with which to query AIDS elegies in particular and AIDS mourning in general. Indeed, I've come to delineate the expression of compounding loss by paying close attention to how the spirituals formalize past and prospective loss, including how they employ a posthumous mood in grammar, privilege metonymy to figure proximate death, and devise a temporality of loss that dissolves the binaries in mourning. Paying such formal attention can give insight into not only how mourning works in *this* lyrical genre, but also how it might work in other forms of lyric mourning, especially in lyrics conceived amid a catastrophe. The spirituals' terms of loss then are generative in reading AIDS elegies across race. An African American poet, Dixon directly appropriates the spirituals to contemplate the AIDS crisis, so the intertextual relationship is evident; Monette, a white American poet, doesn't reference them at all, but still his lyrics can be discerned clearly following the calendar of loss formalized in the spirituals, forecasting the threat of death tomorrow.[26]

"NO ESCAPE, LIKE A HOSPITAL ROOM, OR INDEED A MORTAL ILLNESS"

Paul Monette's two memoirs, *Borrowed Time: An AIDS Memoir* and *Becoming a Man*; his book of poems, *Love Alone*; his two novels, *Afterlife* and *Halfway Home*; and his many essays constitute a rich body of work on the early era of AIDS. My focus here is on the *Love Alone* elegies and the prose preface that introduces them.[27]

Love Alone includes eighteen single-stanza poems with varying numbers of lines, all lacking verse breaks and punctuation marks, the spaces and symbols that order writing and disambiguate meaning. A torrent of words, or logorrhea, is the hallmark of *Love Alone*; this form makes demands on the reader to examine each poem word by word, line by line, in order to comprehend the otherwise undifferentiated outpouring of words. At times, disambiguation proves elusive: even as we imagine breaking up lines with punctuation marks and the long block of the poem into verses, several possibilities for understanding the poem remain. Each line requires the reader to reorient himself, since the tension between sentence and line is multiplied by the lack of punctuation, leading to evocative ambiguities and a headlong rush toward sorrow and rage. As the poem's logorrhea preempts any closure of meaning, it also encapsulates the poet's immediate experience of loss. In the preface to *Love Alone*, Monette explains: "I have let [the poems] stand as raw as they came. But because several friends have wished for a few commas or a stanza break here and there, I feel I should make a comment on their form. I don't mean them to be impregnable, though I admit I want them to allow no escape, like a hospital room, or indeed a mortal illness."[28] The poems' "impregnable" form is not an aesthetic end in itself, but rather a formal way of approximating the poet's immediate axis, the place and time of death around which his life rotates: "a hospital room, or indeed a mortal illness." That the very form of the poems stands in for a hospital room and a mortal illness gives them a meta-metonymic effect. Also, they enact the poet's will to survive through mourning. Says Monette: "These elegies were written during the five months after [Roger] died, one right after the other, with hardly a half day's pause between. Writing them quite literally kept me alive."[29] Like wailing and trembling, lyric mourning becomes an immediate, embodied response to death, the act by which the poet clings to life. "When Roger died," adds Monette in an interview, "I assumed that I would be dead in six months to a year. The burden of the poems that I wrote in those next six months—well, they were written truly as if I were going to be dead the next day."[30] And the exigency of such a calendar—in the wake of Roger's death, the poet's own death arriving "soon soon"—is palpable in *Love Alone*.

"Here," the first poem in the collection, finely illustrates Monette's poetics:

> everything extraneous has burned away
> this is how burning feels in the fall
> of the final year not like leaves in a blue
> October but as if the skin were a paper lantern
> full of trapped moths beating their fired wings
> and yet I can lie on this hill just above you
> a foot beside where I will lie myself
> soon soon and for all the wrack and blubber
> feel still how we were warriors when the
> merest morning sun in the garden was a
> kingdom after Room 1010 war is not all
> death it turns out war is what little
> thing you hold on to refugeed and far from home
> oh sweetie will you please forgive me this
> that every time I opened a box of anything
> Glad Bags One-A-Days KINGSIZE was
> the worst I'd think will you still be here
> when the box is empty Rog Rog who will
> play boy with me now that I bucket with tears
> through it all when I'd cling beside you sobbing
> you'd shrug it off with quietest I'm still
> here I have your watch in the top drawer
> which I don't dare wear yet help me please
> the boxes grocery home day after day
> the junk that keeps men spotless but it doesn't
> matter now how long they last or I
> the day has taken you with it and all

there is now is burning dark the only green
is up by the grave and this little thing
of telling the hill I'm here oh I'm here[31]

From the beginning, loss is aggregating. Monette makes the passing of his lover, who died in October, inextricable from his own impending death. What may appear to be the natural, cyclical figuration of death—a common trope of the genre, particularly the pastoral elegy, which symbolizes the passing of the seasons and the resumption of (normal) time—is undercut by a fixed date: "the final year." In "Here," the poet speaks, literally, from the site/sight of his future grave—"a foot beside where [he] will lie himself soon soon." Death is time-bound and, necessarily, a timed death impinges on the poem's figures and temporality. "[E]verything extraneous has burned away/this is how burning feels," begins Monette, using metaphors that evoke the poet's lost and diminishing world. And Monette pictures his body as a lantern with trapped moths, an image that evokes Kaposi's sarcoma lesions—pejoratively referred to as "AIDS lesions" early in the epidemic—which were among the signs by which a prejudiced public interpellated people with HIV/AIDS and consigned them to social death. But in "Here" as well as in other poems in *Love Alone*, Monette speaks of the KS lesions from an interior position—familiarly, as if gazing at them in the mirror, and intimately, as if touching them on his body. KS lesions are "scatterburst" in the poem "Black XMAS," "bruises like imploded orchids" in "Current Status 1/22/87"; and in *Borrowed Time: An AIDS Memoir*, he writes: "But I could see myself now that KS was something a good deal more dire than skin cancer, its lesions rooted deeper than bruises. They looked like exploded blood vessels under the skin, and sometimes they boiled to the surface like stunted orchids."[32] The lesions are purple not like flowers but bruises, colored not like "leaves in a blue October" but like damaged skin, a scatterburst not of stars or meteors in a dark sky but of lesions on the body. These self-portraits of the poet defamiliarize not only stock metaphors, but the figure of the elegist who has time and health—in short, tomorrow—on his side.

Because death is within reach, time becomes tactile. Monette cannot help but time death metonymically, including with the short lifespan of household goods: "every time I opened a box of anything/Glad Bags One-A-Days KING-SIZE was/the worst I'd think will you still be here/when the box is empty." But now that Roger has died, and the poet can foresee his own death, how does he keep time? With his world coming to an end "soon soon," how does he measure incoming death? On one hand, he shuns time altogether—"here I have your watch in the top drawer / which I don't dare wear yet help me please"—perhaps because of the fear that "putting on" a symbol of time may accelerate what is inevitable: his own ticking death. On the other hand, he characterizes the act of writing these elegies as a form of marking time and prolonging life. Recall the quote cited earlier: "These elegies were written during the five months after [Roger] died, one right after the other, with hardly a half day's pause between. Writing them quite literally kept me alive."[33] In *Love Alone*, there is palpable tension between the poet's determination to mark time and cling to life by writing elegies, and, having lost his lover, his resignation about his own death. As he says in "Here," it doesn't matter how long he lasts. Throughout the collection, there is a greedy plea for more time ("I am so rapacious of time") expressed alongside a resigned attitude toward death ("I put my house in order inch by inch if it comes when it comes").

Just as the timeline of death takes on this and/both dimension in "Here," so too does the space of loss. At the start of the poem, the speaker stands by the graveside of his lover, which he identifies also as "a foot beside where [he] will lie [himself] / soon soon." From there, the poem shifts to the hospital room and the home where Rog lay dying, before ending back again at the graveyard, the borrowed space that houses both the poet and his beloved. This spatial juxtaposition is also wrought by a string of repetitions—"soon soon," "1010," "Rog Rog" "I'm here oh I'm here"—that mirror and measure the two graves just "a foot" apart. The way the poem arrays side by side both existing and preexisting graves as *here* dissolves the absolute grammar that underwrites that word's sense of place or position. No longer adhering to an "either here or there" rule to define the space dividing the living and the dead, "here"—not fixed but a relative term—materializes instead an and/both position that the dead and the dying occupy together. Like the poem's logorrheic form, which forces us to pause with each line and reorient our place in the poem, the disorienting use of the term "here" also makes us pause and reorient our very grammar of space.

Other poems in *Love Alone* make clear the poet's calendar of illness. "Current Status 1/22/87," for instance, first depicts how contingent Monette's life has become, filled as it is with routine doctor visits and lab tests and the intake of pills "like clockwork." As the title puts it so matter-of-factly, the poem is an update on Monette's illness as of January 22, 1987, and it begins by detailing the changes in his vital signs over the several months leading up to that date:

marginal no change T-4 four-sixty-five
as of 12/8 but the labs are notoriously

inexact nerdy white-coat sits eyeballing
his microscope counts the squiggles in a cubic
inch racks them up on his abacus and writes
his apt # on the lab slip thus I'm fifteen
less than August thirty-five more than June
this is not statistically meaningful nor am I
the walking wounded do not count the counting
begins at breakthrough how are my lymph nodes
how are they not a mere three-quarters
centimeter at the neck in the vampire spot
cm and half in the armpit not suggestive[34]

Again, the lack of punctuation demands that we grapple with both the whole unit of the poem and each line as wholeness in order to figure out how the words are related and to discover the tensions between sentence and line. Numbers are the key sounds of this poem—4, four-sixty-five, 12/8, fifteen, thirty-five, three-quarters—as well as the key to the poet's precarious regimen, which includes measuring out and timing the intake of the pills that keep him alive. We gather that not much has changed since his last lab results and, from his body's T-cell count and the size of his lymph nodes, we also gather that his immune system, however compromised, is holding steady for now. Monette goes on to list his daily course of drugs, some that are a bulwark against infection and some to dull pain: "four hundred milligrams *ribavirin*"; "equal dose *acyclovir*/ditto twice a day"; "twenty milligrams *sinequan*"; "add fifteen milligrams *dalamane* 2 A.M. for/the final knock out not the same as sleep." Without a medical "breakthrough," the poet knows that the regimen of drugs currently available will keep him alive only for so long and that he, like his lover, may rapidly fall ill and suffer the onslaught of infections. Just as the will to survive is clear in his tally of life in these small measurements, so too is the feeling of resignation. In spite of the outpouring of numbers in the poem that index living, phrases and lines like "useless measures," "not statistically meaningful," "the walking wounded do not count," "my condition is just a prefix/my vast pharmacopoeia no more than a grave" cannot help but enumerate the poet's resignation about death.

Facing the daily realities of his own illness and life forced Monette to recall Roger's illness and death. Midway through "Current Status 1/22/87," the focus shifts from the poet's present regimen of tests and pills to the awful procedures Roger endured in the final stages of his illness. Monette recalls: "I watched you suffer the six/spinals three broncs your bone marrow sipped by/a ten-inch needle till you had enough numbers / to stump an algebra class." As these lines memorialize Roger's suffering in terms familiar and immediate, they also rack up the poet's presumed fate. Once the poem makes this shift, it cannot help but seesaw between the present and the past, between Monette's current status and Roger's final days:

> Rog I am still in the anteroom of all
> the useless measures leafing old *Peoples*
> reading diplomas deep in my head I hear you
> the night of the third intrusion your larynx
> like slush from an extra milliliter's freeze
> of *xylocaine* quelling your voice to a strangle
> for two three hours *Why is this happening*
> *I don't know* I said all the bells in my voice
> untarnished and thought how no one had better
> try to say why either or ever suppose
> to know the worst take my pills like clockwork
> because you took yours submit to the week's
> bleeding because you fought like Theseus[35]

This movement between the immediate past and the present is part of the poem's timeline of loss and helps to mark at once Roger's dying and death and Monette's illness and life. These temporal shifts are accompanied by shifts in the address of the poem as well. Like "Here" and many other poems in *Love Alone*, "Current Status 1/22/87" eventually turns into an apostrophe and addresses the dead directly, positioning Rog as the example by which the ill poet now conducts his life. But there is another hauntingly intimate dimension to Monette's apostrophes in *Love Alone*, since the poet is addressing the dead whom he is bracing to join "soon soon." Indeed, the lyric intimacy of *Love Alone* is founded on this tension between Monette addressing his lost lover and the fact that this is a *dying* poet calling out to the dead. Addressing both his deceased lover and his future grave, says the elegist in "Here": "I'm here oh I'm here." As a rhetorical device, apostrophe may tend to reinforce the distance between the living poet and the apostrophized dead, but, as we saw earlier, in the mouth of a death-bound poet, "oh" becomes a powerful moan to break down that barrier and bridge the space between the two.[36]

While the elegies in *Love Alone* express the poet's personal, twofold loss, the book's short preface sums up the collective character of this catastrophe. The preface situates Monette's loss amid the deaths of a generation of gay men and urges us to read his elegies—personal as they are—in the context of the AIDS epidemic, collective loss, mourning, and militancy. "I don't pretend to have written the anthem of my people," Monette cautions, but "if these words speak to anyone they are for those who are mad with loss."[37] He adds: "The story that endlessly eludes the decorum of the press is the death of a generation of gay men. . . . We will not be bowed or erased by this. I learned too well what it means to be a people."[38] The collective sense of self that guides the preface— "my people," "those who are mad with loss," "a generation of gay men," "we," "a people"—gives way to a private "I" in the elegies. While the preface signals the collective and political nature of AIDS loss, the elegies encapsulate that loss's personal effects. And yet, as the preface suggests, however much these poems center on the private world of specific lovers, they cannot help but echo the lives of a generation of gay men also contending with the ravages of AIDS.

Love Alone's preface also situates AIDS against the backdrop of another calamity, World War I, and positions Monette's AIDS elegies against the poems of that war. Monette begins the preface with an epigraph by Wilfred Owen, excerpted from Owen's intended preface to his Great War poems: "Above all I am not concerned with Poetry. My subject is War, and the pity of War. The Poetry is in the pity." Following this epigraph, Monette's preface begins in this way:

> Wilfred Owen's *Preface* to the poems he wrote in 1917 and 1918 is the best cau-
> tion I know against beauty and eloquence. He begs us not to read his anthem for
> the doomed youth of his generation as decorous celebration of heroes. Decorum
> is the contemptible pose of the politicians and preachers, the hypocrite slime
> whose grinning hatred slicks this dying land like rotten morning dew. I do not
> presume on the nightmare of Owen's war—may the boys of Flanders be spared all
> comparison—and I don't pretend to have written the anthem of my people. But
> I would rather have this volume filed under AIDS than under Poetry, because if
> these words speak to anyone they are for those who are mad with loss, to let them
> know they are not alone.[39]

Although Monette is careful not to presume on Owen's experience, nor to presume a comparison between the two catastrophes, he nevertheless draws on the words of a poet who elegized the casualties of another mass calamity without recourse to consolation.[40] In his preface, Owen was explicit about the inconsolable character of his elegies and the dangers of justifying the war in the name of one or another grand principle: "This book is not about heroes. English poetry is not yet fit to speak of them. Nor is it about deeds, or lands, not anything about glory, honor, might, majesty, dominion, or power, except War."[41]

Owen refused to use his war elegies as virtue lessons, to reify norms and institutions, or to provide consolation, since to do so would ultimately justify the deaths of millions in the name of something presumably more worthwhile, be it a cause, a deed, an ideal, a nation, or a god.

Owen privileged war over poetry, choosing to resist both poetry's inclination toward "beauty and eloquence," as Monette suggests, and the elegy's inclination toward consolation. An unprecedented event like the Great War demanded its own terms of articulation, terms unbounded by the literary, moral, and mourning codes of the past. Monette appropriated from Owen this provocative gesture, cataloging his poems under an event rather than a literary form. The gesture cautions against decorum, beauty, and eloquence in elegizing the AIDS dead, highlighting the significance of the disease's extraliterary—historical and political—context. Putting AIDS before poetry is imbued further with affective meaning. The gesture is willed by the poet's identification with, as he says, "those who are mad with loss," a collective bound together by grief and rage. It is out of this affective affinity, this solidarity, that Monette's poetic practice is born.

So far, I have discussed Monette's poems apart from race, using mainly the temporal terms of compounding loss. But even in the context of AIDS poetry, there are differences in substance and inflection between the kind of compounding loss expressed in Monette's work and the kind in Dixon's, as we will see. Their works share the calendar of loss that I have outlined, but Monette's underlying view of a pre-AIDS America that was idyllic differs significantly from Dixon's. When Monette looks to other calamities to make meaning of his own, for instance, he goes exclusively to European theaters of war and examples of genocide—Verdun, Ypres, Warsaw, Bergen-Belsen, and Buchenwald. And meanwhile, the American past we glean from the *Love Alone* poems, unlike Europe's, is unscathed by war or any other calamity; it is instead the stage for the poet's blissful life before AIDS. As John Clum has aptly observed, a leitmotif of many white gay AIDS narratives, including Monette's work, is "the encroachment of AIDS on the American dream of beauty, affluence, and immortality."[42] Drawing on an example from *Love Alone*, Clum writes, "Paul Monette's memory in his poem, 'Half Life' that 'once I had it all' refers not only to his beloved Rog, now dead from HIV-related infections, but also to the affluent world he and Rog once luxuriously shared. That world now seems invaded, compromised as AIDS throws into question the values of the 1970s, what Paul Monette calls 'the time before the war.'"[43] Monette's nostalgia for "the time before the war" isn't simply a longing for the sexual freedoms that defined the years between Stonewall

and AIDS, the immediate years after the beginning of the gay liberation movement that saw extraordinary changes in gay life and culture. His nostalgia is also
for the American ideal—of youth, success, affluence, and happy domesticity—
that Monette and Roger embodied before the onslaught of AIDS. What's no longer recoverable, as Monette says in "The Very Same," are "our BMWs our zest
for / winning and half-acre closets," which are now rendered meaningless amid
mounting deaths. And in "Current Status 1/22/87," ironically he laments his
"vast pharmacopoeia" of drugs, which were prohibitively expensive to amass in
the early days of AIDS and which turn out to be "no more than a grave." Also, in
Borrowed Time, Monette's red jaguar is emplotted as if a character, signaling all
the ways in which the poet and his lover had achieved a picture-perfect life of
wealth and status, which was unraveled by AIDS. As Clum says, "The invasion
of the home of Paul Monette and Roger Horwitz by HIV is not only an invasion
of one loving couple, one household, or of gay culture; it is an invasion of the
American dream itself."[44]

Nostalgia for the American dream is uncharacteristic of Dixon's poems and
black poetry more generally. Given how marred America has been with black
death and suffering, black lyric subjectivity has had little recourse in that kind
of nostalgia. Longing for an ideal American past is chief among the affects of
American whiteness, an innocence that helps to evacuate the history of America
as catastrophe. The clear break that AIDS seems to mark for Monette, between
an ideal past and a catastrophic present, is hard to find in black gay AIDS writing, which places AIDS, extraordinary as it is, along a continuum of black death
and disenfranchisement in the United States. As Dixon points out in his keynote speech at *OutWrite '92*, the experience of being disprized is part and parcel
of black life, however new it was to gays who had sought and found protection in
their whiteness: "Some of you may have never before been treated like second-
class, disposable citizens. Some of you have felt a certain privilege and protection in being white."[45] But, amid this calamity, Dixon says provocatively, "we are
the sexual niggers of our society."[46] Dixon collapses the before-and-after AIDS
paradigm common in white AIDS narratives; by way of a single term, he forces
us to think about AIDS and the discarding of gay lives not as an aberration or
an exception, but as something that finds precedent in the long history of black
death and disparagement, a history encapsulated in that word, *nigger*. As Karla
Holloway writes, "Black folk died in mournful collectives and in disconcerting
circumstances. We died in riots and rebellions, as victims of lynchings, from
executions, murders, police violence, suicides, and untreated or undertreated
diseases. In such deaths, being black selected the victim into a macabre frater-

nity."[47] James Baldwin says: "I know how you watch as you grow older, literally, this is not a figure of speech, the corpses of your brothers and your sisters pile up around you, and not for anything they have done, they were too young to have done anything, in any case too helpless."[48] Of course, I don't mean to set up an easy binary between "black" and "white" mourning, or to romanticize black suffering—no. Instead, I am suggesting that, given the persistence of death in black collective life and imagination, black AIDS mourners, including well-to-do poets like Dixon, rarely thought of AIDS as an isolated calamity, but rather saw it as one in a series of calamities that characterized their people and their country.

"UNTIL THERE'S NO ONE LEFT TO COUNT"

Melvin Dixon had found his voice as an author prior to his AIDS writing. Before his premature death, Dixon had published two novels, *Trouble the Water* and *Vanishing Rooms*; a book of literary criticism, *Ride Out the Wilderness: Geography and Identity in Afro-American Literature*; and a book of poems, *Change of Territory*; and he had translated Geneviève Fabre's *Drumbeats, Masks, and Metaphor: Contemporary Afro-American Theatre* and *Léopold Sédar Senghor: The Collected Poetry*. His final work was *Love's Instruments*, a collection of poems and the speech he delivered at *OutWrite '92*, which was published posthumously. This is a sweeping and indispensable body of work, replete with insights into race, sexuality, geography, diaspora, and translation. And in his last book Dixon tallies the mounting deaths around him and measures the close interface between death and life.

Love's Instruments doesn't have a signature form that easily distinguishes it (like the logorrhea in Monette's poems), but in the book's third and last section, the elegies are imbued with recollections of illness and mortality. In these powerful poems, Dixon consistently figures himself as a double mourner, grieving the deaths of others and his own approaching death; and in some he employs African American spirituals to convey his own sense of dying. Here are excerpts from three different poems—"Just Us, at Home," "Wednesday Mourning," and "Heartbeats"—that show how the speaker of the poem identifies his tenuous position as a dying elegist:

His cough now such a part of speech
it is language between us.

When we touch, our bones clatter and clang,
this new music the only song we sing.

Our skeleton dance, our silent screams. ("Just Us, at Home")

My eyes tell it: someone
upstairs inside me is dying
not the first death. ("Wednesday Mourning")

Breathe in. Breathe out.
No air. No air.

Thin blood. Sore lungs.
Mouth dry. Mind gone.

Six months? Three weeks?
Can't eat. No air.

Today? Tonight?
It waits. For me.

Sweet heart, Don't stop.
Breathe in. Breathe out. ("Heartbeats")[49]

Despite the individuality of each poem—despite the differences in form, tone, argument, and personality—there emerges a common portrait of a lyric subject who is experiencing multiple losses: in the first poem, one who draws his "part of speech" and "language" metonymically from the sounds of illness, the "cough" we hear in the enjambment between "part of speech / it is language," and the "silent screams"; in the second excerpt, whose gaze reflects the experience of having witnessed serial deaths; and in the third, who is timing death and measuring the beat of a poem not in weeks or years, but in a rhythm that replicates those felt in the body—heartbeats and breathing. We also gather that this lyric subject is determined to survive. In "Heartbeats," for instance, by reinventing time as a unit of determined bodily function—the two-beat staccato of inhaling and exhaling or of the titular heartbeat—the poet not only extends his lifetime by measuring it in tiny units, but also reclaims sovereignty over his ailing body. Indeed, he gives the lyric voice over to the body, which sounds its agency with heartbeats, breathing, coughs, and screams.

"One by One" is a remarkable poem that shows Dixon's use of spirituals to elegize the AIDS dead and living. He borrows its slowly diminishing refrain, "many thousands gone," from a spiritual that clearly expresses compounding loss. The spiritual—sometimes titled after its refrain, "Many Thousands Gone," other times after its first line, "No More Auction Block"—boldly articulates the insurgent yearnings of slaves. As Richard Newman says, "perhaps no spiritual speaks more directly to the slave experience than ['No More'] because it does not even attempt to hide or code its meaning."[50]

> No more auction block for me
> No more, no more
> No more auction block for me
> Many thousands gone[51]

In subsequent stanzas, the spiritual enumerates the everyday violence that constituted slavery, violence against which the insurgent imperative "no more" is boldly reiterated: "No more peck of corn for me," "No more pint of salt for me," "No more driver's lash for me," "No more hundred lash for me," "No more, no more." This song is remarkable because, in addition to naming and rejecting the forms and "scenes of subjection" that characterize slavery—including auction blocks, whippings, and meager rations—it enumerates this holocaust's casualties indeterminably as *many* thousands gone, not unlike Toni Morrison's accounting of slavery's innumerable dead as "Sixty Million *and more.*"[52]

In "One by One," Dixon takes advantage of the indeterminable, hauntingly elliptical figure of the spiritual and diminishes it further to zero—or amplifies it to infinity. The poem reads:

> The children in the life:
> Another telephone call. Another man gone.
> How many pages are left in my diary?
> Do I have enough pencils? Enough ink?
> I count on my fingers and toes the past kisses,
> the incubating years, the months ahead.
>
> *Thousands. Many thousands*
> *Many thousands gone.*
>
> I have no use for numbers beyond this one,
> one man, one face, one torso
> curled into mine for the ease of sleep.
> We love without mercy.
> We live bravely in the light.
>
> *Thousands. Many thousands.*
>
> Chile, I knew he was funny, one of the children,
> a member of the church, a friend of Dorothy's.

He knew the Websters pretty well, too.
Girlfriend, he was real.
Remember we used to sit up in my house
pouring tea, dropping beads,
dishing this one and that one?

You got any T-cells left?
The singularity of death. The mounting thousands.
It begins with one and grows by one
and one and one and one
until there's no one left to count.[53]

The refrain "many thousands gone" appears initially after the first stanza of the poem, as if trailing its spiritual counterpart: "Thousands. Many thousands / Many thousands gone"; after the second stanza, Dixon worries the line and prunes it down to just the numbers, "Thousands. Many thousands." Finally, in the last stanza, it turns into a new figure altogether: "and one and one and one / until there's no one left to count." The fatalism in the last line may not thwart but certainly calls into question Christian eschatology, the redemption to be had in God's ultimate judgment, which the spirituals collectively prized. In fact, the only consolation Dixon's poem idealizes—"We love without mercy. / We live bravely in the light"—is rooted in fierce loving and living in this dystopic world.[54]

Despite the turn away from Christian eschatology, Dixon adopts the spirituals' apprehension of past and proximate death, incalculable loss, and insurgent mourning. Perhaps it is more apt to call this kind of appropriation a translation—a practice that Dixon defines in another context as the "ability to understand what the work is about, and to imagine another life for that work."[55] I find it productive to think of "One by One" in part as a translation of the spiritual "Many Thousands Gone," since Dixon's poem imagines another life for its precursor and also since imbued in the work of translation is another meaning: reburying the dead. To translate is to "express the sense of (words or text) in another language," "convert or be converted into (another form or medium)," "move from one place or condition to another," and "remove (a saint's relics [i.e., remains]) to another place."[56] Translation's overlapping meanings characterize the intertextual relationship between Dixon's elegy and the spiritual— more than other conceptual terms like "transposition" or "appropriation"— because the word "translation" also conveys the act of carrying the dead from one place (or context) to another. To express his own immediate sense of loss,

Dixon translates the lyrics of slaves, mourning the AIDS dead in an elegiac context that also includes the slave dead.

"One by One," like its antecedent, is decidedly about the disprized. Not only does the first line call out "The children in the life," black vernacular for queer folk, it also promises (with a colon) to take inventory of their lives, which it begins to do, one by one, through a range of speech acts, including questions, gossip, "pouring tea," and testimony. And what's being tallied, we discover quickly, are the incalculable deaths of gay men, including the elegizing subject. The mourning subject's position is inextricable from the objects of loss, and his own "incubating years" are inextricable from the poem's timetable. The poem begins interrogatively, by asking if material and corporeal means of measurement suffice in tallying the incoming calls of death: are the amount of pages, pencils, and ink in his reach and the number of fingers and toes on his body enough to count the dead? We find an answer to this question in the last stanza, as we are abruptly introduced to two new figures—one quantifiable, one unquantifiable—that sum up the inventory of the poem. "You got any T-cells left?" is a jarring question and a jarring figure, since it quantifies mortality by hailing (rhetorically or as direct address) someone whose immune system has deteriorated to the point of bare life. However, unlike a person's T-cell count, which is finite, the second figure—"It begins with one and grows by one/and one and one and one/until there's no one left to count"—exceeds measurement as it calculates the mounting deaths. The immediate juxtaposition of these two figures—one going down and measuring the singular death of a person, the other going up and measuring the collective death of a group—is another incisive formulation of the schema of loss at work in early AIDS elegies.

Dixon's only prose piece in *Love's Instruments*, "I'll Be Somewhere Listening for My Name," which is also the title of a spiritual, demonstrates uses of the spirituals in representing AIDS loss. "I'll Be Somewhere Listening for My Name" is adapted from a keynote address that Dixon delivered—shortly before his death in October 1992—at *OutWrite '92* in Boston, the third annual lesbian and gay writers conference. Again, Dixon translates a spiritual to figure his immediate world, drawing on the insight into proximate death and proleptic mourning that the spirituals provide. At the same time, he withdraws the authority of "calling" that the spiritual endows to God—"When *He* calls me, I will answer/I'll be somewhere listening for my name"—and transfers that power to a worldly audience. After repeating "I'll be somewhere listening for my name" six times in the course of the essay, Dixon reveals at the very end: "I come to you bearing witness to a broken heart; I come to you bearing witness to a broken body—but a witness to an unbroken spirit. Perhaps it is *only* to you that such witness can be brought and its jagged edges softened a bit and made meaningful."[57] Dixon charges his audience with the responsibility and power of calling the dead, and he powerfully illustrates how one goes about doing that. He starts by calling out the names of his lover and many deceased friends: "[Richard] is everywhere inside me listening for his name," "And George is somewhere listening for his name, hearing it among us," "And Greg is somewhere listening for his name," and, ultimately, he adds his own name to the roster:

> As for me . . . I may not be well enough or alive next year to attend the lesbian and gay writers conference, but I'll be somewhere listening for my name. I may not be around to celebrate with you the publication of gay literary history. But I'll be somewhere listening for my name. If I don't make it to Tea Dance in Provincetown or the Pines, I'll be somewhere listening for my name. You, then, are charged by the possibility of your good health, by the broadness of your vision, to remember us.[58]

As he calls the names of the dead, Dixon positions himself among their company. Although alive, he speaks retrospectively, in a posthumous mood, from an anticipated world of the dead. Dixon's proleptic last words in "I'll be somewhere," and the larger enterprise of remembering past and prospective deaths, echo the poem "And These Are Just a Few . . ." discussed above, which ends with the same imperative and poetics of compounding loss: "This poem is for the epidemic living and the dead. / Remember them, remember me."[59]

Both Dixon and Monette include themselves in their poems' roster of the dead, and do so often by using a particular figure of speech: metonymy, a figure of contiguity. Contrast their rhetoric and sense of time with two other remarkable examples of AIDS mourning, expressed from a subject position that differs from Dixon's and Monette's. Let us consider first Jamaica Kincaid's *My Brother*, a memoir in which Kincaid mourns the death of her younger brother, Devon, who died in 1996 of AIDS complications. In these two clear-eyed observations, Kincaid struggles to find a figure of speech for dying and death:

> I entered the house and stood in the doorway of the room in which he was lying. The house had a funny smell, as if my mother no longer had time to be the immaculate housekeeper she had always been and so some terrible dirty thing had gone unnoticed and was rotting away quickly. It was only after he was dead and no longer in the house and the smell was no longer there that I knew what the smell really was, and now as I write this, I cannot find a simile for this smell, it was not a smell like any I am familiar with. . . .

And when I saw my brother for the last time, alive, in that way he was being alive (dead really, but still breathing, his chest moving up and down, his heart beating like something, beating like something, but what, but what, there was no metaphor, his heart was beating like his own heart, only it was beating barely).[60]

Kincaid resists stock metaphors to characterize her brother's dying and makes a much more compelling observation by refusing to substitute other referents for dying and death. In the first excerpt, death defies easy equation, because the author's olfactory memory cannot register it: the smell of a dying body is unfamiliar to her. In the second example, dying again defies description; Kincaid searches for an intermediary for the faintly beating heart—"like something, but what, but what"—only to boomerang back to the same, barely beating heart. These examples of metaphoric aphasia express a limitation Kincaid faces—a limitation made negligible in the writings of death-bound poets like Dixon and Monette, who, as they write, are also voicing their own ailing bodies. Although Kincaid observes her brother's death with enormous care and insight, she does not occupy the same subject position from which Dixon and Monette observe loss. These keenly self-reflexive moments in Kincaid's book highlight how, as mourners, our subject position—by which I mean simply our nearness to our own death—determines our rhetoric and our calendar of loss. Kincaid underlines this very point as she reflects on the difference between her brother's and her own temporal relationship to death: "His death was imminent and we were all anticipating it, including him, but we never gave any thought to the fact that this was true for all of us, too: our death was imminent, only we were not anticipating it . . . yet."[61] The unbounded, unspecified sense of future time that ". . . yet" holds for Kincaid is no longer meaningful for mourners like Dixon and Monette, whose lives and writing are circumscribed by timed death and who draw their parts of speech from their own terminally ill bodies.

Like Kincaid's memoir, Marie Howe's elegies for her brother John, who died of AIDS-related illness in 1989, are a different type of AIDS mourning, illustrating the notable distinction between AIDS grief expressed from the vantage point of a living elegist as opposed to a dying one. In the title poem of her powerful book *What the Living Do*, for instance, the speaker of the poem enacts living by drawing consolation from the very ordinariness of everyday life, from the quotidian rituals that concretize her own aliveness in the wake of her brother's death. The poem "What the Living Do" reads:

Johnny, the kitchen sink has been clogged for days, some utensil probably
    fell down there.

And the Drano won't work but smells dangerous, and the crusty dishes
    have piled up

waiting for the plumber I still haven't called. This is the everyday we
    spoke of.
It's winter again: the sky's a deep headstrong blue, and the sunlight
    pours through

the open living room windows because the heat's on too high in here, and
    I can't turn it off.
For weeks now, driving, or dropping a bag of groceries in the street,
    the bag breaking,

I've been thinking: This is what the living do. And yesterday, hurrying
    along those
wobbly bricks in the Cambridge sidewalk, spilling my coffee down my
    wrist and sleeve,

I thought it again, and again later, when buying a hairbrush: This is it.
Parking. Slamming the car door shut in the cold. What you called
    that yearning.

What you finally gave up. We want the spring to come and the winter to
    pass. We want
whoever to call or not to call, a letter, a kiss—we want more and more and
    then more of it.

But there are moments, walking, when I catch a glimpse of myself in the
    window glass,
say, the window of the corner video store, and I'm gripped by a cherishing
    so deep

for my own blowing hair, chapped face, and unbuttoned coat that I'm
    speechless:
I am living, I remember you.[62]

The power of the poem rests on its reclamation of the everyday as a source of consolation. The unremarkable, mundane routines of the day—house chores, grocery shopping, driving, parking—spark intense self-reflection and self-awareness, reminding the poet that she is indeed alive and able to conduct her life, which her brother can do no more. Living, in and of itself, provides consolation precisely in its capacity to chart a horizon of future time where the repetition of the everyday is possible: the time ahead that will allow the poet to carry on her day-to-day affairs, anticipate the coming and passing of seasons, and, by virtue of living, continue to remember her beloved dead. The act of repetition, the poem reminds us, is essential to living—"again, and again later," "more and more and / then more," "This is the everyday," "This is what the living do," "This is it." The repetition requires an unbounded ". . . yet"—time for living and for consolation's fulfillment. As Sacks has rightly observed, it's by way of repetition that elegists often normalize their world of loss, since "repetition creates a sense of continuity, of an unbroken pattern such as one may oppose to the extreme discontinuity of death. Time itself is thereby structured to appear as [a] familiar, filled-in medium rather than an open-ended source of possible catastrophe."[63] Repetition and time may certainly work in this way for an elegist for whom the future is an ally, but for death-bound poets, for whom time is indeed "an open-ended source of possible catastrophe," the nature of repetition radically changes to figure the seamless relationship between the dead and the dying poet. For poets like Dixon and Monette, repetition becomes an indispensable rhetorical way to rehearse their own approaching deaths and to serialize the more and more and more deaths that characterize their proximate kinship ties to other queer men amid the AIDS crisis.

Compounding death does not loom over life's everyday demands in Howe's poem, in other words, as it does in Dixon's and Monette's. The everyday becomes a source of possible comfort in "What the Living Do" since there is a clear separation between the poem's speaker and its addressee, between the lyric subject and its object of mourning, between the speaker who is "gripped by a cherishing / so deep" and Johnny, for whom "that yearning" for life's everyday prospects has been thwarted. Whereas an elegy like Dixon's "And These Are Just a Few . . ." ends by incorporating the "epidemic living" into the poem's inventory of loss—"Remember them, remember me"—dissolving the difference between the living and the dead, Howe's poem builds that difference throughout and culminates with the evocative last line, "I am living, I remember you."

These two powerful examples, Kincaid's memoir and Howe's poem, attest to the difference between AIDS mourning fashioned by the living and the mourning fashioned by "the epidemic living" or the "still/here," as Bill T. Jones puts it. What distinguishes the poetics of AIDS elegists like Dixon and Monette is their immediate relationship to death, a fact that outweighs other markers of identity in their lyrics. This is precisely why paying close attention to the poetics of AIDS mourning can help to undermine protocols of reading that bank on an overarching identity—say, race or sexuality—to do all the critical work. A "middle passage epistemology," for instance, might lead us to hail together Dixon and Kincaid on the basis of race, and have racial nationalism do all the critical work.[64] Race matters, no doubt about that, but not in the ways we expect it to, which is one reason that I have aligned Dixon's and Monette's poetry with the spirituals: to index how the early AIDS experience placed those living with AIDS, regardless of race, in a situation resembling slavery's ubiquity of the dead. This is also why, however briefly, I align Howe and Kincaid: to illustrate how their shared subjectivity—namely, living—governs their aesthetics of mourning. In the wake of AIDS loss, mourners like Howe and Kincaid, with tomorrow on their side, will themselves to continue living in their work of mourning, whereas those facing impending death, like Dixon and Monette and much like the bards of the spirituals, will themselves to die there.

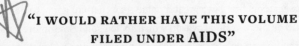"I WOULD RATHER HAVE THIS VOLUME FILED UNDER AIDS"

In "Boon and Burden: Identity in Contemporary Poetry," a 2004 essay about writing and reading poems, the poet Carl Phillips cautions against, on one hand, poetry that wears on its sleeve a particular group identity and, on the other, reading poetry through the prism of autobiography or any other context external to the poem. For much of the essay, Phillips argues against poetry that privileges racial identity—like work by Amiri Baraka and other poets of the black arts movement—since this type of art is exclusionary, fails to transcend the particular identity of the poet, and also fails to resonate with readers whose identity is not the one idealized in the poem. Alternatively, he praises poetry that is not overdetermined by race but instead uses race as mere background, as an instrument to "focus on our more generally human selves,"[65] like the work of Robert Hayden, Yusef Komunyakaa, and Rita Dove, which, Phillips argues, has broader resonance and a more lasting effect because group identity is not the prized subject of their lyrics. Phillips also argues against exegesis that privileges contextual information in order to discern a poem's meaning: readings of poems should be guided not by extratextual context, but by the poem itself. Phillips's advocacy of formalist reading is not new, of course, and in many ways shares the underpinnings of New Criticism. While I am sympathetic to the argument that we should consider poems closely and on their own terms, I find it counterproductive to jettison context, especially given the range of critical modes of inquiry that illuminate how context matters. Context can help to inform, texture, and enrich our experience of reading and interpretation and make us self-reflexive readers, aware of the subject position from which we appraise any work of art.

I bring up this essay not because I wish to rehash the debate over formalist versus contextualist approaches to reading, but because Phillips, in a single paragraph, makes a claim about AIDS poetry and its merits that warrants examination:

> Lest I seem to be confining my argument to African American poetry, I should say that there are parallels to be found in what has come to be considered the poetry of AIDS. AIDS poetry—like Black Arts poetry—has and will continue to have its value (all poetry has value, even when its value is only one of reminding us of what good poetry is not). I suspect that AIDS poetry will be valuable as documentation of, and witness to, the effects of a particular plague on a particular time in human history. Those poems that have greater value than that are going to be the ones that see AIDS as mere context within which to see something more timelessly true about the human condition, namely, that we all come to know death in at least two ways eventually: by losing others to it, and by succumbing, in time, ourselves to the fact of death; reckoning with that act is a crucial part of what it means to be alive.[66]

Phillips is dismissive of AIDS poetry not only in the substance of his argument but also in the way he brings it into the discussion. Whether or not one agrees with him about the uses of race in African American poetry, at least it is an argument buttressed by close readings of several poems, whereas his assessment of AIDS poetry is not supported by a single example. Instead, readers are asked to surmise what AIDS poetry is only derivatively: by way of the simile that "AIDS poetry—*like* Black Arts poetry" is a devalued form. Phillips's claim about the value of AIDS poetry seems untenable since it hinges on not the actual terms of AIDS poems, but on a series of binary formulations that mystify "poetry" and "the human condition": poetry/documentation, timeless/timebound, universal/particular, and so on. I find a paradigm of reading built on such freighted binaries misguided, and what I have sought to do in this book is to analyze the terms of AIDS poetry as closely as possible and to contemplate the particular perspective of mourning that they issue—a perspective, it turns out, that upends the binary ways we have come to think about loss and the elegy form. Phillips is right that "we all come to know death in at least two ways eventually: by losing others to it, and by succumbing, in time, ourselves to the fact of death." But if we sharpen our focus in reading Dixon's and Monette's poetry, we see that the two ways of knowing death so interpenetrate, and the line be-tween losing others and losing oneself becomes so tenuous, that as critics we must seek new ways of conceptualizing loss and poetry that exceed the familiar arguments.

And I wonder: why wouldn't poetry that is a "documentation of, and wit-ness to, the effects of a particular plague on a particular time in human history" resonate as "generally human" in a world devastated by this epidemic? Given the pervasiveness of AIDS deaths—and of plagues and catastrophes in human affairs—why wouldn't AIDS poetry speak to readers across time and place? And why couldn't the particular expression of a disprized group like AIDS mourners resonate universally in a world full of disparaged peoples? Poetry is not mere documentation: it's an art form. And by no means do I wish to mini-mize the *art* of poetry. Nonetheless, we discover more when we consider the art of poems in relation to context, whether that context is generic, historical, political, or personal. As Cavitch points out in his study of the American elegy, for instance, we gain new insights when we consider the cultural and political work elegies perform: the way in which elegies, as works of mourning and com-memoration, participate in the political work of creating ideal or memorable subjects of the nation and narration. The elegy, writes Cavitch, is "an especially politicized genre in the double sense of being 'on the spot' for history: not only present to witness . . . but also implicated in ongoing social struggles over mem-ory and meaning. Elegies seek to extend the lives of individuals and of groups, augmenting personal remembrance and collective heritage."[67] Certainly, whom we choose to elegize, especially whom we elegize collectively and publicly, is an enterprise full of political significance, and we cannot underestimate the politi-cal work that early AIDS elegies carried out, given the general context of silence, indifference, and omission that enveloped the disease at that time. As Zeiger underscores, "the genre of AIDS elegies import[s] a communal politics and an overriding sense of shared catastrophe into the sphere of poetic production."[68] Context matters.

Although his poems bear witness to the personal grief of losing his lover and his own life, Monette stresses that his elegies cannot help but address the broader political context that rendered immaterial the mass deaths of gay men. Monette writes: "The story that endlessly eludes the decorum of the press is the death of a generation of gay men. What is written here is only one man's pass-ing and one man's cry, a warrior burying a warrior. May it fuel the fire of those on the front lines who mean to prevail, and of their friends who stand in the fire with them."[69] He adds: "I don't pretend to have written the anthem of my people. But I would rather have this volume filed under AIDS than under Poetry, because if these words speak to anyone they are for those who are mad with loss, to let them know they are not alone."[70] The immediate, interventionist yearnings of these elegies are clear. They value and articulate what the public deemed insignificant and unspeakable. They are also meant to affirm, encourage, and embolden those fighting for survival. Indeed, Monette's provocative statement to catalog his poems "under AIDS" befits the catastrophic context in which his poems were born. The poems call us as readers to take seriously as well the legitimacy of mourning as an effective instrument of collective action. Amid this catastrophe, to echo Douglas Crimp's words, "mourning *becomes* militancy."[71] Although AIDS elegists "are intensely aware of the tropes and dynamics of traditional elegy," as Zeiger notes, "they deliberately revise them in an attempt to write the dead—and the circumstances of their deaths—into the cultural narrative."[72] Certainly, Dixon and Monette achieve this important revision of the elegy, and in doing so, they inscribe the particular circumstances of the disprized and the death-bound, like the bards of the spirituals, into the work of lyric mourning.

two

A new wave of writing and art by and about black gay men emerged in the mid-1980s. Joseph Beam's *In the Life: A Black Gay Anthology*, Essex Hemphill's *Brother to Brother: New Writings by Black Gay Men*, two literary volumes edited by the black gay writers collective Other Countries, and two more on black gay poetry edited by Assotto Saint—these were the anthologies that inaugurated this renaissance. The poems of Essex Hemphill and Melvin Dixon and the films of Marlon Riggs and Isaac Julien were also key in articulating the experiences of black gay men, while plays like Pomo Afro Homos' *Fierce Love: Stories of Black Gay Life* and one-person performances like Assotto Saint's *Black Fag* embodied those experiences on the American stage. This wave of art represented a self-conscious renaissance that reaffirmed the existence of black gay men as individuals and as a collective group. Yet this was a short-lived renaissance, thwarted by the ravages of AIDS. A decade later, by 1995, many of the movement's defining figures, including Beam, Dixon, Hemphill, Riggs, and Saint, would be dead of AIDS-related illnesses.

Marlon Riggs's 1989 documentary film, *Tongues Untied*, is perhaps the most widely recognized of this body of work. It employs Riggs's signature montage style, mixing together poetry, song, dance, and performance. Mixing forms allows Riggs to punctuate the main narrative of the film, his personal coming-of-age story as a black gay man, with narratives of other black gay men. The film was unprecedented in its candid, unapologetic portrayal of black queer life, and it quickly earned Riggs critical acclaim and won numerous awards and prizes. It also earned him conservative outrage. Politicians like Jesse Helms and Pat Buchanan made the film the focus of their national campaigns against homosexuality and government funding of the arts. Conservative pundits also condemned the film: "*Tongues Untied*, innocently described as a documentary program about black homosexuals, is without doubt the most explicit, profane program ever broadcast by a television network," decried one editorial in the *Atlanta Constitution*.[1] Another in the *Washington Times* went further to suggest that the film belonged in "the bawdy leather bars that litter such gay havens as Castro Street in San Francisco and Christopher Street in New York, but not on public television. Unless the 'P' in PBS now stands for 'Pornographic.'"[2] The obscenity charges against the film were a pretext for the underlying issue that outraged so many conservatives: the national broadcasting of a film that was unabashedly black and queer. Responding to the outpouring of both support and opposition, Riggs observed that "for many this was the real outrage of *Tongues Untied*, and for many, many more, its principal virtue: the refusal to present an historically disparaged community on bended knee, begging courteously for tidbits of mainstream tolerance. What *Tongues* instead unapologetically affirms and delivers is a frank, uncensored, uncompromising articulation of an autonomously defined self and social identity. SNAP!"[3]

Riggs and his film both embody the imperatives of a new black queer counterpublic, whose aims were to assert *publicly* a self-determined black queer identity hitherto excluded from mainstream American culture and from mainstream black and gay subcultures. What Robert Reid-Pharr says of Riggs in his memorial to the filmmaker is also true of several of Riggs's contemporaries, who had "most importantly the courage to speak, to assert the reality of our existence, to cry, 'I am.'"[4] Hence, while a politics of recognition was central to this renaissance, so too was a politics of mourning, as Reid-Pharr's "In Memoriam" suggests. Given that this artistic movement emerged amid the AIDS crisis, its urgent calls for public recognition of black gay life were fused with cries of mourning. Riggs made two films that focused directly on AIDS: *Non, Je Ne Regrette Rien (No Regret)* and *Black Is . . . Black Ain't*, the former focused on the stories of five HIV-positive black gay men, the latter on his own looming death. But even *Tongues Untied*, a film about asserting the *existence* of black gay men, ends with a haunting scene of death and dying. And, to be sure, conservative outrage over the film was meant to stifle not only the self-expression of black gay men on American mass media, but also the broadcasting of their grief over AIDS deaths.

In *Tongues Untied*'s final scene, Riggs synchronizes the sound of a ticking clock and the images of obituaries of black men. The scene begins with a regular pace, an image per second, but then it begins to move faster and faster—so fast that we are unable to keep up a count of the death notices that appear on the screen. After more than thirty obituaries pass, Riggs breaks up the inventory with words about his own pending death: "Faces, friends disappear. I watch, I wait. I watch, I wait. I listen for my own quiet implosion. But while I wait, older, stronger rhythms resonate within me, sustain my spirit, silence the clock."[5] With this ending, *Tongues Untied* presents a clear portrait of the calendar of AIDS loss, death after death, in rapid succession and in contracted spans of time—an inventory that concretizes for Riggs the devastation in his own life and in the lives of countless others like him. Additionally, this scene represents how queer artists and communities arrogated to themselves the authority of the obituary during the early era of AIDS. Queering the obituary and appropriating its powers to grieve gay men who died of AIDS had major formal and extraformal implications: queer obituaries changed the heteronormative underpinnings of the genre and also challenged the nation's interdiction on AIDS loss and queer mourning. What I call "normative" AIDS obituaries—short death notices typically provided by the deceased's family, as well as journalistic obituaries issued by mainstream newspapers—reified the silence around AIDS, often by omitting or censoring three related claims: the deceased's (homo)sexuality, the cause of death from AIDS, and the same-sex lovers or partners who were survivors. In contrast, queer AIDS obituaries upended these interdictions, issuing unpoliced death notices that accounted for AIDS and queer loss, kinship and survival.

Of course, the obituary is an intrinsically political genre, geared toward the dead who are prized, the dead who matter, who have public merit, who are worthy of collective grief and commemoration. As critical studies of the genre point out, the obituary is a popular form of mourning that buttresses the nation with a steady supply of ideal subjects of collective grief and memory.[6] Queer artists and activists in the 1980s and '90s understood full well the authority of the obituary and its uses, and the archive of early AIDS mourning displays a radical appropriation of the genre, transforming it into a forum for—and record of—queer feelings and politics. The crowded obituary pages of gay periodicals like the *New York Native*, ACT UP's mass mailing campaign of AIDS obituaries to the White House, and the work of the artist and activist Assotto Saint all testify that the obituary was an instrumental genre, helping to record and reconstitute the new queer counterpublics that emerged at the time, including the revitalized movement of black gay art and activism that Riggs and Saint helped to define. In this chapter, I consider the different iterations of queer obituaries, beginning with how queer communities broadly deployed the obituary, then centering on how Saint used the form to archive the lives and deaths of several friends. Also, I read Saint's death notices along with Thomas Glave's short story "The Final Inning," which was inspired by an incident that Saint, in his last months of life, recounted to Glave. A story about a funeral, "The Final Inning" draws on the same imperatives of queer obituaries and recreates in fiction the relationship between the rites of the living and the rights of the dead. Since the obituary remains a widely popular form of literary mourning and of public grief and commemoration, part of the aim of this chapter is also to identify a critical way of reading this important genre, as it took on new life and urgency in the early era of AIDS.

THE QUEER OBITUARY AND ITS USES

An obituary is by definition a public (usually published) announcement and record of someone's death. In stripped-down form, it lists the name of the deceased, where and when he died, where he lived, and the surviving kin. The cause of death and funeral arrangements may also appear in shorter notices. Longer, narrative obituaries also include this essential information, but furthermore they can draw evocative portraits of the lives of the deceased. And like their length, the tone and style of obituaries range widely. Some death notices are solemn, some sentimental, some dispassionate, and some tempered with grace. In style, they vary from formulaic to artfully crafted.

In narrative, journalistic obituaries, the lead is the most arresting sentence: it states something ultimate and irrevocable. It's also the signature sentence that identifies the piece as a death notice. The lead usually establishes the merits of the dead in a carefully crafted clause between proper noun and verb. For example, the *New York Times* obituary for Alvin Ailey begins: "Alvin Ailey, who rose from a childhood of extreme poverty in the segregated world of small-town Texas to become a leading figure in the establishment of modern dance as a popular art form in America, died yesterday at Lenox Hill Hospital after a long illness."[7] Readers of this obituary, even if they did not know who Ailey was, could surmise immediately from the lead how much Ailey mattered to the nation, why he merits public grief and memory. This merit clause is an essential feature of journalistic obituaries; it justifies a given obituary and furthermore states the narrative slant. Obituaries then develop and narrate, in effect, the claims stated in the clause between the proper name and the word "died."

Another quintessential feature of the obituary is the kinship sentence, which lists the names and types of the immediate kin who survive the dead. "Mr. Ailey is survived by his mother, Lula Cooper; his stepfather, Frederick W. Cooper, and his half-brother, Calvin Walls, all of Los Angeles."[8] Often placed in the last or penultimate paragraph, the kinship sentence asserts continuity, shifting the focus away from the dead to the living, to what remains: the immediate survivors, to be sure, but also the memory of the dead that survives with the living, of which the obituary is one immediate example and record.

The merit clause and kinship sentence instantly identify the obituary as its own type of literary form. The genre is also distinguished by its unique archival properties. While, like any other form of news, an obituary chronicles an important event of the day, as a record of the dead it also orients itself toward the future, creating an inventory that may be sought out and retrieved by posterity, an index for future generations of the people who made the past. Moreover, like other rites of burial, the obituary has an immediate archival role to play, since it shares the exigencies of materializing death and the dead for the living, providing a form and grammar to identify someone who was just alive, someone just here, retrospectively in the past tense.

Alongside these formal features, obituaries share a common cultural and political power to define whom we grieve publicly. In her essay "Violence, Mourning, and Politics," Judith Butler writes, "I think we have to ask, again and again, how the obituary functions as the instrument by which grievability is publicly distributed. It is the means by which a life becomes, or fails to become, a publicly grievable life, an icon of national self-recognition, the means by which a life becomes noteworthy. As a result, we have to consider the obituary as an act of nation-building. The matter is not a simple one, for, if a life is not grievable, it is not quite a life; it does not qualify as a life and is not worth a note. It is already the unburied, if not the unburiable."[9] Butler's words bring to the fore the larger discursive, political, and ethical implications of the obituary, especially how the categorical exclusion of certain lives from this death record reflects their exclusion not merely from the nation but also from the human.

AIDS obituaries key our attention to both the genre's formal and extraformal properties. In the first decade of the epidemic, the obituary became deeply contested, more so than any other type of literary mourning. In the mainstream press, truthful death notices of gay men who died of AIDS were initially almost nonexistent, but there were scores of normative AIDS obituaries that concealed the cause of death (often as "a long illness," as in Ailey's) and the deceased's sexual identity. The silencing of AIDS and homosexuality in mainstream obituaries did not go unchallenged, however, as gay periodicals issued their own counter death notices that voiced what was being suppressed in the mainstream press. The following pair of obituaries for Paul Jacobs exemplifies the substantive differences between normative and queer AIDS obits. The first notice was published in the *New York Times*:

Paul Jacobs, the pianist and harpsichordist of the New York Philharmonic and an internationally respected authority on contemporary music, died in his New York home yesterday morning after a long illness. He was 53 years old. . . . Surviving is a brother, John Jacobs, a market researcher of Bedford Hills, N.Y.[10]

The second was published in the popular gay newspaper the *New York Native*:

Paul Jacobs, pianist and harpsichordist for the New York Philharmonic and renowned authority on 20th-century music, died on Sunday, September 25, after a long bout with AIDS. He was 53 years old. Although the *New York Times* obituary made no mention of his sexual orientation and attributed his death to "a long illness," Mr. Jacobs was an openly gay man who wanted the nature of his illness to be a matter of public record. . . . He is survived by his brother, John, and by Paul Levenglick, his lover of 22 years.[11]

The differences between these two obituaries clearly point out which claims were publicly contested: Jacobs's homosexuality, his death from AIDS, and his kinship ties. The *Times* obituary illustrates how normative AIDS obituaries reified a heterosexual paradigm, and reinforced the public interdiction on queer/AIDS loss. The *Native* notice, on the contrary, exemplifies how queer obituaries challenged the heteronormative structure of kinship that buttressed the genre, according survival rights to Jacobs's lover in addition to his brother, and how they broke a number of silences, articulating the deceased's sexuality and his illness and death from AIDS. Not only that, in a powerful extraformal statement, the *Native* obit explicitly states its interventionist aims. In going beyond its own purview—by directly challenging the claims of another obituary and, by extension, the public authority of the *New York Times*—it underscores the political and ethical imperatives of queer obits: to break the interdiction on queer/AIDS loss, to state the truth as a matter of public record, and, ultimately, to openly bury those subjects deemed unburiable.

ACT UP's "Clip and Mail AIDS Obits" campaign from 1991 provides another glimpse of how queer communities collectively mobilized the obituary in order to gain public recognition. Here is how ACT UP explained this explicitly political undertaking:

Send obituaries to the White House of those who have died of AIDS or AIDS-related causes. Target either the President or Barbara Bush. [Mrs. Bush is also an appropriate target; she has publicly visited babies with HIV disease in a rare act of political identification. But she should be reminded that ALL people with AIDS are innocent, and that ALL are in desperate need of political advocacy!]

President George Bush or Mrs. Barbara Bush

The White House

1600 Pennsylvania Avenue, N.W.

Washington D.C. 20500

Send the obituary alone, or with a brief note. If the obit doesn't explicitly mention "AIDS," annotate it. Make copies and ask that your friends around the country also mail obituaries. We hope to start a groundswell of response throughout the nation during the summer months, inundating the White House by September. As a first step, send the attached letter. Sign it, fold it into thirds, tape it shut, attach a stamp, and mail it to Washington.[12]

On one side of the attached letter was printed the mission of the campaign and the mailing details; on the other side was a petition. The petition itself was a striking collage of short AIDS obituaries and a brief letter: "Dear Barbara Bush: The AIDS crisis *can* end—and the obituaries can cease—if the epidemic becomes the top priority on the domestic agenda. All people with HIV disease need your public and private advocacy. Please help."[13]

This remarkable fusing of obituaries with a petition meant that the demands of ACT UP's campaign were twofold: a call for urgent government action to fight AIDS and an appeal for public recognition of the dishonored dead. There was also something conceptually significant about this campaign as agitprop: the way the deluge of obituaries arriving in the White House evoked the mass death experience taking place outside its gates. ACT UP targeted Mrs. Bush for a reason. After a nationally publicized visit in 1989 to Grandma's House, a Washington, DC, health center that cared for children with AIDS, where the First Lady was pictured heroically holding a small child with AIDS, Mrs. Bush became a symbol for the nation's ostensibly compassionate attitude toward people living with AIDS. ACT UP appealed to Mrs. Bush, in short, to extend the same kind of sympathy and advocacy she had shown to children with AIDS to all Americans living with the disease, particularly the gay men who bore the brunt of the disease's stigma, shame, and blame.

These subversive uses of the obituary were not lost on individual artists. Riggs's appropriation of the form at the end of *Tongues Untied* is one evocative example. But perhaps it's in the work of Assotto Saint that we see the queer uses of the genre in their sharpest relief, as the obituary became an integral part of Saint's life and corpus. Saint found it shameful when obituaries concealed AIDS deaths; in Riggs's film *Non, Je Ne Regrette Rien* (*No Regret*), Saint even rebukes prominent black gay men who had died of AIDS—including Alvin Ailey;

the renowned fashion designer Willi Smith; and the "King of Gospel," the Reverend James Cleveland—for hiding their illness and having it euphemized posthumously as a "long illness" or as dysentery or respiratory problems, and thus helping to exacerbate the silence and shame surrounding AIDS and gay sexuality. Saint says: "It's a virus. We have to constantly remind ourselves. It is not sexuality that is the problem," and adds with his characteristic sense of defiance and pleasure: "Yes, I was part of the sexual revolution and I have no regrets. I did it all. The baths, the bars, the tracks. In Europe, in Africa, in the United States, in Canada. I did it all and I regret nothing."[14] Such queer reclamations of shame permeate Saint's obituaries, as he records his friends' transgressive lives as acts of great merit and not shame, worthy of public announcement and record, not secrecy and omission. In the face of compulsive erasures of AIDS deaths, mourners like Saint counter with their own unpatrolled death notices, naming their beloved dead truthfully, and stripping the genre of its false trappings.

ASSOTTO SAINT: FIERCE ARTIST, GONE TOO SOON

Assotto Saint (born Yves Lubin), who helped to lead the renaissance of black gay art in the 1980s, died June 29, 1994, of AIDS due to government neglect. Born October 2, 1957, in Les Cayes, Haiti, Saint moved in 1970 to New York City, where he lived until his premature death at thirty-six. He was a charter member of the black gay writers collective Other Countries, founded in 1986, and served as the poetry editor of the collective's signal anthology, *Other Countries: Black Gay Voices*. He wrote two books of poems, *Stations* and *Wishing for Wings*, and a chapbook, *Triple Trouble*; he edited three anthologies of black gay poetry, *Here to Dare*, *The Road Before Us*, and *Milking Black Bull*. His poetry and prose also appeared in landmark anthologies of black gay writing like *In the Life* and *Brother to Brother*, and Saint was one of the five men featured in Marlon Riggs's *Non, Je Ne Regrette Rien (No Regret)*. An artist with a huge arsenal of talent, Saint was a playwright and performer as well. He created three "multimedia theatrical pieces"—*New Love Song, Risin' to the Love We Need*, and *Black Fag*—which he produced in collaboration with his life partner, Jan Holmgren. He performed often in fierce and fantastic drag, and bent gender and reality however he wished. His performances and plays introduced a new cast of characters to the American stage, for example:

> ASSOTTO: 26 years old light-skinned haitian writer/wears black/exotic in his beads, braids, feathered ear[r]ing etc./he is somewhat effeminate/

BLAISE: the writer / 28 years old / black / he wears a red robe embroidered with liz-
ard skin, sun satellites, volcanoes, & salamanders / on one scene, he wears a grace
jones drag /

SPIRIT: she of the dream, the love we need / to be played by an androgynous-look-
ing, black female dancer / she's holder of magic[15]

His plays echo the lyricism of his poems and like much of his work assert
queer desire and black gay personhood. The transgressive imperative behind
his work is the same one that fueled the renaissance of black gay art in the '80s:
the need to "affirm and deliver a frank, uncensored, uncompromising articulation of an autonomously defined self and social identity," as Marlon Riggs puts
it.[16] This renaissance occurred between 1986—the year Joseph Beam's formative anthology *In the Life* was published and also the year Other Countries was
founded—and 1996, by which point many of its central figures had died of AIDS.
It left in its wake an extraordinary body of work, full of courage, vision, and tenderness.

Saint brought to bear his fearless spirit in his AIDS writing and activism. He
insisted on talking about his status as a person living with AIDS and facing the
disease without shame and without regret. He writes in one essay:

> Living with—dying of AIDS is not estimable in itself. However, fighting AIDS pub-
> licly is. I attach the label "person with AIDS" to my name, not as a badge of honor
> (although I am proud and unrepentant that I took part in the sexual revolution
> that raged in the '70s), but because we, the HIV community, especially those of
> us of African descent, must stand up and be counted. Not just as shadows incon-
> spicuously dropping through horrific CDC statistics down into our graves, but as
> flesh-and-blood human beings, standing up for our constitutional rights to life.[17]

Saint prized fighting AIDS publicly. Even as he battled for his own life, he participated in numerous AIDS demonstrations. On April 26, 1993, as part of an
ACT UP contingent, he was arrested at the March on Washington for Lesbian,
Gay and Bi Equal Rights and Liberation. Two days later at his arraignment hearing, he testified, "I unashamedly plead guilty," and delivered a powerful statement of rebuke—of government neglect and medical malfeasance, the true
cause of the catastrophe, he said. It was also a statement of mourning, voicing to
the court his grief over the deaths of close friends and, with an uncanny grammar, his own dying: "May the memory of their suffering, due to the inadequacy,
greed, & stupidity of bureaucracy, finally bring much-needed transformation.

. . . May it have helped to save my own life."[18] Saint lost dozens of friends to AIDS, many of whom he commemorated in eulogies, obituaries, and other obsequies, leaving behind a remarkable work of mourning: committed to remembering the disprized, to breaking the public silence of AIDS, and to archiving a record for posterity.

Spells of a Voodoo Doll—a book of Saint's collected poems, fiction, essays, and plays—was published posthumously in 1996. Saint is survived by close friends and relatives and by all of us inspired by his legacy.

AN ARCHIVE OF MOURNING

The Assotto Saint Papers consists of, the catalog description states, "correspondence and writings by Saint, manuscripts and letters from authors featured in his anthologies as well as other gay writers, printed matter and some personal papers."[19] If the catalog were to further delineate the printed matter, it would list an array of mourning materials: death certificates, death notices, funeral programs, funerary memorabilia, several maps of Evergreen Cemetery, and scores of letters of condolence, which are haunting in their illustration of how much loss punctuated Saint's life and how fast it was compounding. In two years alone, he attended more than twenty funerals for which he kept a clear record; he also participated in several by giving, for instance, a performance at Ortez Alderson's funeral and the eulogy at David Frechette's. And at Donald Woods's memorial service he became a focal point when he disrupted the service to demand that the family voice and not silence Woods's sexuality and his illness and death from AIDS.

Besides actively partaking in funerals, Saint wrote several obituaries for his beloved dead, ensuring that their lives and deaths were a matter of public announcement and record. Some were short notices and announcements, like this one for Alderson, one of the great ACT UP activists, who also performed in Saint's plays:

Alderson, Ortez—Ortez, age 38, actor/activist, died in Chicago on Friday, December 21, 1990 of AIDS complications. Funeral services will be held in Chicago on Sunday, December 30, 1 PM, at the United Church of Rogers, 321-761-2500. Survivors include his life partner, Arthur Gursch; his mother, Mary Alderson; seven brothers and sisters; his best friend, Steve Ballous, all from Chicago, and many other friends throughout the United States. "our martyrdom is no fake slaughter / but terror is a syndrome / which like bleeding black bulls / can act up" / Peace, beloved friend. Assotto Saint[20]

And this one for Frechette, who was a charter member of Other Countries:

> Frechette, David Warren, 43, black gay writer/activist, died of AIDS complications on May 11, 1991 at Roosevelt Hospital. A viewing/wake will be held on Wednesday, May 15, 1991, from 7 pm-9 pm, at Redden's Funeral Home, 325 West 14 Street, 212-242-1456. Departing from funeral parlor at 10 AM, Thursday May 16, 1991, for burial at Evergreen Cemetery in Brooklyn. He leaves behind family and many friends throughout the world and a legacy of poems, short stories and reviews. David, brother to brother, I miss you. Yves Lubin, a/k/a Assotto Saint.[21]

These short death notices were queer in naming AIDS publicly, identifying the deceased's sexuality, and articulating a new model of kinship. They were also queer in referencing the context of mass death and collective activism in Alderson's notice, and the intimate bonds of black gay men in Frechette's, the latter conjuring up Essex Hemphill's mesmerizing refrain in *Tongues Untied* "brother to brother brother to brother brother"—a chant that dissolves the division of blood and chosen family and institutes in its place a queer model of kinship.

Saint's narrative obituaries amply illustrate queer uses of the genre to commemorate the AIDS dead. In addition to the above death notice for Frechette, for instance, Saint wrote a full-page obituary for his friend in *PWA Coalition Newsline*, which he frames with three reflexive paragraphs about the genre, the unique context, and his own "So weird, so weird" feelings about writing this obituary. Rhetorically addressing himself in the second person, Saint begins, "There's something both honorable and absurd about sitting down to write your best friend's obituary. The former feeling comes from a deep sense of respect while the latter emotion acknowledges the ridiculousness of reducing his life and times to a few paragraphs on a newspaper page. In the writing of the obituary, do you only glorify him . . . or do you also testify to the human failings."[22]

This reflexive prologue relays to the reader that Saint is aware of the limits of the genre in which he is grieving. The prologue also underscores the context, that Frechette's death is part of a series of aggregating losses that have exacted a severe psychic and emotional toll on Saint. Again addressing himself in the second person, he says, "your mind constantly flashed back to that morning when you watched his casket in disgust at the whole thing, hating to go through this ordeal *one more time*, burying a part of heart. So weird, so weird."[23] The obituary that follows these self-reflexive paragraphs focuses on Frechette as a prominent journalist, a poet, and an active member of several key black and gay cultural and political organizations; and the kinship paragraph lists Frechette's aunts and "numerous cousins and family of gay and lesbian friends."[24] Saint ends the obituary with this explicitly queer portrait—which would have been unfit to print in a mainstream publication:

> David loved good food (remember his own glorious pecan pies, meat loafs or quiches), good films, good theater, good music, good sex (remember the scandalous pictures that accompanied the tales of escapades): THE GOOD LIFE! As he wrote in the poem, "Ne, Je ne Regrette Rien," these last words capture best his spirit: "Engrave on my tombstone: 'Here sleeps a happy black faggot / Who lived to love and died / With no guilt.' "[25]

The accent on queer desire and intimacy is particularly noticeable in Saint's series of obituaries for his partner, Jan Holmgren. Each obituary has a different iteration depending on its publication context—the funeral program, the *New York Times*, or *PWA Coalition Newsline*. Still, all of the versions share the same lead: "Jan Urban Holmgren, 53, died of AIDS-related complications at NYU Medical Center on March 29, 1993, in the arms of his 13-year life-partner Yves F. Lubin also known as Assotto Saint."[26] I find it moving in its portrayal of care and gay affection, particularly in a context that showed little feeling for the collective deaths of gay men. This was not the same sentimentality as Barbara Bush holding a baby with AIDS, however. Queer sentimentality must not be divorced from politics, a point Saint stresses in other versions of his lover's obituary, saying what he couldn't say in a mainstream paper like the *New York Times*. In the obituaries in both the funeral program and *PWA Coalition Newsline*, Saint writes: "Jan & Yves fell in love on November 9, 1980; the same week that the Reagan-Bush-SHIT government was first elected to the White House with their right-wing politics of greed, prejudice & stupidity. As gay activists, they had both vowed never to succumb to AIDS during a Republican administration."[27] Saint frames both the love encounter and the remainder of their relationship within a broader political context that was deeply inimical to queer love and futurity. Indeed, the horizon of the relationship pictured here entails not a normal sense of time and the future, but a calendar of loss that anticipates both lovers' deaths. The obituary that appeared in Holmgren's funeral program, furthermore, calls for activism and more forms of public mourning. Saint closes that obituary by asking those attending the funeral to "Join one million people on Jan's birthday, April 25, 1993, at the March on Washington for Lesbian, Gay & Bi Equal Rights & Liberation in Washington D.C. . . . A panel quilt in Jan's honor & memory will be delivered that day to the Names Project."[28] Mourning would continue, beyond the obituary, in activism and in other speech acts of grief and commemoration, like the AIDS quilt.

There was yet another context in which Holmgren's obituary was published that underscores how the genre became an integral part of Saint's corpus. Saint published his lover's obituary, along with two other works of prose—a short personal note he submitted to the Names Project when he delivered his quilt panel for Holmgren, and the testimony he delivered in court following his arrest in Washington, DC—in *Wishing for Wings*, his last book of poems. He titled these works, respectively, "No More Metaphors (Part One)," "No More Metaphors (Part Two)," and "No More Metaphors (Part Three)."[29] These prose works disrupt the formal cohesion of a collection of poems, gesturing to the limits of poetry as the only means of AIDS mourning. It's deliberate that Saint chose these particular prose pieces, which are themselves conjoined to other speech acts of mourning—obituary/funeral, personal note/quilt, court testimony/demonstration. In gathering a variety of mourning forms in a book of poems, Saint's provocative gesture seems to say that AIDS mourning must reach beyond the elegy to include other public expressions of grief, like the obituary, the AIDS quilt, and collective activism.

When Saint delivered to the Names Project his quilt panel, he also enclosed a copy of Holmgren's funeral program and a moving note he had penned by hand, an intimate death notice of his partner *and* himself. "No More Metaphors (Part Two)" starts off by making Holmgren's illness and death inextricable from Saint's illness and life: "I made this quilt for my 13-year life-partner, Jan Urban Holmgren. He was my Jan & my man. Born in Alno, Sweden, on April 25, 1939, he died in my arms on March 29, 1993. We both found out in late 1987 that we were HIV-positive. Jan came down with full-blown AIDS in early 1990. I came down with full-blown AIDS in late 1991. Yes, it is a strange phenomenon when both life-partners in a relationship are fatally ill."[30] This is a stirring statement, evoking the dead with the intimate language of lovers ("He was my Jan & my man") and creating a haunting symmetry between the dead and the bereaved ("Jan came down with full-blown AIDS in early 1990. I came down with full-blown AIDS in late 1991"). It is indeed "a strange phenomenon" to see imbricated in the same obituary Holmgren's past death and Saint's pending one, measured with the timeline of a fatal illness that includes both the dead and the living. Saint adds, "Because of my disbelief in God & a spiritual after-life, it gives me great pleasure to know that at least we will be physically reunited in the same grave at The Evergreen Cemetery in Brooklyn, NY."[31] In enmeshing his lover's and his own death in this way, Saint takes the obituary to its furthest limits, his death-bound position confounding the genre's key assumptions, including the difference between the object and the subject of mourning, and the life of the survivor that is assumed in the genre's signature phrase "survived by": Saint is a mourner who cannot complete the cycle of mourning by surviving the dead.

Along with its heightened reflexivity, this death notice also stands out for the way it embodies Saint and Holmgren's interracial relationship. Unlike the formal obituaries, which focus on Holmgren's life, this informal obit centers on the couple, celebrating the relationship they forged out of multiple differences: "Our pictures appeared in the pages of many national & local lesbian & gay magazines. We even graced some covers. We were a 'hot' couple. In many ways, our relationship symbolized how common ground can be found in 'difference.' Jan was 53 when he died. I am 35. Jan was white. I am black. Jan was born in Sweden. I am from Haiti. Jan believed in God. I don't. The list goes on & on; but we shared similar taste in music, exotic cuisine, traveling, political activism, & sexuality."[32] Why Saint names these differences here but leaves them out of the other obituaries may be a matter of form—in an informal note he could improvise and make the dead and dying or the couple the focal point, whereas in a formal obituary he could focus only on a death that had already occurred and squarely on the life of the deceased. But there may be another reason that Saint chose to deemphasize the interracial relationship in the published obits. As Marlon Ross incisively observes:

> [D]espite the politicizing of queerness in Saint's obituarial activism, there are other ways in which Saint depoliticizes the life of the beloved in a manner similar to conventional obituary. The interracial aspect of the relationship between Saint and Holmgren was not lacking in controversy, but Saint absents this matter from the obituary composed for the newspapers—appealing instead to the beatific image of the survivor holding the beloved in his arms. . . . Saint's depiction of his Swedish lover's death in his arms is no doubt intended to portray "care and gay affection," but it also is intended to defeat the common slurs and hostilities aimed at interracial lovers *within* many gay and non-gay contexts. This was, of course, famously at stake in the filmography of Saint's friend and colleague, Marlon Riggs, who was also beset with controversy due to the fact that his lover was white. How could he understand or voice true brother-to-brother love if his lover is not a brother? It may be that, in the face of such loss, such rumblings appear to be trivial, but this is exactly the point: just as Saint reduces to triviality the calls for shame in his portrait of gay love, so he seeks to reduce the slurs against interracial love that could easily overwhelm a beatific portrait of a black gay man holding his dying white lover in his arms.[33]

The recurring feature in all of the obituaries that Saint wrote for Holmgren is the image of his lover dying in his arms, as Ross rightly notes, which champions "the transcending love of queer equals" and contests derogatory terms like "snow queen" and "dinge queen," which were common references to black-white gay couples. Although in the formal obits he doesn't articulate their interracial relationship with words, he does so with a powerful "beatific portrait of a black gay man holding his dying white lover in his arms," normalizing that relationship with a transcendent image whose value rests not in racial or sexual identity, but in the gesture of ultimate care and intimacy expressed between two lovers.[34]

From the range of death notices and obituaries Saint wrote, and the different contexts in which they appeared, it's easy to surmise how much the genre mattered to him and how he used it productively and for multiple ends, including to mourn others and himself; to amplify the silenced subjects of AIDS and gay sexuality; to create an ideal picture of queer love; and to bear witness to a mass calamity. These queer feelings and imperatives Saint brought to bear on other obsequies as well, best exemplified in his improvised, insurgent eulogy at Donald Woods's funeral, where he rose up and began to shout at Woods's family for masking the deceased's sexuality and how he died from AIDS. That defiant act would inspire Thomas Glave's short story "The Final Inning," a brilliant work of fiction written about AIDS.[35]

"THEY WAS GONE BURY HIM WITH—WITH A *LIE.* CAN YOU IMAGINE?"

A remarkably performative short story, "The Final Inning" is set in the living room of a small apartment in the far reaches of the Bronx in 1980s America, where AIDS silently raged. The parlor or living room is certainly a classic locus of American drama, featured in Arthur Miller's *Death of a Salesman*, Eugene O'Neill's *Long Day's Journey into Night*, Tennessee Williams's *The Glass Menagerie*, and Lorraine Hansberry's *A Raisin in the Sun*, among others. The setting and Glave's ear for how people actually speak—not just his uncanny ability to render the intricate subtleties of black urban vernacular on the page but also the manner in which he foregrounds speech—give this short story its performative power. It reads as if it were meant to be acted on the stage; the physicality of the characters is that palpable.

In form it may be different, but the same questions that prompt an obituary —questions laden with ethical import—also preoccupy the narrator and characters of "The Final Inning." How shall the dead be remembered? What parts of their lives do we remember and reify? Who has the rights of survival? What's the ethical link between the rites of the living and the rights of the dead? And how about that battered word "truth"? The narrator of "The Final Inning" is eager to find out. Here is how the story begins:

—And whether or not Duane had really made a beautiful or even a fly corpse with all of his fingernails and fierce teeth intact beneath the lid of that closed coffin, and why the fuck his mother had just had to wear that shit-colored crushed-velvet or whatever it was tacky suit (to match her just-as-tacky crushed-velvet also shit-colored hat with that old cheap-looking St. Patrick's-green fake daffodil on it), and if it was true that Uncle Brandon McCoy had made a Goddamned fool out of himself again by crying like a big old droopingass baby in front of all those people instead of acting like a grown (old broken-down) man should even in the midst of all that grief for the fallen brother, and what it was exactly somebody had said to the minister (Reverend Dr. Smalls, old pompous fire-and-brimstone drunkass) about going on and eating up all the (greasy-nasty, Cee-Cee had said) greens so that there wasn't none left for nobody, not for nobody, honey—when it was all over and they were all over it and just dying to get home and take off heels and panty-hose and loosen up bra-straps and whatnot, those things, they all agreed, weren't even really the issues: by then they just wanted to leave it behind (especially what had happened in the church) and get back to where they were now, which was back in Tamara's house in the most northeastern (and inaccessible, the people who lived there cursed and praised) Bronx neighborhood, Sound Hill; in her living room, with the heat on because it had gotten even colder, hadn't it, she said, and the television on too because it always was and like always now was showing some dumbass sitcom about two high yellow girls as usual who couldn't even keep their trashy-looking hair straight, do you believe the shit they were putting on TV these days, Jacquie said, but it couldn't get no worse than that other show about that black family that was all doctors and whatnot, Cee-Cee said, 'cause I ain't never seen nobody like that acting like all we got is fly furniture and no problems, did you? Nicky said; and all of them, even Jacquie's husband Gregory sitting off real quiet in the corner with two-year-old Gregory Jr. asleep on his knee and the Sports Illustrated open on the side table in front of him, said they hadn't and laughed.[36]

Not only does the story begin in medias res, the lead sentence is more than 400 words and voiced by a narrator who demands the reader's full attention; only limited punctuation guides this leaping monologue that introduces the drama of the story and its main characters. From the outset, the story's time frame is clearly formulated, as the narrator (and, later, the characters) provides "narrative information *après-coup*, or after the event, which we can use for a retroactive interpretation of the story."[37] The story begins with a dead body—which has engendered the funeral and, in turn, the story—and asks us to imagine what lies hidden inside the closed coffin. At Duane's wake, something extraordinary has taken place; and now, after the funeral, in the private retreat of a living room, five of the six main characters—Cee-Cee, Tamara, Nicky, Jacquie, and Gregory—try to piece together "especially what had happened in the church" and that event's bearing on their relationship to their dead friend.

Cee-Cee is the one who insists on rehashing the proceedings of the day, talking about it as if it's juicy gossip—"Cee-Cee was not through," exclaims the narrator at one point.[38] Tamara cannot bear to hear the truth and ultimately forces Nicky out of her apartment for daring to voice it. Jacquie is neither as intolerant as Cee-Cee and Tamara nor as fearless as Nicky; she feigns innocence instead. Her husband, Gregory—not unlike their son, Gregory Jr., who sleeps on his father's lap from the beginning to practically the end of the story—is silent throughout much of it; in fact, he pleads with them several times to change the conversation: "I wish y'all would *stop*—"; "Why y'all gotta keep going on and on about this damn funeral?"; and "I just can't stand—."[39] As a married man who has had sex with other men covertly, without the knowledge of his wife or the others gathered at Tamara's house, he is deeply conflicted about his own sexuality. We soon gather that he was fully aware of Duane's sexuality and illness—and Duane in turn knew about Gregory's secret life. Gregory therefore is invested in keeping the story from being revealed, since he fears the telling will somehow implicate and "out" him. We learn more about Gregory than about any of the other characters although he hardly speaks, because the story displays his interior thoughts with a dazzling technique that allows Glave to convey simultaneously the character's outward silence and interior turmoil. Certainly, he and Nicky are the characters who build much of the story's suspense. And it's through Gregory's silent ruminations that, at last, James, the sixth major character, enters the story, partly as a distinct character and partly as Gregory's opposite. Although he appears only once, James is the linchpin of the story, each turn of the plot auguring his militant mourning at the funeral.

In the interim, what pushes the story forward and provides its tension is Nicky's persistent challenge to her friends' selective and normative memory of Duane, her resolve strengthening with each decisive pivot in the story. She first breaks the spell—with some trepidation—when she responds to Cee-Cee's trivialization of the funeral as a "freak show":

"It wasn't all that, Cee-Cee. You got a real problem when it comes to . . ." It was the first time Nicky had spoken since they had left the kitchen. . . .

"It wasn't even all that," she said.

"What you mean?" Cee-Cee said.

"I *mean*, you got a problem."

"What kinda problem?"

All eyes in the room drove toward the marshes and stopped there.

"I mean . . . like, you . . . —you don't like them."

"Them who?"

"You . . . well . . . umh . . . homos." (but oh no, now she thought, she could be stronger than that with the Olde English. Braver and maybe even—)

"*Gay* people," she said.[40]

This is the first pivot, since Nicky not only names and demystifies what Cee-Cee proscribes as taboo, but also calls into question (if we follow her reasoning) Cee-Cee's relationship to Duane. Since the "freaks" at the "freak show" stood up to claim Duane as one of them—as "a freak"—then Cee-Cee is forced to reconcile her own relationship to Duane's queerness posthumously. Nicky's fearlessness isn't presumed. She's a triumphant character precisely because we see the gradual process by which she triumphs, rather than a polished end product. Her yearnings to "tell it like it is" are tempered initially—as suggested in the ellipses and the faltering moment when she refers to Duane's "city" friends at the funeral as "homos"—but by the end of the story, her tongue is so precise and lacerating that she is ejected from Tamara's house. "Get out!" Tamara tells her, unable to bear the truth. "Get the fuck out!"[41]

Unlike Nicky, the other friends vie to discredit what James defiantly announced at the funeral: Duane's gayness and his illness and death from AIDS. "He ain't never *told* me," Jacquie says, to which Cee-Cee responds conclusively, "He ain't never *tell* nobody." Here, again, Nicky intervenes: "That's a lie, Cee-Cee. He told me."

"Yes, he did. Said he thought his mother mighta said something. Yes, he did. Couple months ago. Oh yes he did."

"You lying!" Tamara said.

"Girl, you ever see me up in here lying?"

"His *mother*? Ain't that some shit? I ain't ever even know she knew!"

"Hell yeah she knew." Nicky turned toward her cigarettes, lit one and sat back, closing her eyes for a moment. The Olde English had begun to feel reckless in her veins, as it had in everybody's.

"She just didn't want to say nothing, that's all," she said.

"Um-hmm. But see—I'm sorry—I can't blame her," Tamara said.

"I can."

"What you mean?" Cee-Cee said. Luther was still singing.

Nicky's eyes opened again and turned—flickered, ever so slightly—toward Gregory. The marshes were black as the night now descending, revealing only the shape of small scurrying things before the moon's glide.

"Because"— (her voice soft as the marsh-darkness he didn't turn his head to see, shimmying out toward him as if seeking a partner for that step-and-feint they might both have recognized on some other night—the most elusive, most interlocking dance of all) "—because, y'all . . . —they was gone bury him with—with a *lie*. Can you imagine?"

"Imagine what, girl?" Tamara said.

"She bugging," Cee-Cee said—but she was sitting very still.

"Naw, I ain't bugging. I know just what I'm saying. It's like—he lived his whole life— . . . see, y'all don't know, y'all didn't know Duane the way I knew him."[42]

This second turn reveals the ethical dilemma upon which all other issues pivot. Nicky articulates out loud and for the first time that the truth, too, is susceptible to death; her friends are now actively collaborating to inter the truth along with Duane's corpse, just as the family had sought to do earlier in the day. Their tacit collaboration forces her to realize the ethical implications of their actions and hers. The ethical fault line is clearly drawn: she has to intervene, or else she's no different from them. She must violate their silence, or acquiesce to it and inter her friend (enter him into narrative), against his wishes, with a lie, which she characterizes as a fundamental wrong, as another kind of killing: "they was gone bury him with—with a *lie*. Can you imagine?" Nicky's tone radically changes from this point on, her outrage stemming partly from their hypocrisy and partly from their killing of Duane's character and memory, which she finds an egregious act, a failure of ethics and imagination, indeed a failure of the human. To Nicky's decisive question, Tamara can only say, "Imagine what, girl?"

We soon reach James's powerful testimony, which the reader has been anticipating for some time. It was never a given that James would enter the present tense of the story: chronologically, his role is past, and midway through the story, the characters and setting have been firmly established. Suspense nonetheless lingers; we would like to find out what exactly happened at the funeral, since the other characters have provided merely innuendo. Nor could we have anticipated the powerful way James enters. Gregory's interior life takes center stage immediately following Nicky's ethical injunction. As Gregory's interior world opens up, James's testimony takes over, finally allowing us to judge for ourselves what Cee-Cee and Tamara have contemptuously dismissed as "a goddamn freak show," "A damn shame," "goddamn disrespecting blasphemy," and "shit like that."[43]

Though silent, Gregory's anguish is palpable. The irrevocable loss of his friend is certainly part of it; he seriously broods over Duane's death, and in part we read his pleas to change the conversation as a feeble attempt to prevent his friends from turning the loss into gossip, into spectacle, into something that denies the full expression of grief. His anguish, however, is also born out of the desperate need to distance himself from the queers of the story: the friend he mourns, James, the "Village downtown faggots," and—himself.

> (—holding his son verytight on his lap, tighttight like back in the church, and sitting, staring, at that too-shiny coffin; he, sitting there senseless, staring but not believing (no!) that what had been Duane was *in there* ninety pounds lighter than what Duane had used to be: that ain't even you in there, he had thought, O my God: not even no you with all them purple marks on your face (:the coffin had been closed:) and your hands with them purple marks on them and up on your chest too O my God Duane even on your eyes and in your mouth and you skinny like a damn rail with your hair all funny too (chemotherapy, radiation, drugs: had made what had been hair into—*that?*) O my God Duane: remembering and holding still on his lap tighttight his son not even you *wasn't even you* he had thought[44]

Gregory's inward grief, his silent weeping, is turned outward. He is the first character who heeds the narrator's opening demand and confronts Duane's dead body, a body that has suffered the onslaught of AIDS-related illnesses. And he heeds Nicky's injunction to imagine what's rendered unburiable, and yet that imagination—that grief—is stifled. He can't voice it.

Right before the narrative transitions to James, we are made fully aware of the deep recesses of Gregory's shame and unarticulated life, which are further illustrated with typographical marks of enclosure, ( ) and (: :). Enclosed between parentheses and colons, Gregory is trapped in his own silence, his voice sealed "tighttight" with the same typographic marks that represent Duane's coffin: "(:the coffin had been closed:)." These marks signify not merely Duane's final inning, but also Gregory's. Indeed, the story's narrative chiasmus is that it begins with one form of burial (Duane's body) and ends with another (Gregory's sexuality). While posthumously Duane's personhood remains a living memory—given voice by Nicky's defiant tongue and James's sanctified shout—Gregory's life is kept safe from the truth; his closet is a coffin.

James's voice and fearlessness are contrasted against Gregory's silence and shame. Also, well before James appears in the story, the other characters have already named his difference; indeed, they have declared it anathema to them. Prior to his own testimony, James is prefigured as a nameless "Village downtown faggot," "boggered up," with "hair all shaved off and zigzagged and earrings and nose rings"; he's a "white looking ass," a "half-breed," and "no real black man [would] do some shit like that." But here is how he appears in the story, in the left column, on his own terms:

and my name (then louder) is JAMES MITCHELL SCROGGINS and no you won't make me SHUT UP 'cause I'm PROUD to be here today as a GAY friend of DUANE'S and a (*shouting over the rage*) HUMAN BEING GODDAMNIT just like DUANE WAS TOO and now why won't you SAY IT he died of AIDS of AIDS (*Lord God the screaming remember how their eyes looked everybody shouting*   SIT DOWN WHERE YOU THINK YOU AT SIT DOWN) say it AIDS we all KNOW IT because I know some of you know I HAVE THE DISEASE TOO and I took care of him so I know many of you KNOW ME and what you're doing today is WRONG WRONG Duane wasn't ASHAMED of it either but all of you people YOU'RE KILLING US you won't STOP you keep right on KILLING US like you didn't even want us to come today to SAY GOODBYE to our friend our LOVER and then we came but you made us wait out in the COLD RAIN and then SIT WAY BACK IN THE BACK BACK OF THE CHURCH how can you KEEP ON DOING THIS when is it going to STOP now how can you bury him and say you LOVE HIM and not say one

They, thinking: everybody yes with hands up in the air over hats and balding heads; hands fluttering to the top of the church and O my God Lord Sweet Jesus what is happening God who is this boy standing up there where's the minister well why don't you stop him what kinda going on is that and (faggot shit: growls: sissy shit: abomination: growls) O Jesus Jesus Jesus Jesus! No my son ain't no homosexual no my cousin ain't no faggot no my nephew didn't have no damn AIDS the devil's disease don't you say that in this church and O you you filthy:— and the screaming and the children Mommy who's that man and look: O God Almighty the women the ladies crying and the men their nostrils flaring and saying muttering growling We should kick his motherfucking mulatto-looking ass and getting ready to do it too: but then you could see some people thinking from what you could see in their eyes the way their heads nodded soft and slow and the ladies' dark eyes so dark revealing that way showing so much so little under those tacky hats their eyes saying only in part You speak the truth up there boy but O God Jesus but still you speak it all the same word about how HE LOVED OTHER MEN he loved all of us and WE LOVED HIM yes he had AIDS   it KILLED HIM we us here now we should SAY IT SAY IT you're trying to IN him I'm bringing him OUT again for God's sake please I'm asking you for once won't you just SAY IT SAY IT

The faggot continuing Jesus

—I want all of you now who were proud of Duane as a proud out open GAY MAN to stand up WITH ME STAND for a moment of silence STAND

because it's all true all of it: under three hats three ladies in particular Yeah we sure do know how he died but ain't nobody saying nothing 'cept "a long illness" and that boy is right rightright: could even be my grandson my godson or: but something and no it can't keep going on because He the One knows don't He: knows the truth about all of it and if we sitting right here with the dead boy's mama and can't even speak the truth now so damn late in the day when are we ever gone speak it and now just think about it what in the hell kinda going on is that?

James is fierce. Unwelcomed, he makes his presence felt. Sequestered in the back, defiantly he rises to the pulpit. They try to gag the truth, but he shouts it out. They try to shame him and the dead, but he shames them instead. And try as they might, they fail to bury Duane with a lie, and James, at last, inters him—and enters him into the story—truthfully. It's hard to read the left column and not feel James's presence embodied in his eulogy of rage and grief. James's queer eulogy not merely articulates, but amplifies those subjects the family seeks to suppress and bury—that Duane was proudly gay and loved other men and that he died of AIDS. It asserts moreover that Duane's death was not caused by AIDS alone, but by the very silence the family kept while he was dying and keep on keeping at his wake. James incriminates them directly, that their silence = death: "YOU'RE KILLING US you won't STOP you keep right on KILLING US." These words also make palpable the collective thrust of James's queer eulogy, demanding that we see Duane's death in relation to other AIDS deaths and in relation to those living with the disease, including the eulogist standing right there in the pulpit, whose survival hinges on breaking the fatal silence, on mourning openly.

James's testimony presses the story to its climax, and the form of its expression enhances the story's third and last inning. The suspense of what happened in the church can no longer be contained, either semantically or typographically. It finally bursts out, and the form of its expression is as significant as its content. The split narrative is a wonderful visual illustration of call-and-response, a root mode of communication in African and African Diaspora traditions. "Call and response," writes Robert O'Meally, "refers to the Sunday service: 'Say "Amen" somebody'—'AMEN!' This interaction between preachers and congregations all over black America has become an integral feature of cultural expression in the United States. Born in West and Central Africa, where one experiences it in exchanges among singers and instrumentalists (as well as dancers and sculptors), in the U.S. this pattern occurs in church songs and sermons and also in work songs, play songs . . . blues, rag, and in jazz. You say something; I say something back."[45] Thus, in the contrapuntal narrative above, James gives his testimony on the left-hand side and on the right-hand side we hear the visceral emotion he elicits from the congregation, including awe, shock, and hate, but affirmation and identification too. Toward the end the "three ladies in particular Yeah" not only corroborate his testimony but also claim him as one of their own. Unlike Cee-Cee and Tamara, who use his otherness to cast him out, the elders imagine James as kin—he "could even be my grandson my godson."

The contrapuntal narration also represents how truth—the idea of bearing witness, of testifying—can have both secular and religious meaning. For James, truth is mostly a secular endeavor. The open and unapologetic expression of himself and his sexuality (one truth) allows him to embrace openly and publicly Duane's identity as a proud gay man (another truth). Furthermore, he realizes the crucial role of bearing witness, being a truth teller and demystifying AIDS so that those living with the disease, like himself, are afforded the proper care, support, and respect. He testifies, too, so that he, Duane, and other queers like them are accepted on their own terms as gay men and as equally human. At the same time, at the bottom of the right column, we see taking shape a religious understanding of truth. The three women affirm James's testimony because they can't remain silent before God, knowing that what James is saying is true and what he's doing is righteous, "right rightright." It's as if we hear a blues statement of truth on the left and, echoed on the right, the spirituals' truth. Still, while James's eulogy assumes the form of a secular transgression—naming the disease and the sexuality associated with it—in a sacred place of worship and at a sacred family rite, it also sounds the sanctified shout in the black church. Possessed by the spirit, the shouter can amplify truths others dare not voice and, in that moment, can supplant the ordained authority of the preacher and deacons with his righteous discontent. James's testimony does just that, assuming a sacred quality, the substance and form of which are too powerful, too sanctified to be questioned by a congregation confronted by its lies and hypocrisy.

There's another important relationship that the double narration signifies. Glave uses call-and-response to signal the true-life anecdote that inspired his story. Here is how Glave distinguishes between "The Final Inning" and the other stories that appeared in his debut collection, *Whose Song?*:

> So far as I know, I haven't written anything in *Whose Song?* that directly responds to contemporary news, except for "The Final Inning." That story was inspired, in part, by the death of a black gay poet named Donald Woods, who was very out in his personal and political life. I heard [about it] from a friend, the late Assotto Saint, another black gay poet who died of the disease. Assotto said that he felt so stricken during the service that he got up and began to shout at Donald's family about their hypocritical silence. Assotto recounted all this to me in the last year of his life, then said, "There's the story, my dear. Now go write it." All the characters were completely invented, but I can trace one of them to Assotto, I guess. That's the only story in the book that I can trace to a direct, identifiable source.[46]

Although Glave is formally experimental throughout his collection of stories, this split into columns is the only instance where two distinct narratives are taking place concurrently. That such a split takes place at the precise moment that James speaks accentuates the imaginative manner in which Glave defers to the anecdote recounted to him. We can trace James's character to a "direct, identifiable source," to Assotto Saint—who not only provides Glave with a powerful character and a dramatic anecdote, but who charges him to write the story, to imagine it and to reconstruct it anew. We can hear signified in the break a call-and-response between Saint's anecdote and Glave's short story, between truth and fiction, between the real incident and the imagined story.

QUEER BURIALS, QUEER ARCHIVES

The subject of the anecdote, Donald Woods, another icon of the renaissance of black gay art, was cut down by AIDS in his prime. When he died on June 25, 1992, he was only thirty-four years old. He was a member of Other Countries and, as one of its editors, oversaw the publication of *Sojourner: Black Gay Voices in the Age of AIDS*—the most important anthology of black gay writing on AIDS. As a poet, he was featured in the signal black gay anthologies *In the Life* and *Brother to Brother* and was well known for *The Space*, a collection of poems and illustrations published on broadsheet. His collaborations were many. He worked with Riggs on *Tongues Untied* as the film's production assistant; and, along with Saint, he was one of the five men featured in *Non, Je Ne Regrette Rien (No Regret)*, Riggs's film about black gay men openly living with AIDS. So, given who Woods was, given his writing and activism and how he lived privately and publicly, it was indeed a violent act for his family to try to bury him with a lie and to disenfranchise him posthumously.

Who knows what sparked it, what exactly it was that struck Saint at the funeral, what prompted him to go into militant mourning. Maybe it was hearing something discordant in "Amazing Grace" or "There Is a Balm in Gilead," the spirituals sung at Woods's funeral. Or maybe it was what the Reverend Robert Benjamin did not say in his eulogy, what family members left out in their remembrances. Or perhaps it was reading Woods's obituary in the funeral program, which had completely erased Woods's personhood, drawing a portrait of him instead as a devout Christian with all the normative bona fides. At his own funeral, in his own obituary, Woods was no longer recognizable as himself, and maybe these omissions triggered in Saint his anger at what he had read, and cut out, and saved the day before: Woods's obituary in the *New York Times*, which stated, "He died of cardiac arrest, his family said."[47] Something triggered it and at some point, as he told Glave, "he got up and began to shout at Donald's family about their hypocritical silence."[48]

Saint later wrote about Woods's funeral in a letter he sent to a mutual friend of his and Woods', rebuking the friend for not joining him in his defiant eulogy. Succinctly, the letter captures the significance of his transgression, the imperative behind his "truthful daringness":

> There are occasions, when raging against the madness, the hypocrisy, and the plain foolishness that overshadow [our] lives and deaths as gay black men, our truthful daringness serves as an empowering tool for discussion, learning, and change in ourselves as well as others. Moral of the story: When I asked you at Donald's funeral to make a statement, with me, regarding the friend we knew, but whose involvement with our lesbian and gay community was completely ignored by his family to the point of denial, you should have embraced that responsibility and not avoided it. We should *never* let our lesbian and gay friends be sent to their graves in the closet.[49]

Saint's words evoke the intertwined politics of recognition and mourning that defined the renaissance of black gay art and writing and, more broadly, queer counterpublics in the 1980s and early '90s, how the speech acts precipitated by death—funerals, obituaries, elegies, and other obsequies—became necessary vehicles of self-expression and survival. Saint's defiant mourning—his "truthful daringness"—was meant to protect the identity Woods had fought for and earned while alive, and prevent it from being snatched away from him posthumously. While the family wished to discard Woods's queer life along with his corpse, Saint's intervention rescued it, committed it to a posthumous afterlife. The body was buried, but the queer life was preserved as sanctioned memory, as a record for posterity. Saint reprimanded his friend who had not stood up partly by using the very politics that defined their counterpublic—at all costs, the open recognition of black gay identity—but partly too by under-lining a fundamental human claim from which the queer dead and living were being excluded.

Ultimately, there were two memorial services for Woods: one arranged by his family, which sought to suppress his queerness, and another by his friends, which openly embraced it, a contrast clearly reflected in the two memorial pro-grams. The program for the family funeral makes no mention of Woods's queer identity or his personal struggle with AIDS, but states that he was "Executive Director of AIDSFILMS where he carried out the organization's goals of creat-ing educational films on AIDS." The phrase "organization's goals" is sly in char-acterizing this part of Woods's life only as his occupation, not to be conflated with his personal life. The language used in the family funeral program further-more indexes a level of repression and even compensation for what must have been an open secret, saying, "In the past year, Donald sought earnestly to renew his relationship with Christ." The second program doesn't seek to normalize Woods or cleanse him of his sins, but instead celebrates him for the man he was: someone who professionally and personally embodied queer life and AIDS ac-tivism. The way Woods is pictured in each program also sends a striking mes-sage. The family's ideal image of Woods—a respectable young man with short cropped hair, attired in a white collared shirt and a dark tie—is hardly recogniz-able as the sensual man in the other program, who wears dreadlocks and jew-elry, and meets the camera's eye with a disarming queer gaze. In both words and pictures, Woods's friends were adamant about righting the wrongs the family had committed in the obituaries that appeared in the *New York Times* and the funeral program, and drawing a portrait of Woods that spoke truthfully to how he lived and died.

In "The Final Inning," Glave conjures up brilliantly the ethics of burial that are paramount in Saint's act and the anecdote Saint recounted to him. In Glave's story, Duane's family, entitled to control the burial rites, try to use that prerogative to contravene the rights of the dead and his queer survivors. James's defiant act is in response to the family's abuse of their power over Duane at his most vulnerable—a violent act, a "killing" that James articulates as a breach of the essential claim to burial, indeed to what it means to be human. When he first introduces himself, James says, "I'm PROUD to be here today as a GAY friend of DUANE's and," he adds, "a HUMAN BEING GODDAMNIT just like DUANE WAS TOO." James voices his and Duane's identity as proud gay men and, it had to be restated, their identity as human beings. Along with a particular politics of identity, what James exercises here is a fundamental right to bury one's dead and to mourn. For to bury Duane against his wishes, according to the normative terms of the family, would have meant interring him under a false persona, leaving him in effect unburied and unburiable. James's words testify that the family's false burial amounts to desecration, a breach of the ethics of burial, a breach of the human.

As Nicky's rhetorical question—"they was gone bury him with—with a *lie*. Can you imagine?"—strongly evokes, burying Duane with a lie would have been comparable to not burying him at all, violating his constitutive claim to what it means to be human. If we follow Giambattista Vico's etymology, the word "human" originates from the act of burying. In his incisive study of burial, which builds on Vico's *New Science*, Robert Pogue Harrison writes: "To be human means above all to bury. . . . The human is bound up with the humus and burial figures as the generative institution of human nature."[50] Burials, he argues, constitute "the humic foundations of our life worlds":

> A humic foundation is one whose contents have been buried so that they may be reclaimed by the future. The humic holds in its conserving elements the unfinished story of what has come to pass. If it is true that we move forward into the future only by retrieving the past, it is because, through burial, we consign the future of our legacies to this humic element, with its vast, diversely populated underworlds. Thus burial does not mean only the laying of bodies to rest in the ground (although religion and matrimony are more likely to disappear among humans than burial customs are). In a broader sense it means to store, preserve, and put the past on hold.[51]

Harrison aptly captures how burial constitutes us, a characterization that also illuminates what's at stake in AIDS burials like Duane's. Without James's intervention, the family would have inhumed Duane under a false persona, performing what would have been a deconstitutive act—disarticulating the corpse from its queer embodiment, leaving the dead without a posthumous or humic trace. As James and Nicky suggest, burying Duane with a lie would have meant a breach of burial itself, of what Harrison calls the "humic foundation," since it would have prevented the dead from having the posthumous afterlife that burials institute. James's characterization of the burial as a killing resonates here in that the family's silence was also a way of killing Duane's queer afterlife, fore-closing the memory of queer Duane.

Ultimately, the defiant act embodied by James in Glave's story and embodied by Saint in real life protects the rights of the queer dead from the normative rites of the living. The imperative that informed Saint's militant eulogy—"to *never* let our lesbian and gay friends be sent to their graves in the closet"—informed the mourning he undertook in other acts of speech, like the obituary. These expressions of grief became a vehicle for Saint to carry out his work to inter/enter the queer dead truthfully, ensuring that they were survived by the living and consigned to posterity. In all of its forms, Saint's queer mourning broke not only the public silence around AIDS but also the silent funerals and obituaries that effaced the lives of gay men from the record. Instead, Saint left behind an archive of loss where we can look for the disprized dead—and find them.

three

Visions of Loss
Hip Hop, Apocalypse, and AIDS

Within the deceptively clean black borders, on a wide canvas coated in cadmium yellow—apocalypse. A fantastic, multilimbed creature stands in the center. Between its thighs are linked together male and female sex organs and a cow's udder. Two headless bodies extend out of each hip, forming the creature's sturdy thighs and legs, anchoring its enormous weight. Up on each shoulder and facing one another are two more bodies, whose heads have morphed into the creature's single head, with untamed hair like Medusa's that whips and twirls into restless limbs—or coils into a snake whose tail is Mickey Mouse's gloved and pointing finger. The creature's arms are spread wide open, and from each hand dangle two inverted male figures, hanging by their own stretched and looped genitals. Seven angels hover above the creature's head, but unlike the winged cherubs that look benignly down on churchgoers, these ominous angels loom like bomber pilots masked in respirators. Drawn in black ink, this foreboding scene stands in relief against the yellow background, as does the pendant hanging from the creature's neck, which is emblazoned with a red X. The expression on the creature's face is weary: it has weeping eyes and a gaping mouth, like those of the angels above it, arrested in a relentless howl. This could be an image of Walter Benjamin's angel of history as it faces the debris of catastrophes.[1]

The image is Keith Haring's, one among many in which the artist wrestles with apocalypse as a theme in his oeuvre. This painting is notable for the stark manner in which it reveals Haring's tragic temperament. He completed it in 1985, well before his own diagnosis—although that distinction seems arbitrary when we talk about Haring, since his short career is indelibly marked by the AIDS epidemic. Unlike many of the posters he designed for AIDS health and political activist groups, his paintings often incorporate AIDS into a vision of history perennially under siege, replete with catastrophes, a tragic sense of history

Keith Haring, *Untitled* (1985), acrylic and oil on canvas, 120″ × 120″. © Keith Haring Foundation. Used by permission.

he shares with African American artists, who figure AIDS deaths not as an exception, but as part of a continuum of black death and disparagement in American life. Haring's perspective is closely linked to his critique of whiteness, a vantage point that allows him to embrace and to hone a visual vernacular inspired by the budding hip hop culture of the late 1970s and early '80s. While jumping off from an emerging urban and primarily black art form, Haring does not succumb to an easy white exploitation of that art, eschewing the pitfalls of what Toni Morrison calls "American Africanism": "the process of organizing American coherence through a distancing Africanism, . . . the fetishizing of color, the transference to blackness of the power of illicit sexuality, chaos, madness, impropriety, anarchy, strangeness, and helpless, hapless desire."[2] On the contrary, Haring's critical relationship to his whiteness and his affinity with urban black life and aesthetics allowed him to develop a unique visual idiom, through which he expressed the tragedy of AIDS, along with the tragic character of history.

GRAFFITI, POP, AND VERNACULAR

There have been numerous posthumous retrospectives of Haring's work, and the appraisals have been consistently in his favor. Although Haring achieved unparalleled fame during his brief career, critical attention and acclaim, especially from the American fine arts establishment, eluded him because, on the one hand, his work started out in the subway and was associated with graffiti, and on the other, he was being penalized for having achieved fame and international stature without going through the proper channels that are supposed to confer status. "What happened to me," says Haring, "is that [my work] started in the subways, it began in popular culture and was absorbed and accepted by the popular culture before the other art world had time to take credit for it."[3] Robert Farris Thompson, one of Haring's key interlocutors, underscores the point: "The fact that [Haring] fluently and powerfully combined the voice of the street and the voice of the gallery system was threatening to those dependent upon a clear sense of ladder, a reassuring braille of social hierarchy. And so 'they' bracketed his work as 'subway.'"[4]

In hindsight, and in the context of this book, I find it productive to read Haring's work under the heading of graffiti art (and, more broadly, hip hop culture), since that reading reveals the deeply racialized discourse of the arts establishment in the 1980s, which could not conceive of art being the proper domain of New York's racial underclass. In addition, Haring used the graffiti art form to develop his aesthetic and to draw insights from a culture where the deathbound subject is a ubiquitous figure. However different hip hop may be from its antecedent vernacular forms, like the spirituals and the blues, it shares their preoccupation with compounding loss, a perspective that Haring brought to bear especially as he faced his own imminent death.

Before analyzing the influence of hip hop culture on Haring's articulation of loss, it is necessary to first demystify the racialized discourse attending graffiti and Haring's work. Unlike other forms of visual art that emerged in the 1970s and '80s, graffiti entered discourse as a problem of public policy rather than as the subject of art criticism.[5] As early as 1972, New York City mayor John Lindsay had concluded that the "rash of graffiti madness" was "related to mental health problems," and his administration coined the phrase "the graffiti epidemic" to characterize the proliferation (and containment) of tags by black and Latino youth.[6] And as graffiti began to spread, the discourse around it quickly adopted the vocabulary of "American Africanism," investing these tags with "the power of illicit sexuality, chaos, madness, impropriety, anarchy, strangeness, and helpless, hapless desire."[7] The sociologist Nathan Glaser describes graffiti in his influential 1979 essay, "On Subway Graffiti in New York":

> The subway rider is assaulted continuously, not only by the evidence that every subway car has been vandalized, but by the inescapable knowledge that the environment he must endure for an hour or more a day is uncontrolled and uncontrollable, and that anyone can invade it to do whatever damage and mischief the mind suggests. I have not interviewed the subway riders; but I am one myself, and while I do not find myself consciously making the connection between the graffiti-makers and the criminals who occasionally rob, rape, assault, and murder passengers, the sense that all are part of one world of uncontrollable predators seems inescapable. Even if the graffitists are the least dangerous of these, their ever-present markings serve to persuade the passenger that, indeed, the subway is a dangerous place—a mode of transportation to be used only when one has no alternative.[8]

It is as if graffiti has some intrinsic, bewitching power to thrust its viewer into a state of chaos and violence. It's endowed with such brutal force that it becomes in effect a real act of violence, as if the inscriptions actually leap off the walls of the subway and begin assaulting, robing, raping, and killing passengers. And the difference between signifier (graffiti) and signified (violence) is not the only one that's obliterated here; so is the one between noncriminal and criminal: assumed to be all black and Latino, those tagging subway cars and those assaulting subway passengers are, in Glaser's mind, one and the same.

Like the people who produce it, graffiti entered discourse as "a problem" to be solved within the field of sociology, rather than as an art form to be appreciated within art criticism/history. A racialized sociological framing of the art was so prevalent that it determined how art critics initially made graffiti coherent to the fine arts establishment. In one of the first profiles of graffiti in a major arts periodical, critic Suzi Gablik suggests that "to many people, the presence of graffiti in the environment has come to symbolize violation, social anarchy and moral breakdown. They see it as vandalism, pure and simple—a crime signifying that we can no longer take orderly society and orderly change for granted."[9] Gablik goes on to underscore her observation with quotes from other, presumably "legitimate" artists who are contemptuous of graffiti. Says Mark Lancaster: "I think [graffiti's] a kind of theft, an assault on the right to feel that public transport is a reasonable means for getting from one place to another. I think it's frightening to a lot of people. I can't separate it from fear, from someone pulling a knife on you and robbing you in a public place. You have to have an immunity to violence if you use the subways. The presence of graffiti increases the sense of lawlessness and danger."[10]

Although an artist, Lancaster echoes Glaser's sociological perspective and considers graffiti to be both personified menace and omnipresent threat: imbued with such ominous power, graffiti is indistinguishable "from someone pulling a knife on you and robbing you in a public place." Curiously, both Glaser and Lancaster incriminate those who tag the subway cars not mainly for acts of vandalism, but for seizing control of public space. Ultimately, what they find disturbing is that even in their physical absence black and Latino youth are always present, embodied in the subway system in their tags and thus preventing commuters from riding the train ensconced in white immunity and innocence.

The subtext of race appears in sharper relief in Gablik's article when the author discusses particular graffitists. While she relies on the terms of sociology to characterize artists of color, she shifts to another idiom to profile Haring. On the one hand, of the black and brown graffitists who were gaining recognition, she writes:

> It's difficult at this point to judge the long-term results of suddenly catapulting individuals who are ill-prepared socially and economically into a higher income level—since, as the sociologist Emile Durkheim has pointed out, poverty exerts its own disciplines and limits, but affluence, by its nature, usually does not. Affluence breaks down these limits, and substitutes for them a set of expectations which rise almost constantly. Are these artists being encouraged beyond any reasonable evaluation of their talents? How, finally, are we to define the underlying meaning of an experience which, to the uninitiated, appears as sheer nasty babble—at best a hermetic Morse code of hieroglyphs, at worst a violent assault?[11]

But, on the other hand, Haring—who's "a special case," "something of an anomaly in the graffiti world," Gablik is keen to note, "because he [is] white and middle-class (from Kutztown, Pa.), and because he [has] been to art school (the School of Visual Arts in New York)"[12]—requires no sociological explanation. His whiteness is proof positive of his artistic merit.

In retrospect, it's clear to see how the *idea* of Keith Haring played a pivotal role in shifting the discourse of graffiti from sociology to art history. For the critics, Haring brokered this transition not because graffiti shifted the general perception of its personified menace, nor because Haring etched, between 1981 and 1985, some 5,000 remarkable drawings in New York City subway stations (which he considered works of graffiti),[13] nor because he collaborated with the graffitists LA II (Angel Ortiz) on several pieces, nor because Haring was a skillful graffitist and contributed to the genre in the manner of "wild style" artists like Futura 2000, Fab 5 Freddy, Lee Quiñones, and others.[14] Rather, a naturalized faith in his whiteness extracted the threats of graffiti. It was his race that helped to give intelligence to his art and, by way of synecdoche—for he too painted in New York City's subway system—to graffiti art in general.

Not surprisingly, some of the posthumous attempts to redeem Haring as a non-graffiti artist rely on a variation of the logic that earlier critics used to bracket Haring's subway art. For instance, Barry Blinderman argues: "It is important to note that Haring did almost all of the subway drawings during the day, unlike the graffiti writers who preferred to work by flashlight in desolate train yards in the middle of the night."[15] Blinderman fails to see that it wasn't simply that graffiti writers "preferred to work" undetected, but rather, unlike Haring, they were not afforded the security of whiteness. Young men of color tagging in broad daylight increase their chances of arrest and police brutality, whereas Haring's skin was ample protection.[16] Robert Pincus-Witten's take on Haring and graffiti is another example:

> Characteristically, Haring's graffiti—what a misnomer—were drawn in white chalk on black paper. The black ground of these drawings was the surface of the clean, matte paper regularly pasted up in the subways to provide fresh backing for each subsequent change of advertisement. Keith always respected the format of the mount. This restraint points to his marked classicism in distinction to the messy expressivity of the spray-can graffitists. However offensive the graffitists' abuse of public space—and Keith was alive to its adverse aspects—one still remembers the pleasure, even security, that Haring's drawings introduced into an otherwise noisy and threatening netherworld.[17]

Respect versus contempt; restraint versus messiness; classicism versus primitivism; pleasurable versus offensive; secure versus threatening—it's only through binary oppositions that pit his work against racial others' that these critics can make meaning of Haring's art.

Perhaps we should take heed of what Haring himself had to say about the role of graffiti in his development as an artist:

> Almost immediately upon my arrival in New York in 1978, I had begun to be interested, intrigued, and fascinated by the graffiti I was seeing in the streets and in the

subways. Often I'd take the trains to museums and galleries, and I was starting to see not only the big graffiti on the outside of the subway trains, but incredible calligraphy on the inside of the cars. This calligraphic stuff reminded me of what I learned about Chinese and Japanese calligraphy. There was also this stream-of-consciousness thing—this mind-to-hand flow that I saw in Dubuffet, Mark Tobey, and Alechinsky. The forms I was seeing were very similar to the kinds of drawings I was doing, even though I wasn't making the voluminous letters and the aggressively fluid lines, which were done directly on the surfaces, and without a preconceived plan. They were really, really strong. Well, I felt immediately comfortable with this art. I was aware of it wherever I was. So the time spent en route to a gallery or to a performance or to a concert was just as interesting and educational as that which I was going to see. Sometimes I would even get on the first train. I'd sit and wait to see what was on the *next* train. Graffiti were the most beautiful things I ever saw. This being 1978–79, the war on graffiti hadn't really begun yet. So the art was allowed to blossom into something amazing, and the movement was really at its peak. These kids, who were obviously very young and from the streets, had this incredible mastery of drawing which totally blew me away. I mean, just the technique of drawing with spray paint is amazing, because it's incredibly difficult to do. And the fluidity of line, and the way they handled scale—doing this work on these huge, huge trains. And always the hard-edged black line that tied the drawings together! It was the line I had been obsessed with since childhood![18]

It was during the winter of 1980 that I started to actually draw graffiti on the street—and I did that with a marker. . . . I felt there was a reason to draw on the streets, because what I was drawing was communicating information. I had developed a language made up of pictographs, and I'd draw these with a big black Magic Marker, which was what other graffiti artists used. The way it began was to draw my tag—tag, meaning signature or what graffiti artists called their name. So my tag was an animal, which started to look more and more like a dog. Then I drew a little person crawling on all fours, and the more I drew it, the more it became The Baby. So on the streets, I'd do various configurations of the dog and the baby. Sometimes the baby would be facing the dog—confronting it. Sometimes, it would be a row of babies, and the dog behind them. I was using these images, always bearing in mind the [William] Burroughs / [Brion] Gysin cut-up ideas. And I juxtaposed these different tags or signatures or images, which would convey a different meaning depending on how you combined them. But those first things I did on the streets were just these rows of babies and dogs. I would add that I made these drawings where I saw other people's tags, and I did them so that they would be acknowledged by other graffiti artists.[19]

Haring's emphasis on aesthetics—beauty, line, scale, color, technique, instrument, intertextuality—bespeaks a mode of interpretation unburdened with extraformal "American Africanist" criteria. Rather than signs of terror, graffiti inside subway cars are calligraphy for Haring; rather than seeing graffitists as violent criminals or as Durkheim's déclassé, Haring considers them fellow artists with "incredible mastery of drawing" with whom he seeks a creative exchange; rather than seeing his subway art as an exception, he calls it "graffiti" and his own signature a "tag"; and rather than making a clear divide between the art he sees in museums and galleries and the art he sees in the subway system, he expresses equal interest and sees the educational value in both.[20]

Along with Haring's words, we should also listen to what other graffitists say about Haring's role. Recalling an important show from 1980, the first to bring together people from both the graffiti and downtown art scenes, the pioneer graffitist Futura 2000 says: "When Keith created the *Beyond Words* graffiti show at the Mudd Club—the show that Fab Five Fred and I curated—people in the art world realized the genius, naïveté, simplicity, and simple truth of graffiti art. It wasn't about traditional ideas—it was a fresh spirit—something people hadn't seen before. I think that most graffiti artists will agree that Keith Haring probably gave the movement its greatest exposure—he kind of pushed it forward right from the start. Without Keith there at the beginning, a lot of this wouldn't have happened the *way* it happened. I'll say this, Keith affected our lives single-handedly. It wasn't Andy and it wasn't Jean-Michel. Keith was the catalyst!"[21] The significance that Haring assigns to graffiti and the significance that other graffitists assign to Haring need a more in-depth study than I can offer here, but I hope it's clear that we must first free graffiti from the cluster of associations that denigrate it before we can make meaning of that art form and of Haring's work.

"The story of Keith's art," writes Thompson, "bears witness to a rising multi-traditional state of affairs where Europe-derived art history and criticism must hack it, democratically, in terms of competing streams of influence from Africa, Asia, Oceania, and the Americas. Adieu Euro-American insularity, hello world beat. His work, I think, helped 'deterritorialize' art and criticism, pushing as far into the vernacular, as far into academic idioms, and as far into commerce as he wished, all at once."[22] Influenced by a range of traditions, Haring's art also asks us to query another category under which his work is often cataloged and explained—pop art. Lawrence Alloway states in his signal essay, "The Long Front of Culture," that pop art is an "aesthetics of plenty [which] opposes a very strong tradition which dramatizes the arts as the possession of an elite."[23]

Pop art draws its inspiration from mass and consumer culture, which provides for its practitioners and proponents a slew of references from which they can draw. Iconic brands and consumer goods like Coca-Cola, Campbell's soup, Tareyton cigarettes, Chryslers and Fords, and comic books and their heroes hold aesthetic meaning, as do specific Americans, including the Kennedys, Elvis Presley, John Wayne, and Marilyn Monroe. As Dick Hebdige points out, "the significance of pop lies beyond the scope of traditional art history, in the way in which it posed questions about the relationship between culture in its classical conservative sense—culture as, in Matthew Arnold's words, 'the best that has been thought and said in the world'—and culture in its anthropological sense: culture as the distinctive patterns, rituals, and expressive forms which together constitute the 'whole ways of life' of a community or social group."[24] It is this blurring of distinctions between not only high/elite and low/popular cultural output, but also between the often conflicting claims of "culture as a standard of excellence [and] culture as a descriptive category"[25] that pop art instigated.

In principle, Haring is pop, for he too considers a paradigm of art and life built on such binaries—high versus low, appreciation versus description—to be artificial and politically misguided. However, Haring takes the irreverence that fuels pop art much further. Perhaps we should not conceive of Haring as simply a pop art successor to Warhol, the artist with whom he's often compared. Haring's oeuvre goes so significantly beyond the reach (in terms of aesthetics, ideology, or audience) of his pop art predecessors that it represents a new, more self-consciously populist or "vernacular" art tradition.[26] The term "vernacular" seems especially suitable here because Haring's visual language is inspired by his immediate everyday world of New York City in the 1980s. Haring's art expresses a vernacular, as opposed to a pop, aesthetic because it not only incorporates the images and themes of American pop and mass culture, but also takes its cues from a variety of local subcultures—gay, downtown art, hip hop, which often became one culture for Haring—and synthesizes these influences into an art that has become an icon of late-twentieth-century American civilization.

The burgeoning hip hop culture evoked such fascination in the artist that it ended up constituting one of the most explicit influences on his art. It's easy to see in all of the different media that Haring uses—from graffiti to painting, mural to sculpture—that signature moves from break dancing, like the baby freeze, the windmill, and the back bridge, influence his pictographs. Haring was able to transform what he saw and heard around him into a vernacular visual idiom because he experienced this world firsthand and not vicariously. As Haring says, "See, there was this incredibly raw energy in the air—and it lasted for a good two or three years—and the energy was called Hip-Hop. This Hip-Hop scene included 'scratching,' which meant moving the record back and forth so that it would be making a sort of electronic scratching noise. And it also included break dancing and spray graffiti, because the graffiti scene was really the visual equivalent to the music. . . . Well I began incorporating all of this into the images I was making."[27] His muse was a subculture that had yet to become mass or popular and was often maligned. Had Haring come of age two decades later and honed his vocabulary in the new millennium, after hip hop came to be part of mass and consumer culture, then perhaps we could establish a clear continuum from the pop artists of the 1950s and '60s directly to Keith Haring. But he didn't; he died in 1990, well before hip hop popped.

THE DEATH-BOUND SUBJECT IN HIP HOP

From hip hop culture Haring was able to glean an incredible sense of life as well as an acute sense of loss. As scholars have pointed out, hip hop emerged in the 1970s and '80s in the death-dealing world of a post-industrial urban borough—the Bronx (specifically, the South Bronx)—deprived of economic stability and government attention, and faced with widespread homicide, suicide, drug use, and police violence.[28] Hip hop was indispensable in reckoning with these deadly dangers and in providing a sense of self-worth amid the detritus of New York City. In the classic song "South Bronx Subway Rap," Grandmaster Caz rhymes:

> Look past the garbage over the trains
> Under the ruins through the remains
> Around the crime and pollution
> And tell me where do I fit in?
>
> South Bronx New York that's where I dwell
> To a lot of people it's a living hell
> Full of frustration and poverty
> But wait that's not how it looks to me
>
> It's a challenge and opportunity
> To rise above the state of debris
> You've got to start with nothing
> And then you build
> Fire low your dream until it lits fulfilled.[29]

A rap like Caz's emphasizes both the reality of living in extreme hardship and the yearning for a better life. Against this backdrop, early rap offered also an interior gaze at a life under the constant threat of death. One of the greatest songs of hip hop, Grandmaster Flash and the Furious Five's "The Message," underscores the sense of impending loss felt by young people of color in the '80s. As the song's powerful refrain puts it: "Don't push me cause I'm close to the edge / I'm trying not to lose my head / It's like a jungle sometimes it makes me wonder / How I keep from going under / It's like a jungle sometimes it makes me wonder / How I keep from going under."[30] Contemplating the relationship between death and hip hop, Michael Ralph observes that since death is "a constant force in their lives . . . many rappers 'flirt with death,' in fact, one could argue rappers of the crack and post-crack era are obsessed with it."[31] From early rap songs like "The Message" that express wonderment at being still here, to songs from a decade later like Notorious B.I.G.'s "Respect"—"Umbilical cord's wrapped around my neck / I'm seein' my death and I ain't even took my first step"—to twenty-first-century music like the Roots' *Undun* (an album sung from the vantage point of a death-bound man), one defining feature of hip hop has been acknowledgment of imminent and premature death.

Hip hop emerged in tandem with AIDS art and activism, both movements amplifying the lives and deaths of those disparaged by the nation, and both articulating compounding loss. Haring keenly observed these overlaps. In an evocative journal entry dated March 20, 1987, Haring first discloses his HIV diagnosis and relates his illness and pending death to the deaths of black people. First, ticking off the calendar of loss that marked the early era of AIDS, Haring says: "The odds are very great and, in fact, the symptoms already exist. My friends are dropping like flies and I know in my heart that it is only *divine intervention* that has kept me alive this long. I don't know if I have five months or five years, but I know my days are numbered."[32] Later in the entry, Haring frames his own prospective death and the AIDS crisis in relation to the police killing of Michael Stewart, a twenty-five-year-old graffitist who was brutally and fatally beaten by New York City transit police officers.[33] Haring draws an association between the evils of white supremacy and AIDS, and between his looming death and Stewart's killing:

> Most white men are evil. The white man has always used religion as the tool to fulfill his greed and power hungry aggression.
>
> Business is only another name for control. Control of mind, body and spirit. Control is evil.
>
> All stories of white men's "expansion" and "colonization" and "domination" are filled with horrific details of the abuse of power and the misuse of power.

I'm sure inside I am not white. There is no way to stop them, however. I'm sure it is our destiny to fail. The end is inevitable. So who cares if these pigs kill me with their evil disease, they've killed before and will continue to kill until they suck themselves into their own evil grave and rot and stink and explode themselves into oblivion.

I am glad I'm different. I'm proud to be gay. I'm proud to have friends and lovers of every color. I am ashamed of my forefathers. I am *not* like them.

Today I read in the *New York Times* that all of the officers who killed Michael Stewart were *again* dismissed of charges.

Continually dismissed, but in their minds they will never forget. They know they killed him. They will never forget his screams, his face, his blood. They must live with that forever.

I hope in their next life they are tortured like they tortured him. They should be birds captured early in life, put in cages, purchased by a fat, smelly, ugly lady who keeps them in a small dirty cage up near the ceiling while all day she cooks bloody sausages and the blood splatters their cage and the frying fat burns their matted feathers and they can never escape the horrible fumes of her burnt meat. One day the cage will fall to the ground and a big fat ugly cat will kick them about, play with them like a toy, and slowly *kill* them and leave their remains to be accidentally stepped on by the big fat pig lady who can't see her own feet because of her huge sagging tits.

An eye for an eye . . .

I'm not afraid of anything I'd ever done.

Not ashamed of anything.[34]

Through a series of paratactic statements, Haring defines whiteness as profoundly immoral and malevolent: however naturalized as a good—under the guise of religion, industry, or civilization—whiteness is an apparatus of control, an abuse and misuse of power. Hence, he rejects a sense of whiteness predicated on a hierarchy of race; he says, "I'm sure inside I am not white," as if to divest from whiteness its essentialist claims to racial difference and superiority. Instead, Haring accentuates and takes pride in his disprized difference, his identity as an HIV-positive gay man with a multiethnic assortment of friends and lovers. Given the default privileges that come with white skin, of course, this does not mean that Haring stopped benefiting from his whiteness, however much he sought to disavow it.[35] Because of his skin, he could paint in the subway system and get arrested (as he was several times), but not be brutalized and killed as Stewart was for doing exactly the same thing. Still, I take this to be a significant journal entry since it indexes Haring's desired sense of self, and also, by way of juxtaposition, identifies a relationship between the deaths of gay men from AIDS and the deaths of black and brown people from police brutality, which hip hop culture amplifies.

That the AIDS crisis was sanctioned by the government is a recurring theme in AIDS narratives. But what stands out about Haring's characterization is that, like many black gay artists, he places the AIDS crisis against the long backdrop of black death and disparagement, refusing to see AIDS, like many of his white counterparts do, as an isolated American calamity. For instance, Haring charts a calendar of loss in which "today" becomes a point of intersection for two types of calamities—he begins to mark his imminent death from AIDS ("I don't know if I have five months or five years, but I know my days are numbered"), and he records the racially motivated death of a young black man from police violence ("Today I read in the *New York Times* that all of the officers who killed Michael Stewart were *again* dismissed of charges"). With the exception of Haring, it's hard to think of another white artist who sought to make meaning of his own imminent death and the AIDS crisis chiefly through the perspective of black loss.

In '80s New York, the Stewart case epitomized the extreme forms of police brutality against people of color and the gross failure of the legal system to administer color-blind justice. Stewart was arrested in the middle of the night on September 15, 1983, tagging inside New York City's First Avenue and Fourteenth Street subway stop. Between the time of his arrest and when his unconscious body arrived at the hospital less than an hour later ("hogtied—his ankles bound together, pulled behind his back and tied to his hands with elastic cord"[36]) the police had beat him so badly he was covered with bruises, and they had choked him until he went into cardiac arrest, which left him in a coma for thirteen days before he died. After a series of legal mishaps, in November 1985 an all-white jury acquitted the eleven white officers involved in the incident; also, after running its own investigation, in March 1987 the Metropolitan Transit Authority determined that none of its officers were responsible for Stewart's death and suspended only one on charges of perjury. It was in reaction to the MTA's decision that Haring wrote the above entry and then conjured his own retribution on Stewart's killers, who are metamorphosed into stunted birds, caged, tortured, and killed by their ghoulish caretaker.

Two years before he penned that journal entry, Haring made a powerful homage to Stewart, titled *Michael Stewart—U.S.A. for Africa*. At the center of the apocalyptic painting is an image of a man being strangled. He's naked, arms splayed out in the posture of a crucifixion, his right wrist bound by metal

Keith Haring, *Michael Stewart—U.S.A. for Africa* (1985), enamel and acrylic on canvas, 116″ × 144½″. © Keith Haring Foundation. Used by permission.

handcuffs to a skeleton holding a key, and his left wrist to a serpent striking a dove. Clamping him down further, someone is stepping on his left foot, while two arms reach down and pull a garrote tight around his neck. The pressure of being bound at the extremities and strangled from above has distorted his neck, almost disarticulating his head from his body. Lacking air, the man's face has turned a deeper shade of red than the rest of his body. His eyes are wide open with pain and terror, his mouth also agape, howling. Two signs accent his distorted neck—an upturned cross is tumbling toward the man's left shoulder, and from the other side of the painting the hand of money (a dollar sign morphed into a human hand) reaches for his nape. Meanwhile, in the upper right corner of the painting, blood gushes out of a globe cleaved in half, drowning scores of people below, while the remaining figures shield their eyes from the scene of lynching and apocalypse.

Michael Stewart—U.S.A. for Africa is stark in its indictment of American civilization. In calling attention to the immediate forms of police brutality in the '80s, the painting echoes the long-standing American tradition of lynching. The disfigured image of Stewart in the painting recalls pictures of Emmett Till's corpse, narratives of Sam Hose's remains, the sound and imagery of black bodies depicted in the song "Strange Fruit," and countless other examples that reverberate in black American psyches. The painting extends its indictment of the United States also by troping Africa. Two X's dot the bleeding globe—one on the United States, the other on South Africa—signifying racial apartheid as their common denominator. Furthermore, the title conjoins two contradictory images of America in the '80s—American apartheid, exemplified by the killing of Michael Stewart, and American charity, exemplified by the famous logo/campaign U.S.A. for Africa, whose goal was to bring relief to millions of Ethiopians during the 1984–1985 famine—the former belying the latter. This critical view of race is a leitmotif of Haring's work, a political temperament that distinguishes his art from that of his pop art predecessors of the 1950s and '60s. Under the guise of celebration and nostalgia, "the aesthetics of plenty" had turned the American optimism of the postwar boom years into a virtue, sidestepping the currents of racial violence and terror in the United States. But Haring, although a product of the high commercialism of the 1980s,[37] insisted on exposing the underside of Reagan's morning in America. He had no illusions about the tragic character of an era rife with both sudden and protracted deaths.

APOCALYPSE

Apocalyptic imagery is central to how Haring presents the manifold devastations around him, imagery that was cemented in his imagination while he was an adolescent. In his teen years, Haring briefly joined an evangelical group called Jesus Saves, which, he says, was "obsess[ed] with the concept of the Second Coming—and the 'End of the World,' and that everything that was happening in the world was a sign that these *were* the last days."[38] Although he severed his evangelical ties shortly thereafter, he acknowledged the durable effects of the imagery of apocalypse (and more broadly religious imagery) in his work: "Still, all that stuff stuck in my head and even now there are lots of religious images in my work, although they're used in a more cynical way—to show how manipulative those beliefs and images can be."[39] Apocalyptic and religious imagery can be seen not only in the paintings described above, but in his entire oeuvre, beginning with his early drawings, which juxtapose in the same panel scenes of cataclysm (spaceships zapping the earth, nuclear plants emitting disaster, men brandishing crosses and batons) and scenes of ecstasy and renewal (men engaged in oral and anal sex; radiant babies; animals, humans, and humanoids dancing with abandon). Vivid imagery of awesome destruction and aberration, the sense of human frailty, the dispensation of righteous rage and justice, the calendar of death, and the possibility of regeneration—these are all key motifs that Haring borrows from the idea of an apocalypse, even as he subverts with irony its strict evangelical and fundamentalist meaning.

"Part of [the] extraordinary resilience" of the biblical concept of apocalypse, Frank Kermode observes, is its power not only to prophesy time's ultimate end, but also, in the interim, to explain history's long line of calamities as examples of minor and false apocalypses, as preludes and proofs of the coming end of the world.[40] Also extraordinary about this notion is its ability to conjure up a set of binary worlds—this world and the next; heaven and hell; the familiar and the unfamiliar; the normal and the aberrant; the logical and the illogical—all in one vivid vision, which is why artists often appropriate it. Indeed, while they often dispense with its literalism, Kermode rightly notes, artists still retain the intensity of apocalypse's imagery, affect, and timeline of loss:

> Great artists know too much about the relationship of their fictions and images to historical reality to be seduced by figures or promises of Armageddon, Rapture and Judgment; but apprehensions of terror, epochal change and possible renewal are still strong, and it is not difficult to see the history of the twentieth century as providing more than adequate confirmation of the horrible events imagined as preceding the end. . . . Modern artists, in giving precise expression to a vaguer, more general, less acute anxiety that all may share, find themselves repeating the old figurations of Apocalypse. Even when the old thought is modernized the old imagery recurs, and is potent because Apocalypse still has a date in the calendar.[41]

These words certainly resonate with Haring's use of the idea of apocalypse to give "precise expression" to the different catastrophes converging on him, as one way to visually formalize his own death date and also take inventory of the mass devastation around him. With respect to the AIDS crisis, an apocalyptic timeline of imminent death speaks to artists like Haring and many others for whom that calendar was a reality, for whom *today* was a marker of more deaths, including one's own imminent final day. The torrential quality of apocalyptic expression can also give voice to the compounding suffering and death borne by people living with AIDS; the intensity of emotion in those images can amplify the keening and rage of AIDS mourners battling against the silence and false moralism of a society colluding in their mass suffering and death.

In the hands of Haring, the figure of the apocalypse is freed of its literalism and moreover exposes the very people who exploited the book of Revelation for homophobic ends. In the early era of AIDS, a cadre of moralizers had taken to the airwaves, using apocalyptic language to license the suffering and deaths of gay men from AIDS, and to propagate the belief that AIDS was a sign of the literal end of the world. Emblematic of that discourse is the following remark by Jerry Falwell, who was head of the Moral Majority and a personal confidant of President Ronald Reagan:

> What we see is a commitment to spend our tax dollars on research to allow these diseased homosexuals to go back to their perverted practices without any standards of accountability. If homosexuals are not stopped they will in time infect the entire nation, and America will be destroyed. If the Reagan administration does not put its full weight against this, what is now a gay plague in this country, I feel that a year from now, President Ronald Reagan, personally, will be blamed for allowing this awful disease to break out among the innocent American public. ... When you violate moral, health, and hygiene laws, you reap the whirlwind. You cannot shake your fist in God's face and get by with it.

Such apocalyptic language about AIDS and homosexuality was common among evangelicals, conservative politicians, and pundits, who manipulated that language to gin up fear, panic, and hatred; to deny government funding for AIDS research and care (or, for that matter, any kind of care for people suffering from the illness); and to conjure up a reborn America cleansed of its "diseased homosexuals." Against such violent exploitations of the concept of apocalypse, Haring's transgressive uses of the imagery take on heightened meaning.

Mixed in with the Christian references is the etymology of the word "apocalypse": "to uncover." And Haring's adoption of apocalyptic imagery encompasses both the Christian and secular senses of the word, both the time of time's end and the act of unveiling. There is a clear yearning in Haring that in the end judgment and justice will be meted to those in power, those who are responsible for the devastation around him, and he often wills that outcome on canvas. His sense of apocalypse is not trapped by religious literalism, and how he uses the imagery to unveil the underside of America imbues it with a radical political character and a historical rather than providential temporality. Some of Haring's imagery resembles strongly the angel of history that Benjamin envisions in "Theses on the Philosophy of History." In his rich ekphrasis of Paul Klee's painting *Angelus Novus*, Benjamin writes:

A Klee painting named "Angelus Novus" shows an angel looking as though he is about to move away from something he is fixedly contemplating. His eyes are staring, his mouth is open, his wings are spread. This is how one pictures the angel of history. His face is turned toward the past. Where we perceive a chain of events, he sees one single catastrophe which keeps piling wreckage and hurls it in front of his feet. The angel would like to stay, awaken the dead, and make whole what has been smashed. But a storm is blowing in from Paradise; it has got caught in his wings with such violence that the angel can no longer close them. The storm irresistibly propels him into the future to which his back is turned, while the pile of debris before him grows skyward. This storm is what we call progress.[42]

This passage also aptly characterizes Haring's vision and tragic temperament. His work is "fixedly contemplating" a world compounding with loss, visualizing figures in distress (like the ones in *Untitled* and *Michael Stewart—U.S.A. for Africa*) and agents of God who operate in historical time, endowed not with the power of divine intervention but with the human act of bearing witness. There is a simple but powerful "self-portrait" of Haring made a few months prior to his death that reflects the posture of Benjamin's angel. On a photograph someone had taken of him (he's sitting on a chair, facing the camera, and we see his full body), Haring has drawn wings sprouting from his shoulders—with a black felt pen and with typical Haring lines and outlines—and a halo above his head; but he has also put ropes around his body and drawn shackles around his feet. "Whoever understands this photograph," says Haring of the portrait, "understands what my work is all about."[43] A roped and shackled angel—one who yearns for flight and transcendence, but is bound to the earth and history— bears the same burden as one whose power to "awaken the dead" has been irredeemably lost. All he can do, to quote James Baldwin, is "to try [to] bear witness to something which will have to be there when the storm is over. You have to get through the next storm, storms are always coming."[44]

In two of Haring's late works—a collaboration with William Burroughs titled *Apocalypse*, and a book titled *Eight Ball* that he created by going through a drawer of saved and found items—we see how Haring articulates the two meanings of "apocalypse" as catastrophe and revelation. *Apocalypse* consists of twenty silkscreens, ten of Haring's images and ten of Burroughs's cut-up statements. Both Haring's leaping association of images and Burroughs's aleatoric literary technique lend themselves to conjuring up a figure that "radically suspends logic and opens up vertiginous possibilities of referential aberration."[45] Haring's compositions recall his earlier panels of apocalyptic imagery, but

 Keith Haring, *Glory Hole* (1980), acrylic, spray enamel, and ink on paper, 48″ × 35½″. © Keith Haring Foundation. Used by permission.

these are more minimal and disconsolate. They are not densely filled with lines, sharp outlines, or brilliantly colored backdrops, and there are no exuberant figures nor clear signs of renewal and regeneration. For example, what once radiated with life-giving energy—the penis in *Glory Hole*—in *Apocalypse* oozes out what looks like a mushroom cloud and is surrounded by sperm cells with horns (the most repeated pictograph in the series). All of Haring's silkscreens in this collaboration include a collaged iconic image, including *Mona Lisa*, the sacred heart of Jesus, and postwar pictures of the white American family, which Haring accentuates or disfigures with his signature black felt line. And almost all of the compositions include a visual fragment of calamity: breaking and melting skyscrapers; a volcano about to devastate a city; piled-up bodies; a body tortured, tied up, and hung upside down. Haring's humanoids are here too, but in

One of ten panels from *Apocalypse* by Keith Haring (1988), silkscreen, 38″ × 38″.
© Keith Haring Foundation. Used by permission.

this series they are much more menacing. While the compositions in *Apocalypse* distill Haring's long-standing apocalyptic vocabulary, through which he visually apprehends terror and devastation, they do so without the sense of rapture and radiating life that animated his earliest works. Apocalypse looks and feels different to a budding artist in the early '80s than to a dying one in 1988, who was a witness to a decade awash with death.

In the very last panel, Burroughs arrives at a definition of apocalypse that strikes me as true of Haring's last works: "The final Apocalypse is when everyman sees what he sees, feels what he feels, hears what he hears. The creatures of all your dreams and nightmares are right here, right now, solid as they ever were or ever will be."

This sense of apocalypse as heightened awareness and revelation is illuminated clearly in *Eight Ball*. In the book's preface, Haring writes:

> [*Eight Ball*] comes at a time in my life when I am searching for answers. Having spent thirty years here, each day seems to provide only more questions. This book is a testament to that search.
>
> It was constructed like a kind of game. First, I went through drawers of old mementos, newspaper clippings and drawings that I had saved and found ones that were particularly interesting to me. Then, they were randomly glued onto the 20 sheets of paper which had each been measured to correspond to the size of a double-page spread in the book.
>
> After this, I painted the papers with red and green gouache. Finally, with black sumi ink, I "finished" each of the drawings. The black line ties together all the other elements already on the page. It constructs relationships and reveals meaning. It is during this process that the drawing is brought to life. Change and intuition play major roles at every stage of its development. Slowly, as if uncovering a hidden treasure, the group of drawings begins to reveal its meaning. The juxtaposition of image, text, and color cross-reference each other from page to page and the book is born.
>
> This book is about the mysteries of love, life, death, and art (not necessarily in that order). It attempts to reveal certain truths. However, as I have found in my own life, each revelation brings with it many more new questions. After 30 years, I am exactly at the same point where I started.[46]

Haring's statement can't help but reflect the calendar of loss brought about by AIDS, as a thirty-year-old man is forced to reckon with his own imminent, premature death. Made in the last year of Haring's life, *Eight Ball* illuminates the artist's death-bound revelations as well as his fundamental relationship to the line. As the title signals, the book can be read as a metaphor for Haring's life in its last round. Faced with a final date on the calendar, he's looking back at life, sifting through old mementos and keepsakes, piecing them together freely, allowing meaning to leap from minimal and aleatoric juxtapositions of image, color, and line. And as the preface underscores, Haring sees his life trajectory achronologically. In much the same way that the book uncovers meaning through a cut-up technique that thwarts linearity and reveals "the mysteries of love, life, death, and art" in no particular order, Haring acknowledges that there is a similar, open-ended and associative quality to life as well. Truth and revelation are not culminations, end points, or ways of summing up life once and for all, but instead are pathways for examining life unflinchingly.

An apt metaphor for the artist's searching is, of course, the line, which for him, like life itself, resists any clear beginning and terminal points. Haring says, "with black sumi ink, I 'finished' each of the drawings," putting scare quotes around the word to signify the open-ended character of his line. "The black line ties together all the other elements already on the page. It constructs relationships and reveals meaning. It is during this process that the drawing is brought to life," he adds, characterizing his lifelong fascination with the line as the very instrument by which connections are made and meanings unveiled. "After 30 years, I am exactly at the same point where I started," says Haring, and where he started, at least as an artist, was in graffiti, and what had arrested his attention then about the art was this same line. "And always the hard-edged black line that tied the drawings together!" Haring said of graffiti, adding, "It was the line I had been obsessed with since childhood!"[47]

ART AND ACTIVISM

While works like *Untitled*, *Michael Stewart—U.S.A. for Africa*, *Apocalypse*, and *Eight Ball* display Haring's sense of loss, the many posters he designed for AIDS health and political activist groups show how he used his art explicitly to fight AIDS. Haring produced perhaps the most widely disseminated series of works devoted to AIDS prevention and the theme of "safe sex"—artwork that was unapologetic in its explicit portrayal of sex (especially gay sex) and that was determined to break the silence surrounding AIDS in its early years. One of the artist's safe-sex drawings features two men masturbating each other. Images like those utilize Haring's cartoon-style figures to represent, explicitly and graphically, the taboo of gay sex. Indeed, the cartoon-like drawings ultimately suggest that sex between two people is, after all, innocent and harmless, and that it can also be, and should be, safe. His AIDS graphics use cartoon figures to diffuse the subversive and transgressive for a more mainstream audience, and they also temper the apocalyptic scenes that permeate his later works.

The ACT UP logo was a black backdrop with a pink triangle at the center and at the bottom the words/equation Silence = Death. This powerful AIDS graphic was first produced in 1986 by members of the Silence = Death Project and then given to ACT UP to use as its symbol.[48] The image would end up serving as a visual manifesto of AIDS activism, and today it serves as a powerful reminder of the turmoil of the epidemic's early years. In Haring's 1989 appropriation of the image, there are generic, identical little Haringesque bodies covering the entire surface of the composition, giving a sense of ideological homogeneity and mass hysteria. The bodies actually move off the picture's edges as if the crowd contin-

Keith Haring, *Untitled* (1985), synthetic polymer on canvas, 60″ × 60¹⁄₁₆″ × 1¼″.
© Keith Haring Foundation. Used by permission.

ues and extends infinitely beyond the drawing's frame—representing millions and millions of people. The figures shield their eyes and ears in defiant evasion and silence about the death and suffering of AIDS. But the fact that the anonymous figures surround and are included in the pink triangle—a symbol of gay liberation and gay pride—suggests that the silence is not only about disease and plague, but also specifically about the fear of homosexuality and gay sex (terms that became almost synonymous with AIDS during this period of time). The pink triangle's dominance in this composition also recalls the Holocaust. During World War II, the Nazis mandated that Jews identify themselves with the Star of David and that male homosexuals identity themselves with a pink triangle. The early gay rights movement reclaimed this historical marker of shame and internment by reappropriating it as a symbol of liberation and visibility. But in this artwork—explicitly addressing death and silence—the pink triangle

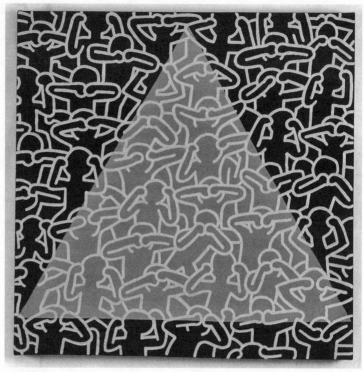

Keith Haring, *Silence = Death* (1989), acrylic on canvas, 40″ × 40″. © Keith Haring Foundation. Used by permission.

haunts. Haring's use of the pink triangle—which can be read as an allusion to the oppressive regime and concentration camps from which it is derived—suggests that AIDS is itself a kind of genocide or holocaust.

The vivid color juxtaposed with the black background creates a separation of the generic little bodies into two distinct groups: those outside the pink triangle, who are silhouetted against the black background, and those inside the triangle, who are highlighted in the neon pink. The suggestion is that those included within the symbolic pink triangle are gay and perhaps reckoning with AIDS. And their conspicuous visual incandescence—against the neon pink—suggests that they have somehow been identified, exposed, and shamed by the public. These figures therefore shield their eyes and ears not only from the truth, but also from the hysterical, paranoid public gaze of phobia and judgment. But what is perhaps most striking about this drawing is that Haring's generic little men—who are usually represented in his works with motion strokes drawn into the images themselves to evoke a sense of movement, dance, or

Keith Haring, *Ignorance = Fear* (1989), poster, 24″ × 43¼″. © Keith Haring Foundation.
Used by permission.

energy—in this composition are strikingly immobile: there are no motion
strokes whatsoever. Haring therefore augments the mood of melancholy, silence, and evasion with a pervasive sense of paralysis. The social protest is chilling and clear. Haring uses a limited, yet striking set of images and symbols to tell
a story of and for an entire generation of Americans. The contrasting colors, the
basic and stark triangle, the seemingly innocuous yet highly symbolic generic
bodies—all come together in a painting that brilliantly breaks the very silence
it critiques.

Haring's AIDS graphics vocabulary also is evidenced in another poster he
made in 1989, this one specifically for ACT UP and titled *Ignorance = Fear*. At
the center of the composition are three figures, one covering his eyes, another
his ears, and another his mouth, a pictorial demonstration of the maxim of the
three monkeys: see no evil, hear no evil, speak no evil. Slogans of AIDS activism
frame the picture; the header reads Ignorance = Fear, and the footer references
three key ACT UP texts: Silence = Death, the pink triangle, and Fight AIDS / ACT
UP (the latter a line drawn from the group's famous chant, "ACT UP! FIGHT
BACK! FIGHT AIDS!"). Haring aligns the proverbial image with AIDS activism,
signifying both the public's act of willed ignorance, fear, and evasion of AIDS,
and the countervailing forces of knowledge, power, and engagement that AIDS
activism brought to bear.

As we have seen, Haring was well attuned to the social issues of his time and brought those issues into his art. In addition to the numerous AIDS prevention and AIDS outreach artworks, he made a famous mural called *Crack Is Wack* and used his art to make social statements about apartheid in South Africa, gay pride and National Coming Out Day, and UNICEF, among many other causes. Given Haring's thorough and almost spiritual involvement in the culture and politics of his time, it's important that we examine the cultural world he existed in. The 1980s was a decade of cold war, which included the threats of the nuclear age (recall the Three Mile Island accident, which occurred at a nuclear plant less than fifty miles from the town in which Haring was born). The '80s were also a time of Republican leadership, conservative backlash, and urban decay, in which the proliferation of crack cocaine and large decreases in federal social welfare spending contributed to the development of an increasingly alienated, predominantly black and Latino urban underclass. Violence from without and within compounded the devastation experienced in many an inner city. And it was out of this desperate situation that hip hop, with its new art and cultural forms, emerged.

At the same time, the '80s was a decade of great prosperity for the American upper class, especially in New York City, where the Wall Street culture became a breeding ground for the über-rich and powerful. The great wealth of certain parts of New York City subsequently resulted in a new kind of Lower Manhattan art world industry in which artists became big-money moguls themselves. And of course, against this backdrop, one of the most cataclysmic historical events of the twentieth century began to unfold. AIDS would turn America's urban gay communities upside down. But AIDS would also reinvigorate these gay communities to fight back and push forward for increased acceptance and visibility. The cacophony of symbols and images in Haring's visual language certainly draws on this sociocultural landscape and on the manifold calamities of the decade, which Haring also dared to portray.

four

Epistles to the Dead
AIDS Orphans and the Work of Mourning

In a simple but haunting untitled painting created in 1998 or 1999, Trevor Makhoba, the late South African painter, captures the havoc wrought by AIDS in his country and in many other parts of the global south. The canvas depicts a burial procession, which is not an unconventional subject for a painting. What's disturbing about Makhoba's burial scene, however, is that the people carrying the casket and watching the procession are all toddlers. Innumerable, the children file out to the horizon carrying caskets grossly disproportional to their bodies, the white diapers they wear in sharp relief against the muted tones of the painting. With gripping simplicity, Makhoba conjures the plight of the masses of children who have lost their parents to AIDS, and he does so by centering the grief that these AIDS mourners must bear. The idea of young children as pallbearers is both haunting and confounding. Since children cannot physically carry coffins, Makhoba's painting compels the viewer to ask, then how do they bear their loss? How do children mourn without recourse to the funerary rites and mourning conventions that buttress adults? What is their vocabulary of death, their grammar and calendar of loss? Furthermore, how do these particular children stigmatized by AIDS—orphaned not just by their parents, but by the world around them—carry out the work of mourning? These are the urgent questions that Makhoba's painting has asked of me since I came across it in a small gallery in Cape Town, South Africa, a decade ago. I have sought to answer these questions by studying closely the works of mourning produced by AIDS orphans themselves.

When considered in AIDS discourse, AIDS orphans in Africa are often presented in a lump sum—as statistics or as objects of western charity, pity, and spectacle—but rarely do they enter the field as subjects capable of articulating their own experiences. One way of mitigating the myopic view of AIDS orphans is to foreground the children's own experience of the loss of their parents and, more broadly, of the AIDS calamity. Foregrounding the perspective of the children also allows us to expand the scope of AIDS studies in the humanities, which has focused almost exclusively on adults, and to reframe the terms of queer studies, which in recent iterations has constructed queerness in direct opposition to the figure of the child. Given that AIDS scholarship and activism in the 1980s and '90s helped to constitute queer studies as a scholarly field, I believe that queer studies should also think about other subjects queered by AIDS, in addition to gay men. While children are often pitted against homosexuality— as vulnerable creatures in need of protection from the homosexual menace—I use the resources of black queer studies to break the negative ties between the concepts about children and those about homosexuality promulgated by politicians and queer theorists alike. The figure of childhood that we glean from the narratives of AIDS orphans jars against the stereotypical figure of the child that helps to prop up heteronormativity; and the world of these children, suffused with multiple losses, clashes with the rosy future that children symbolize in most cultures.

The materials of mourning I draw on here are from Sudden Flowers, the first AIDS art collective in Ethiopia, which was founded in 1999. Sudden Flowers emerged at a decisive moment in the timeline of AIDS in Ethiopia. The mid-1990s, when HIV/AIDS became a crisis that demanded public attention, can be seen as the early era of the epidemic in the country. It was only in 1998 that the Ethiopian government first issued a national policy on HIV/AIDS, and in 1999 that the country held its first national forum on the subject.[1] It was in the mid- to late 1990s that AIDS deaths began to compound exponentially, even as the silence surrounding the crisis and the stigmatization of people living with the disease went unchecked.[2] Amid the rising death toll and deafening public silence, people living with HIV/AIDS began to organize, founding two pioneering organizations, Mekdim Ethiopia and Dawn of Hope (in 1997 and 1998, respectively), which aimed to empower people living with HIV/AIDS.[3] In 1999, Sudden Flowers followed as the first organization to use art to counter the stigma and silence surrounding HIV/AIDS, and it did so by amplifying the voices of AIDS orphans.

Sudden Flowers began as a unique collaboration among Eric Gottesman, an American in his early twenties, and Salamawit Alemu, Yamrot Alemu, Biniyam Mesfin, Hana Mesfin, Amsale Shiferaw, and Asrat Tessema, Ethiopian children between the ages of nine and seventeen.[4] A graduate of Duke University and the recipient of a Hart Fellowship, the young Gottesman arrived in Ethiopia in 1999 with little knowledge of the country and with no set plans of what he would do during his fellowship year.[5] His decision to travel to Ethiopia was fortuitous, enabling him to come of age as an artist and also to forge a deep, enduring connection with Ethiopia.[6] Upon his arrival, Gottesman partnered with local nongovernmental organizations that were confronting an issue swathed in silence—HIV/AIDS. He recalls being struck by the absence of any discussion of AIDS, in spite of the extraordinary toll both the silence and the disease were taking on the country: "I knew the virus was having a tremendous effect on Ethiopia but I rarely heard people talking about it, and I found little in the media about it."[7] The absence of public discussion of HIV/AIDS led him to embark on his first creative, socially and politically committed endeavor: to make a series of photographic portraits of Ethiopians living with HIV/AIDS as one concrete way of countering the silence and mitigating the public erasure of those living with the disease. Given the extent of the stigma experienced by Ethiopians with HIV/AIDS at the time, it was difficult to find willing participants who would publicly declare their seropositive status. So Gottesman began to work closely with counselors at the few organizations that were providing support and care for people with HIV/AIDS, and he soon found volunteers willing to be photographed, which became the first portraits of Ethiopians living with the disease.

While making these portraits of adult Ethiopians with HIV/AIDS, Gottesman met Yawoinshet Masresha, a trailblazing social worker affiliated with the Medical Missionaries of Mary (MMM), who later founded Hope for Children; these were two of the first NGOs to focus on the plight of AIDS orphans. He learned that Masresha had just begun counseling Salamawit, Yamrot, Biniyam, Hana, Amsale, and Asrat, and that all six "were left alone when their parents died. Some remained in the hospital, some with abusive guardians, some on the streets. [Masresha and MMM] collected them, found a small two-room home and a caring foster mother . . . [and provided] food and basic services for them until each graduate[d] high school or turn[ed] 18."[8] Encouraged by Masresha and moved by the orphans' extraordinary stories and resilient spirit, Gottesman asked the group to collaborate with him and, he explained, "they all agreed to make photographs and texts with [him] for a local exhibition of the work."[9] He began by teaching them how to use a camera and asking them to photograph and write about their lives. The group gelled quickly, brought together by their similarities (like their age and inexperience as artists) and differences (like language and cultural experience). Gottesman recalls, "I was 23 and yes, I do think that my age allowed me to relate to young people at that time. I also think my naïveté, my inability to speak the language, my lack of knowledge about the place or about photography all had benefits as well as costs. I learned about

Ethiopia from young people. I learned by listening and therefore I learned to listen. Also, with my photography, I learned photography by teaching it and doing it with people who had just a little less photographic knowledge than I did at the time."[10] Sudden Flowers blossomed out of this ethics and practice of collaboration, where the children in the group had as much to teach Gottesman as he had to teach them, rather than a hierarchy of power relations. Individually and in collaboration with each other, the group began to generate a variety of striking photos and texts that documented the realities of AIDS in ways that resisted the one-dimensional view, the spectacle of AIDS in Africa so pervasive in the west. Soon after their collaboration began, in August 2000, the group held an exhibition of their work, the first art exhibit on AIDS ever held in Ethiopia.

Since their first exhibition, Sudden Flowers has grown significantly, holding numerous shows both inside and outside Ethiopia. Using a variety of media— letters, photographs, films, public installations, performances—this pioneering collective has produced remarkable narratives of AIDS that give insight into how children have borne this calamity. It is a body of work that transcends the overdetermined discourse—governmental, NGO, public health, news media— that has narrowly framed the experience of AIDS orphans, often obscuring the agency, resilience, and depth of perception with which they have confronted this catastrophe. If disprized children are allowed to speak, their voices, Toni Morrison reminds us, present "a chance to interrupt, to violate the adult world, its miasma of discourse about them, for them, but never to them."[11] In their work, the children of Sudden Flowers certainly interrupt a discourse of AIDS in which they have no say but are there merely as objects of adult knowledge and sentiment; they violate that arrangement, much like the children in Makhoba's painting, by carrying out a queer act of mourning: in their letters, photographs, films, and performances, they manifest and mourn the AIDS dead whom their compatriots have refused to recognize and grieve.

EPISTLES TO THE DEAD

Between 1999 and 2004, the children of Sudden Flowers wrote over fifty letters addressed to their deceased parents. In their extraordinary intimacy, these epistles to the dead became a powerful form of mourning and self-expression for these children, as well as an integral part of the group's creative repertoire. I call these texts "epistles" because they are letters addressed to someone in particular and because of their literariness; many of them read like verse. My English translations do not fully capture the poetry and lyric intimacy of the original letters in Amharic, partly because I have opted for translations that closely follow the original grammar and wording of the letters in order to maintain the integrity of the children's own utterances of loss. Nor can the translations convey the experience of reading the original letters in the children's own handwriting and language. Since many of these epistles are by budding writers whose penmanship and literacy have yet to settle—because of their young age and intermittent schooling—there are many mischaracterizations of the Ethiopic alphabet and vocabulary: there are words missing characters, words that are not legible, and sentences and paragraphs without punctuation marks. On the first pass, these flaws might bring the reader to a halt. I had to reread many of the letters word by word, modifying characters and tweaking diacritics in order to capture the intended sound and meaning of a word; and line by line, disarticulating strings of sentences. Despite these constraints in translation, I hope the English renditions still impart the children's expressions of loss, longing, and life.

Salamawit Alemu was nine years old when she drafted her epistles, three letters that embody her personal loss and anguish and also exemplify common themes and terms of loss expressed in many of the children's letters. Salamawit stood out as a member of Sudden Flowers, not merely because at nine she was the youngest founding member of the collective, nor because of the incalculable hardships and trauma she endured as a child—"she was begging on the streets with her mother when she was four, six when her mother died."[12] Despite all this, she had a strong sense of her own agency and was keenly reflexive and performative. She renamed herself at age seven, changing her first name from Rut to Salamawit, meaning She Is Peace. And she assumed another persona, Beti, in Gottesman's portfolio of portraits of her, as well as in her own self-portraits. When writing to her dead parents, she crafted letters as both Rut, the name given to her at birth, and Salamawit, the name she gave herself, each version imbued with grief and empowered self-expression. The epistle that she authored as Salamawit reads:

To My Dear Mother

My dear beloved mother how are you? Except for the thought of you and longing for you I am fine. Because now you are not living by my side with such intense feeling my stomach gets very very disturbed. Now when a mother hugs her boy or her girl I wish my mother was here I could also be hugged like this I say. Because you are not here by my side now no one cheers me up and because I always get jealous I cry. If my mother and father were here, like this, there is no one to cheer me up, to hug me, to console me. I wish I could find a mother like you and be happy. Mommy, you were the one who gave me advice. But now both you and my father are far from me and I am far from you. Who comes close to me?

Separated from my side before I was full of your love separated from me my mother.

Your child,
Salamawit Alemu[13]

Salamawit's letter exhibits the pathos and vexed grammar typical of these epistles to the dead: a form in which bereaved children hold an intimate conversation with their deceased parents and mediate the interface between life and death. Salamawit's epistle, like several others, begins with a generic salutation—"My dear beloved mother how are you?"—and, more specifically, with the generic salutation of Amharic letters addressed to a beloved the writer has not seen for some time: "Except for the thought of you and longing for you I am fine." These are two basic conventions of letter writing in Amharic with which these children would have been familiar. But there is something disconcerting about these salutations in the children's letters. Although standard in addressing the living, in these letters they hail the dead. Delineated from the start is the tension between the present orientation of the letter as a form of communication among the living, and the irrevocable absence of the recipients of these letters, who are dead addressees incapable of replying. Even as they rehearse the basic greetings of the Amharic letter, these epistles conjure an absent addressee who has departed, troubling the fixed distinction between the living and the dead.

Throughout the collection of letters, the children repeatedly characterize the relationship between themselves and their dead parents as a separation that is not ultimate. Although in reality the separation may be final and irrevocable, in the letters that separation is still tentative, in flux, unfixed. The reiterated term and trope for death is "separation," while the term "death" appears, astonishingly, in only one letter. Amharic has a repertoire of phrases that use separation as a euphemism for death—*kezee alem bemot teleye* (from this world by death he's separated), *kezee alem teleye* (from this world he's separated), and, pruned down further, *kealem teleye* (from the world he's separated)—but the separation is qualified to signify, categorically, another world the dead inhabit. When the word "separation" shows up in these letters, however, it is never in the context of these common adult expressions that mark the divide between the world of the living and the world of the dead. Furthermore, none of the letters use the most popular Amharic euphemism for death: *maref*, "to rest." Thus,

Salamawit Alemu's letter in Amharic

when Salamawit closes her letter with the lyrical words "Separated from my side before I was full of your love separated from me my mother," we have to consider closely what "separated" denotes in this loaded line and not presume that the term signifies in the same way it does for adult speakers of the language.

It is worth noting how these epistles account for the separation between the living and the dead. The children measure the space that divides them and their parents in terms that are contiguous—"not living by my side," "not here," "far from me," as Salamawit writes—but give no indication as to where their parents have gone. Given the deeply religious temperament of Ethiopians, and the almost automatic use of religious condolences in speaking about death, one expects to see the children resort to that vocabulary and imagery to characterize their parents' posthumous abode, but they don't. Their letters employ a trope of separation that is relative rather than absolute, eschewing the language of scripture and religious condolences that are conclusive about where the dead dwell. Consider, for instance, how Salamawit, in another letter to her mother (this one signed as Rut) inscribes death as a tentative separation. Addressing her mother, she writes: "But you having left begging you are now in a better place. Mommy now will you not come to see us?"[14] Rut imagines her mother to have gone to "a better place" where she is no longer a beggar enduring that life of extreme hardship. Nevertheless, "a better place"—a common Christian phrase to signify heaven—is not used here in a religious sense; in fact, the question that immediately follows defies Christian eschatology, since it conceives of the dead as inhabiting a contiguous space and time, as capable of being summoned back and physically reuniting with the bereaved.

Some of the most arresting portions of these letters are precisely the moments when the children demand that their deceased parents materialize themselves either in person or as embodied tokens of familial care and affection. In her letter, Amsale says to her mother: "What I want to tell you after this is about my school. I have good grades. Now in the first semester I came in second. And in the second semester, well, I think I will come in between first and third. Make sure you send me the prize, okay, Mommy?"[15] Bereket Muluneh asks of his mother, "Today you know is a holiday. Give me money."[16] Heywot Umer, in one of her two letters, makes an insistent plea for her mother's material care and embodied presence: "Now the reason I am writing this letter to you is because my clothes are wearing out and I want you to buy me clothes. And shoes and everything, just come and I will tell you, don't you think? If you came and we talked or played how thrilled I would be. Therefore before spending a day or night hurry and come. I love you very much. I will wait for you, ok?"[17] The conflation of the living and the dead may stem partly from the conflation of the grammar of letter writing, which is the present tense, and the grammar of loss, which is geared toward the past tense or the subjunctive. But that conflation also reflects these children's particular, unfixed sense of the interface between the living and the dead, which is why they make these kinds of temporal and material demands on their parents.

Along with a provisional sense of separation, the letters share other notable features. One is their characterization of loss in somatic terms as the loss of intimacy with the parent's body. Salamawit says, "Now when a mother hugs her boy or her girl I wish my mother was here I could also be hugged like this I say. Because you are not here by my side now no one cheers me up and because I always get jealous I cry." This is a striking scene, to which she returns in each of her three letters. Writing to her father, she says, "now because you are not near me when everyone hugs his child I begin to covet and because you are not near me I am very mournful."[18] And as Rut, she writes to her mother: "And now when a father hugs his child, when a mother is going to the market with her child, at that time, I remember you."[19] Seeing other parents physically intimate with their children triggers a range of intense feelings in this author: longing, jealousy, crying, coveting, and mourning, all prompted by the absent parental touch the child craves. There is another telling context in which the word "hug" shows up, this time as a metaphor to characterize the new caretaker in the children's lives. Amsale writes: "My name is Amsale Shiferaw. I am a student in the 8th grade. I don't have a father and a mother. I live hugged by an organization."[20] These children yearn for the physical care and affection expressed by a parent's hug, so much so that they extrapolate from that embodied act to other forms of caregiving, like that provided by the organization that now sponsors them.

Another striking characteristic of the loss in these epistles features time, perhaps best expressed in Salamawit's closing line—"Separated from my side before I was full of your love separated from me my mother"—with its eloquent articulation of the calendar of bereaved children. The temporality of loss that Salamawit expresses is intimately linked to a foreshortened horizon of time that comes with youth. I read the phrase "before I was full of your love" to signify the author's reflexive sense of her own age, that her youth has somehow delimited the amount of her mother's love she could absorb. In another letter, Rut reiterates this same sentiment of lost futurity, delineating further the different temporal effects of loss on the child versus on the parent: "Before I could finish your love you left. You were finished with my love."[21] The regret and resentment expressed in these lines suggest that the child feels betrayed by her age. As her intricate timeline of love and loss indicates, she feels that when her mother died she had not yet reached a certain threshold of time necessary to consummate a child's love for her mother, whereas her mother had been afforded that time. Others echo Salamawit's lament of lost time: "leaving her without finishing her love," writes Hana, describing herself in a missive to her mother, again characterizing loss partly as the loss of the future time necessary to forge a deeper bond with the parent.[22] Other letters point to different temporal aberrations brought about by the loss of parents. Asrat had to leave school when her mother died and was held back when she eventually returned. She connects her grade retention and her mother's absence in the same line: "Isn't it sad, Mommy, if you were here, my education level and my age would have matched."[23] Specifically, what Asrat is mourning in these lines—what's "sad"—is that her mother's absence has interrupted the normal progression of her development, misaligning the symmetry of age and grade level, a temporal tool by which children often evaluate themselves. Hence, there is a particular loss of time—a lost future to consummate love or a lost past to be in school—that is mourned in these letters in addition to more tangible losses.

The epistles take inventory of a range of losses experienced by these young children: as they lament the loss of their parent's physical body, as well as the care, affection, affirmation, and advice the parent provided, they also bemoan the loss of the old routines that structured the child-parent relationship. In Bereket Muluneh's letter, he strikes up an intimate, lyrical conversation with his mother, recalling the kinds of exchanges that once mediated their lives:

[From] Bereket Muluneh

Mother, how can I help you? Mother, I am about to go to school. I am about to go to school give me breakfast Mother. I just got back from school, give me lunch. Buy me a book and a pen. Buy me a ball. Mother, can I go and play ball? Mother, can I run an errand for you? Can I draw water for you? Watch the store for you? Brew coffee for you? Go and buy something for you? Mother, can we sleep together? Mother, at school our math teacher has given us an assignment, who's going to help me? I'll spank whoever comes to class without doing his homework, he said. Mother, where are you going? Are you going to Addis Ababa? To buy things? Take me with you. I will help you carry things. Today you know is a holiday. Give me money.[24]

While most of these epistles open with the formal greetings of letter writing—which at the very least index a physical distance or separation between author and addressee—some, like Bereket's, eschew those conventions, breaking down further the barrier between the living and the dead. Here, the mother isn't merely the absent addressee of the missive, but a present interlocutor, however silent, partaking in the intimate colloquy of the lyric. The string of questions and the repeated apostrophe to his mother give Bereket's epistle an evocative aural rhythm, at the same time evoking the daily patterns of life. The action-oriented letter reprises not only the mother's authority and the essentials she provided her child (food, school supplies, toys, pocket money, physical comfort, protection) but also the roles and duties the child fulfilled

Bereket Muluneh's letter in Amharic

for his mother (doing errands, performing household chores, helping her carry things). While the child's actions may seem routine and perfunctory, they are imbued with formative feelings. The desire to please and help one's parent by taking on certain duties, the delight to be had in running to the kiosk to fetch an item, the sensual experience of a coffee ceremony—say, the aroma of frankincense and roasting coffee beans—are among the everyday experiences, sensations, and pleasures the child is losing out on now, bereft of his mother.

Along with relaying the children's articulations of loss, the letters also convey the outcast status of these bereaved authors, who are of very poor background and moreover disparaged as AIDS orphans. The missives that I have referenced so far only gesture at the social status of these children. Salamawit asks, for instance, now that both her parents are gone, "Who comes close to me?"—which could also be translated as "Who dares comes close to me?" or "No one dares come close to me!" uttered in a tone that encapsulates the pariah status of people with AIDS at the time, including children. But there are letters that explicitly portray the authors' social standing both before and after their parents' deaths. Even before they were orphaned, these children were no strangers to hardship. They lived at the very margins of Ethiopian society, often in the care of destitute mothers eking out an existence. Asrat's epistle draws a moving portrait of the life mother and child once shared:

For My Dear Mother,

Mother, I can never find someone like you. Because I know how burning with hardship you raised me. Ever since the day you left my father, without leaving me, without boredom, as long as your ability and age allowed it, you raised me. And, without being full of you, without you seeing me like this grown up, that you were separated from me makes me very sad. Mommy, let me remind you how you raised me back then. Carrying me on your back, when the rain pounded on you, selling boiled potatoes to raise me until I believe I was one or two years old. And you didn't rest when I got a little older. You'd take any day job you can find, that's how we began to live. After a long time, my father came again and saw us. But, Mommy, what kind of person is he? Why is it that people don't pity each other, love each other? My father is one of these people. Do you remember, per month 30 birr, he'd give us and leave. But you never waited for his handout. When we found food, we ate, when we didn't, we ate roasted chickpeas and drank water, and slept nestled together as if we were a single person. Isn't it sad, Mommy, if you were here, my education level and my age would have matched.

Yours, your loving,
Asrat[25]

Asrat's epistle has all the hallmarks of mourning—the trope of separation, the loss of old routines and the loss of futurity, and the recollection of and longing for the parent's touch—at the same time that it foregrounds the bare conditions under which many of these kids lived before they became orphans. Despite their remarkably difficult circumstances, Asrat feels that her mother's care and affection for her never faltered, and so she writes this epistle of mourn-

Asrat Tessema's letter in Amharic

ing and praise. Meanwhile, other letters speak of the new hardships borne by these children during the precarious intervening time between the deaths of their parents and their current foster care. In an expressive letter, Heywot Umer portrays the perils of life during this interim:

> To my very beloved mother, how is your health, how are you? Me, praise to God, I am doing very well. Yeshi-Hareg [her mother's name], when you left you did not leave me in the hands of a good person. If you ask why, a motherless child is always a thief,

Heywot Umer's letter in Amharic

always a liar, that's what people say. Mom, from the beginning of my childhood until now, I have been spanked, beaten, cursed at. Mom, my ear also hurts. What shall I do to it? Mom, during my childhood, I did not live like a child. If you ask why, you have passed me on and given me up to a mean person. I am told that I steal, when I don't steal, I go hungry, I go thirsty, that's how I've come here. More than that, she made me leave her house. After leaving the house, I began to live on the streets, in people's houses. But at this time, praise God, I am in an organization called Tesfa le Hetsanat [Hope for Children], and living now in a house rented for us, nine of us, we go to bed on a full stomach, on a comfortable bed, comfortable seat, table, and several other comfortable things, they are caring for us. I am going to school. Mom, for today, let me stop here. In my next letter, I will send you what follows in my history.

Your child,
Heywot Umer
For Yeshi-Hareg[26]

Heywot draws a gripping picture of her life in the wake of her mother's death, linking her newly disparaged identity to the fact of being orphaned—a "motherless child," whom people distrusted, stigmatized, harmed, and abandoned. And unlike Asrat, who lionizes her mother, Heywot harbors deep resentment toward hers for entrusting a child to an abusive caretaker. While letters like Asrat's conjure up the hardships these children encountered while their parents were alive, ones like Heywot's portray the new dangers that awaited them in the wake of their parents' deaths. They were left behind to live in abusive homes or were forced to live in the streets. Although they don't articulate this concern in the epistles they write to the dead, in their other writings, these children express an acute sense of an uncertain future. While they are cared for now (as they compose these letters), they know that their present domicile is only temporary, since once they reach eighteen, they'll no longer be eligible to receive support from their foster organization—in effect, leaving them without a home.

In a letter addressed to prospective sponsors, for instance, Amsale writes:

> First of all, thank you for giving me this opportunity. My name is Amsale Shiferaw. I am a student in the 8th grade. I don't have a father and a mother. I live hugged by an organization. The organization aids you until you are 18. After 18, they let you go. Us, me, we don't have anyone else assisting us. If they let me go, I don't know where I'll go. But now the organization is helping me. The organization has hired a nanny to supervise us. We appreciate anyone who would respond back to our letter. Amsale, ciao ciao[27]

From the lives they led with their mothers (as glimpsed in Asrat's letter), to the lives they endured alone (in Heywot's), to the precarious future that awaits them (in Amsale's)—in each stage of their short lives these children have faced a series of losses, and Heywot concludes, "during my childhood, I did not live like a child."

Below, I consider the queer figure of childhood that emerges from these complex and deeply interior narratives, as Heywot's self-reflexive words conjure up: a figure of the child that belies the normative symbols of childhood's innocence and futurity. For now, though, I frame the discussion of these letters by speculating on their extraliterary function as proxies for burial. This was

በመጽ መቤያ ዒሀ ህጹል ቀሰተ ሰጦኝ በጣም አመሰግናለሁ፡፡
ስ ዌ እ ምላ ኽ ፌ ሬ ወ እ ግላ ካ ሁ የ ፀ ፉ ን ፍ ለ ተ ማ ሪ ነ ን
እ ኔ ም እ ባ ፋ ሕ ሩ ፤ የ ኩ ኝ ም የ ም ሮ ሮ ም ለ ፍ ቄ ፩ ተ ው እ ን ተ ቄ ፪ ነ ወ የ ም ሮ
ለ ወ ፉ ር ፃ ተ ም እ እ ካ 18 አ መ ኧ ፉ ሬ ለ ነ ወ የ ሚ ሬ ዖ ወ 18 አ መ ኧ ካ ሚ ላ ኝ
ያ ከ ሪ ሏ እ ኘ ም አ ፩ ም ም ን ም እ ሬ ዖ ተ የ ከ ኝ ም ካ ገ ሬ ኝ ም የ ተ አ ን ዖ
ም ዖ ዖ አ ካ ወ ቶ ም እ ሁ ን ግ ን ዖ ር ፃ ተ ም እ የ ሬ ዖ ኝ ነ ወ ያ ለ ሁ ተ ፉ ር ፃ ተ
ም ም ግ ዘ ተ ተ ቀ ፖ ኖ ወ የ ሚ ያ ለ ተ ዖ ዖ ሬ ኝ እ ኘ ዐ ህ ን ዖ ለ ነ ፉ ጨ እ ን ከ በ
መ ሏ ለ ለ ካ ሏ ኝ ነ ም ጣ ም እ መ ሰ ግ ና ለ ሁ እ ም ላ ኸ ፇ ወ ፇ ወ

Amsale Shiferaw's letter in Amharic

Gottesman's answer when I asked how these epistles came to be a part of Sudden Flowers' repertoire:

I know that we [Yawoinshet Masresha and Gottesman] were trying to come up with ways to get the kids to talk about their experiences of grief. We were both interested in providing some avenue for the kids to process their parents' deaths. The first exercise we tried was this: each child took a tape recorder, went into a room by themselves and just tape recorded their stories alone in a room. They did that and most of those tapes are filled with weeping. This was the first chance to process what had happened to them. So after Yawoinshet and I heard these tapes, Yawoinshet came to the conclusion that the kids, because they were not invited to their parents' funerals and because no one explained what was going on to them, never had a chance to say goodbye or to slowly adapt to the idea that their parents were going to die. It was all very sudden. Also, while NGOs at that time were focused on providing food, clothes and material support for AIDS orphans, again and again in these tapes the kids talked about how they missed hugging their parents, missed talking to them, seeing them.... they didn't only need food and shelter, they needed to *feel* the relationship with their parents. At that point, one of us (and I honestly can't remember who) came up with the idea that if the kids could talk to their parents, perhaps that would provide them with the opportunity to feel that relationship and would assist them in processing their grief. I also must have thought at that time (correctly, as it turns out) that these would provide intimate portraits of what the kids felt.[28]

Perhaps it's because these children were deprived of funeral rites that the feelings and prerogatives of mourning become insistent in their narratives, why their oral stories are punctuated with weeping, why their letters are fixed on the body, why they want to materialize the dead. Since they couldn't observe their parents' burials, these children use the resources of narrative to reckon with death, concretizing the dead on a piece of paper or an audiotape, giving their loss and longing a material presence. Burial, Robert Pogue Harrison writes, "does not mean only the laying of bodies to rest in the ground. . . . in a broader sense it means to store, preserve, and put the past on hold." He adds, "humans bury not simply to achieve closure and effect a separation from the dead but also and above all to humanize the ground on which they build their worlds and found their histories."[29] Surely, we can think of these epistles as undertaking the imperatives of burial, not only in humanizing the living world and holding onto the past, but also in establishing the bases for the children to found their histories. Like the pallbearers in Makhoba's painting, who despite their age insist on interring the dead in the ground, the children of Sudden Flowers commit themselves to archiving their dead, entering them into narratives that otherwise would not exist. By mourning the dead, by way of this humanizing act, the children of Sudden Flowers authorize themselves, using narrative to reclaim their inheritance and perpetuate their survival.

SUDDEN FLOWERS AND THEIR REPERTOIRE

It is worth considering these letters alongside other works by Sudden Flowers that also characterize the early era of AIDS in Ethiopia. Among the collective's initial projects, Gottesman's interviews with and photographs of adult Ethiopians with HIV/AIDS powerfully capture the specter of AIDS. When he began the project in 1999, the fear surrounding AIDS was so profound and the government silence so deafening that people living with HIV/AIDS were harmed with impunity. Interview after interview that Gottesman conducted details evictions, firings, imprisonments, and other legal and extralegal violence inflicted on men and women living with the disease. "When my brother found out," says one interviewee, "he kicked me out [of] the house. He said he didn't even want me coming to the house. That I should send somebody to pick up my clothes."[30] When the landlord of another interviewee found out that he and his girlfriend were HIV-positive, he evicted them, locked them out without notice, and put their belongings in the sewer.[31] Another recalls the conditions under which she was expelled from her home when she disclosed her status: "One Wednesday, I spoke in public about having AIDS and that Sunday, while I was walking home, some people mocked me. The owner of the house I rented heard the news and asked me to leave her house. I agreed to leave but, at the time, I was sick; I had lesions on my head and could not see properly for 15 days. . . . Even with the condition I was in, the owner of the house cut off my water . . . then she cut off the electricity. This lady was working at Menelik Hospital as a nurse. I felt sick because she so poorly misunderstood her profession."[32] Accounts of gross harm and cruelty abound in these testimonies, as encapsulated in another powerful example:

> My family hates me. In 1995, my family won the diversity visa lottery and I began the process of moving to the United States. For one of the steps of the process, I have my blood [drawn]. I was told that I was HIV+. My mother asked me about it. I told her. She cried at first. Then, little by little, she began to ostracize me, telling me, "Don't touch that." When they heard I was HIV+, they falsely accused me of stealing things around the house and took me to the police. I was in prison for 41 days. They concocted this dramatic plot so I would spend the rest of my life in prison. They brought in three witnesses, all from my family, and the police believed them. . . . My friends rejected me. Everyone understands that if someone wins the DV lottery and doesn't get the visa, that it would be because of HIV. I don't know what they are saying about me behind my back. I do know my mother asked, "Why doesn't he commit suicide?" My sister told me this. I became strong in spirit and decided to live. If everybody wants my death, then I will not die.[33]

The news of this man's HIV status foiled his chances of moving abroad and put him in peril at home. Although he won the coveted diversity visa lottery, as an HIV-positive person he was "inadmissible" to the United States after the 1993 immigration ban. Because of his seropositive status, he was unwelcome abroad and unwanted by his own state and kin, who conspired against him and wished him dead. In such a violent context, people rarely disclosed their illness publicly or privately, since the consequences of disclosure, even among family, were immediate and severe. In a very religious country like Ethiopia, furthermore, people with AIDS were afraid of disclosing their status for fear of being condemned by the church and excluded from burial rites,[34] which is partly why it became common to euphemize AIDS deaths as pneumonia, malaria, tuberculosis, as anything but AIDS, to shield the dead and the surviving family from disgrace.

The violence that people living with HIV/AIDS encountered in all quarters of Ethiopian life only helped to perpetuate their invisibility. It's telling that when Gottesman began his portraits in 1999, all of the adults who participated did so anonymously by covering their faces. He worked on this series until 2004, deciding to end it only when, he explains, "two HIV+ people allowed me to photograph them and show their faces. At that point, I considered this series of photographs finished."[35] Entitled *If I Could See Your Face, I Would Not Need Food*, the series of portraits reflects on the early years of HIV/AIDS in Ethiopia, and it does so not by using the common trope of representing AIDS in Africa as spectacle, but instead, like the interviews, by attending to and evoking with care the experiences of those living with the disease. Given the high stakes of disclosure, Gottesman realized that he had to work closely with his subjects in order to produce images that ensured their anonymous safety while giving them a public platform. Of the collaborative process, he writes:

> I wanted to make portraits of people living with HIV but the stigma surrounding the disease at the time prevented anyone from feeling comfortable going public with their disease. This guided me toward a different way of making portraits. I picked up a Polaroid camera and used "positive-negative" film, which produced both a print and a negative. Through local organizations, I solicited people interested in sharing their stories. I invited them to sit for interviews. I told the subjects I would make a picture without showing their faces. We set up the picture and I would expose the film. One minute later, the subject and I would look at the images together. If the subject approved, he/she would keep the print and write me a permission form allowing me to publish or exhibit a photograph produced from the negative. If not, we destroyed the negative on the spot. The results of this process, collectively, provide a very different image of people affected by [this] disease than do the images produced by aid organizations or by the media.[36]

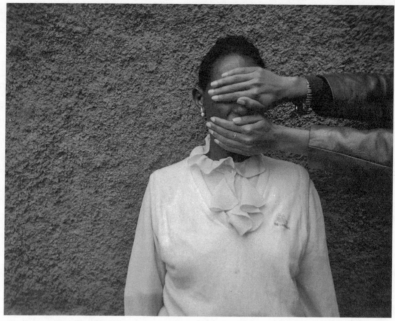

Eric Gottesman, *Beletu* (2000), toned silver gelatin print, 20″ × 24″

Gottesman's photographs clearly represent the entangled feelings of fear of and daring for public recognition. Fear of being recognized as someone living with HIV looms large in the series, as each portrait shows a face that is partially or fully covered—by hands, by a shawl, by a painting, and so on—or turned away from the camera. And yet fear is not the only feeling conveyed by these pictures. However veiled and tacit, by virtue of being photographed, the men and women in these portraits also dare to embody people living with HIV/AIDS, making the agency of that decision, the yearning to be recognized without repercussion, equally visible in the images. Unlike aid organization materials and media photos—of emaciated bodies that turn a person living with AIDS into an object of spectacle and pity—these muted but resonant portraits reveal a different kind of image of people living with HIV/AIDS, illuminating the subject's interiority and a complex set of feelings that thwart mere sensationalism.

The texts and photographs produced by the children, as well as Gottesman's portraits and interviews, became the first and among the most viewed art representations of HIV/AIDS in Ethiopia. Sudden Flowers' work was exhibited in leading galleries and museums and in everyday public spaces in Addis Ababa and other parts of the country. In their widely effective public installation—*Abul Thona Baraka*, named after the three rounds of coffee during a traditional

Eric Gottesman, *Yonas* (2000), toned silver gelatin print, 20″ × 24″

Eric Gottesman, *Hiwot* (2000), toned silver gelatin print, 20″ × 24″

Eric Gottesman, *Metasebya* (2000), toned silver gelatin print, 20" × 24"

Ethiopian coffee ceremony—the collective designed a mobile gallery of their work in 2006 that traveled to different neighborhoods in Addis Ababa and other cities in the country, reaching thousands of Ethiopians far beyond the limited audience of an art gallery. The installation was made up of waterproof banners and metal frames that created ten large panels, which were arranged to enclose a wide circle. On the outside, each panel had an enlarged image of one of Sudden Flowers' texts—including Gottesman's photographs and interviews and the children's epistles—which were striking enough to catch the attention of any passerby; and on the inside, more than a hundred smaller pictures and letters were arrayed to be viewed and read up close, in a kind of intimate enclosure that drew viewers "inside" these stories. At each location, the installation

Eric Gottesman, *Wondimu* (2004), toned silver gelatin print, 20″ × 24″

attracted large crowds who were captivated by the interviews, epistles, and portraits, privy to narratives and images otherwise invisible in the public sphere.

"The installation," says Gottesman, "recalls the circular shape of the Ethiopian coffee ceremony. . . . We used the ritual of the coffee ceremony because
we were interested in how local traditions could provide guides for how to deal
with an epidemic."[37] In Ethiopia, the coffee ceremony is an everyday gesture of
hospitality toward strangers and of care toward family and friends; it is a ritual
to celebrate both secular and sacred holidays. And often it provides the choice
atmosphere for deliberating difficult matters. The elaborate preparation of the
coffee—first washing the raw beans, then roasting them, grinding them, slowly
brewing the coffee, letting it settle, and finally serving it in three spaced-out
rounds: *abul*, *thona*, and *baraka*—provides time, ease, and intimacy for real talk.
In their installation, Sudden Flowers insightfully appropriated this familiar
ritual—its gesture of hospitality and its means of candid dialogue—to broach
a publicly explosive issue like AIDS and lay bare the provocative and evocative
testimonies of those living with the disease.

Further expanding their repertoire, Sudden Flowers began making films in

Sudden Flowers, *Abul Thona Baraka* (2006). Photos by Eric Gottesman.

2006. "For our first videos together," Gottesman explains, "I asked the children to write scripts about their lives. From these scripts, we made four movies. In addition to the scripts, the children made decisions about the masks that they wore, wardrobe and location. I made decisions about camera angle and lighting. We edited these films together and produced and displayed them publicly in Addis Ababa. I subtitled them in English for foreign audiences."[38]

One of these collaborative films is *Yabat Ida Le Lij* (The Debt the Father Owes the Child), which is incisive in its characterization of AIDS stigma, and poignant in its performance of grief. In a series of tightly woven vignettes, the short film portrays a family contending with the sudden catastrophe of AIDS. Alemu, the film's protagonist, is the husband of Emu and the father of three young children. When he is diagnosed with AIDS, his troubles compound quickly once his neighbors find out, and the *edir* resolves to revoke his membership. An *edir* is a formative Ethiopian institution, a " 'burial society' to which members make monthly contributions and receive a payment to help cover funeral expenses in return. Nearly every modern Ethiopian is a member of at least one *edir*, either a neighborhood association, one based at work, or operating along age or gender lines."[39] Along with providing financial support, an *edir* plays an important cultural role in facilitating the public rites and recognitions of loss. For instance, a neighborhood *edir* is charged with publicizing the death throughout its streets; raising a tent in front of the bereaved home to accommodate the influx of mourners; and, in some cases, hiring a professional mourner for the wake. So, to be cast out from an *edir* has serious consequences, not only leaving the bereaved family without financial support, but also divesting them (and their dead) of the public rites/rights of loss authorized by this binding civic institution. When faced with such a threat of disinheritance, Alemu, in the film's penultimate scene, takes matters into his own hands. Before the *edir*'s measure can take effect, he commits suicide, preemptively securing his family's due. The film ends with a haunting scene of Emu and her children hovering over Alemu's corpse, keening and thrashing their bodies.

Yabat Ida Le Lij offers, on the one hand, powerful social commentary. What brings about Alemu's death, the film is keen to point out, is not the disease but the stigma of AIDS: it's the *edir*'s fiat that leads to his premature death. The film spotlights the *edir* in part to signal the stigmatization of people living with AIDS and their ultimate exclusion from civic life. Indeed, if the *edir*, the most egalitarian and inclusive civic institution in the country, fails to safeguard the welfare of people living with AIDS, and even colludes in their suffering and death, then it's easy to surmise that other institutions do the same and more. In choosing the *edir* as its context, the film also signifies how people with AIDS are so disparaged that they are kept out of civic life while alive *and* when dead, barred even from being objects of public mourning and memory. Amid this violent context Alemu's suicide takes on heightened agency, not only as his final living act but also as an act of necropolitics; he kills himself to defy and defeat the *edir*'s grievous measure, and posthumously to provide for his family.[40] On the other hand, the film offers a performance of mourning that forcefully grabs our attention. In the intense last scene, Emu and her children begin their mourning, phrasing their keening and moving their bodies in an expressly Ethiopian manner of grief—clasping their arms behind their heads, beating their chests with their palms, and heaving their bodies rhythmically.[41] The sight of young children immersed in grief, performing the role of mourners, makes for an affecting ending; the scene evokes the aberration conjured up in Makhoba's painting of children as pallbearers.

Together, the early works of Sudden Flowers—the epistles, interviews, photographs, public installations, and films—provide insight into the initial years of AIDS in Ethiopia, illuminating both the public attitude toward the disease and the interior life of those dealing with its loss and stigma. As I noted earlier, these texts were among the first in Ethiopia to present public narratives of people affected by AIDS, which in addition to breaking the silence around the disease also thwarted the dominant representations of AIDS in Africa as spectacle and statistics. While it is true that when Sudden Flowers was founded in 1999, HIV/AIDS had "infected an estimated 3 million of Ethiopia's 62.8 million people" and "killed the parents of an estimated 903,000 Ethiopian children,"[42] the statistics can never capture the complex individual and collective experiences of the people impacted by AIDS. "Numbers alone do not make death meaningful. Rather, they create a spectacle that captures attention for a moment before alienating its beholder in a realm of fact."[43] Because Sudden Flowers' work eschews an externalizing gaze, and focuses instead on the interiority of individual lives, it is able to render a textured and nuanced picture of AIDS. The success of Sudden Flowers' intervention also has rested in giving extraordinary agency to children, allowing them to voice their experiences and make their losses meaningful in their own ways, rather than having their identity governed by adult projections of childhood and how children should feel.

"Narrative is radical, creating us at the very moment it is being created," assert the children in Toni Morrison's short fable to their adult interlocutor.[44] In

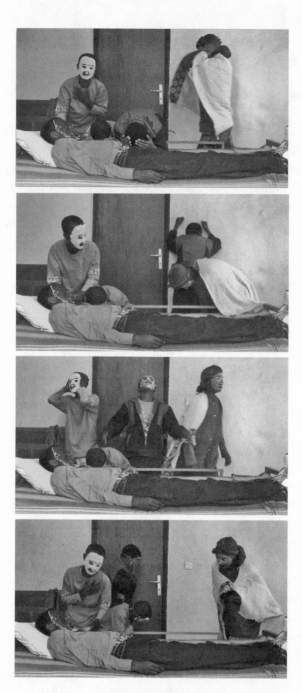

Film stills from *Yabat Ida Le Lij* (2006)

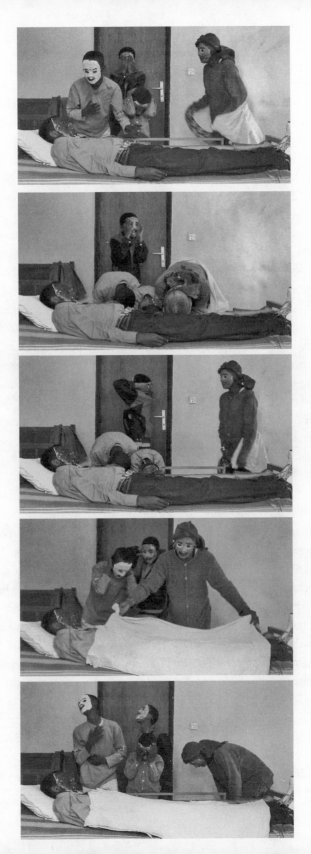

reading their letters or watching their films, we glimpse the fundamental truth of that claim in the work of Sudden Flowers; in the process of working through their grief, these children re-create themselves, materializing artifacts that mirror for them and the world a self-willed image. This fundamental agency, which inheres in the process and the product of narrative, is evident in these children's texts. Also clear are other forms of radical agency: these texts openly grieve the dishonored dead, and they are produced by subjects themselves disgraced by HIV/AIDS. But even before they were queered by AIDS, as street beggars some of these kids were already deemed abject by the public; "begging [was] no different than being a thief," sums up Beti, one of Salamawit's personas. Further compounding their abjection, some were left without a caretaker after their parents' deaths. When her mother died, Yamrot recalls, "since [my sister and I] had no place to go, we stayed there in the hospital." The same thing happened to Asrat: "Knowing I had no relatives to help me, the hospital allowed me to stay." Perhaps it is their experience of life on the margins, bereft of parents and "put outdoors"; or perhaps it is the experience of a childhood not fully circumscribed by adult moralizing and shame; or even the experience of remaking their kinship ties in a foster home of others bereaved and stigmatized like them—some combination of experiences in these children honed in them an uncommon courage to voice their disprized lives publicly.[45]

FIGURES OF CHILDHOOD

I have presented the work of Sudden Flowers so far by closely heeding their own terms, paying careful attention to how the children have used the resources of narrative to mourn their parents and enfranchise themselves. I have done so in part to counter the overwhelming discourse about AIDS orphans in Africa that has figured them, and children more generally, without substantive agency and as objects of adults' knowledge. From the series of texts discussed above, however, it's easy to glean a picture of these children as powerful agents, as subjects capable of reflection on and articulation of their own experiences. Also easy to glean from the work of Sudden Flowers is a figure of the child that belies the normative symbols of innocence and futurity with which we interpellate children. Shunned by the world and deprived of protection, these children rely not on idealized figures of innocence and purity to characterize their own experiences, but instead on queer figures of abjection, disparagement, and fearlessness. They issue a calendar of loss, furthermore, that thwarts the naturalized figure of the child as the very embodiment of futurity. Contemplating his mother's illness and death and his own contingent present and future, says Biniyam,

"I don't want to worry about the future too deeply as I have got experience from watching my mother." Indeed, the unorthodox figure of childhood we derive from the work of Sudden Flowers refutes not only the normative symbols of childhood prevalent since the Romantic period, but also more recent critical theories that pit figures of the child and the queer against each other.

As Philippe Ariès, Anne Higonnet, James Kincaid, and others have pointed out, the idea of the innocent child that crystalized in the Romantic period transformed the child into an empty surface on which adults carve meaning, in effect erasing the complexity of children.[46] If children are idealized only as a tabula rasa—as a "white paper void of all characters"[47]—then they become simply the stuff of adult overdetermination, a repository of normative ideals and feelings, like innocence and purity, coveted by adults. Although it coalesced in the nineteenth century, this idea of the innocent child still wields enormous discursive and affective power in our own time. It is hard to imagine twenty-first-century American culture, for instance, bereft of this figure. What would advertisers do without this spectral child, their default visual ploy to arouse the happy feelings of consumers? What would happen to politicians and preachers emptied of their rhetoric to protect "our children" and "our children's future"? Lee Edelman has argued that this idealized child has in fact become the organizing force behind heteronormativity. This figure warps our perception of reality, Edelman contends, because it naturalizes our understanding of the future *as* "reproductive futurism." By conflating futurity with procreation, reproductive futurism delimits and regulates not just homosexuality (as a category ostensibly excluded from that enterprise), but more broadly how we construe social and political relations. The figure of the child that underwrites reproductive futurism, writes Edelman, "impose[s] an ideological limit on political discourse as such, preserving in the process the absolute privilege of heteronormativity by rendering unthinkable, by casting outside the political domain, the possibility of a queer resistance to this organizing principle of communal relations."[48] He adds: "The consequences of such an identification both of and with the Child as the preeminent emblem of the motivating end, though one endlessly postponed, of every political vision *as a vision of futurity* must weigh on any delineation of a queer oppositional politics."[49] Consequently, Edelman formulates a queer figure that is antithetical to "the Child" and its future: if "the Child" stands in for the future, then, negatively defined, the queer has no future and is propelled only by the death drive and the search for pleasure. For Edelman, to hold the future as the horizon of queer politics is to reify a future already delimited by the logic of procreation cum reproductive futurism, whereas the death drive, "the negativity opposed to every form of social viability,"[50] provides queerness a temporality that is outside the timeline of the idealized child and, by extension, the temporal trappings of heteronormativity.

Of course, this ideal is not the only figure of childhood that has had political and cultural value; so too has its counterpart, the figure of the black child. From its inception, the figure of the innocent child was never meant to refer to children of color, but only to those children who were already prized in the modern world for their whiteness. As Higonnet writes, "In the shadows of ideal childhood we have been confronted with the issue of race. How very white the Romantic child has been, so dominantly white that race did not even seem to be an issue."[51] The figure of the black child that gelled in the nineteenth century, at the same time as the idealized white child of Romanticism, stood not for innocence, purity, and futurity, but for repulsion, abjection, and social death. Robin Bernstein shows in her superb book, *Racial Innocence*, that the "pickaninny," the prevailing characterization of black children as insensate was born alongside the Romantic child.[52] Valued as commodities of slavery, for their potential for work and prospects for sale, black children of the nineteenth century could not figure innocence, purity, and futurity, since these were qualities intrinsic to whiteness only. Like its normative white counterpart, the devalued figure of the black child continued into the twentieth century and, albeit in attenuated form, continues to plague black children today. As Kathryn Bond Stockton observes, "children, as an *idea*, are likely to be both white and middle-class. It is a privilege to be protected—and to be sheltered—and thus to have a childhood. Not in spite of privilege, then, but because of it, the all-important feature of weakness sticks to these markers (white and middle-class) and helps to signal innocence."[53]

In discussing figures of childhood, therefore, the idealized child has to be qualified significantly since it was never meant to interpellate black and other disparaged children, and since that prized figure doesn't exist in a vacuum but competes with another powerful symbol: the soiled child that has mediated modernity. So while a queer critique of the normative child, like Edelman's, is instructive, it's also quite narrow in scope, omitting in its analysis the undesirable figures of childhood. To theorize queerness in relation to the figure of the black child, as opposed to the normative white child, would generate very different claims than those Edelman posits. Emptied of innocence and futurity, the black child figures a radically different affect and temporality and thus cannot be a marker against which queerness can be negatively defined. As José Esteban Muñoz notes in his incisive critique of Edelman's thesis: "The future is only the stuff of some kids. Racialized kids, queer kids, are not the sovereign princes of futurity. Although Edelman does indicate that the future of the child as futurity is different from the future of actual children, his framing nonetheless accepts and reproduces this monolithic figure of the child that is indeed always already white."[54]

The canon of African American literature is brimming with figures of childhood that are emblematically queer; Pecola Breedlove in Toni Morrison's *The Bluest Eye* is one powerful example. In Morrison's chilling allegory, Pecola is the very figure against which the society defines its norms: "all of us" need and use her to polish and perfect our normative lives.

> All of us—all who knew her—felt so wholesome after we cleaned ourselves on her. We were so beautiful when we stood astride her ugliness. Her simplicity decorated us, her guilt sanctified us, her pain made us glow with health, her awkwardness made us think we had a sense of humor. Her inarticulateness made us believe we were eloquent. Her poverty kept us generous. Even her waking dreams we used—to silence our own nightmares. And she let us, and thereby deserved our contempt. We honed our egos on her, padded our characters with her frailty, and yawned in the fantasy of our strength.[55]

If the figure of the innocent child is a prized commodity (like the white doll in the novel), Morrison insists, then so too is the figure of the abject black child, as the underside of innocence. Furthermore, given the extreme risk of death that black children have faced and continue to face because of their skin color (the killing of seventeen-year-old Trayvon Martin in 2012 being only one recent example), black parents and caretakers cannot afford to cling to a figure of childhood innocence and not impart to their children at a very young age the realities of a hateful world. Recalling his own upbringing, James Baldwin says, "The Western idea of childhood, or children, is not at all the same idea of childhood that produced me. To put it very brutally—to exaggerate it a little bit, but not much: white people think that childhood is a rehearsal for success. White people think of themselves as safe. But black people raise their children as a rehearsal for danger."[56]

When it comes to representing African children, the caricature of the black child is exacerbated by the image of the starving baby, a spectacle that has dominated western media since the 1984–1985 Ethiopian famine and that has become the default visual vocabulary for representing African children in our postmodern age. Turn on any western television news, open the pages of any western daily paper, and there they are: African children, almost always in a state of bare life, stripped of their personhood, rendered only as objects of pity and charity. I bring up these figures of childhood because they frame our perception of children and also prevent other figures of childhood from coming into view. When we look at the work of Sudden Flowers, on the other hand, we can gain perspective on both the actual historical lives of children and a queer figure of childhood. The child as public mourner is an aberration that dislodges our conventional views of childhood; furthermore, the child as political figure, publicly taking on one of the most urgent issues of our time, also departs from the norm. From the corpus of Sudden Flowers emerges a figure of the child who mourns and fights for survival.

conclusion

Tallying Loss

A few years before the children of Sudden Flowers penned their epistles to the dead, another artist, in another country, and in another AIDS-riddled context, employed the same form to express multiple losses. In 1993, while anticipating his own death, Marlon Riggs wrote five short missives collectively titled "Letters to the Dead" that sound the mourning gathered in this book.[1] Three letters were addressed to close friends who died of AIDS—Gene, Chris, and Lewayne; one was to Harriet Tubman, the fearless anti-slavery crusader whom he considered to be immediate kin; and a final parting letter was to "comrades, lovers, girlfriends, and family." The letters Riggs writes to his deceased friends are in many ways a stark reflection of his own precarious life. To Gene, he says: "I studied you as I might study a mirror, witnessed the reflection of my own probable future, my not too dissimilar past."[2] And to Lewayne: "Sweet Lewayne, who first lost sight, then life, to the raging virus, were you nonetheless my witness? Did you see over the ensuing months of my recuperation what happened to my kidneys, my sight, my tongue? Did you see how slowly, gradually, my kidneys once again started to work, how slowly, gradually I began to see the consequences of silence, and how as a consequence of this insight, my tongue unhinged from the roof of my mouth, dislodged from the back of my throat, slipped—free?"[3]

The way Riggs worries the line between the living and the dead—by charting his own dying on a calendar of past and prospective losses—is a central feature of early AIDS mourning. As is the political imperative to openly mourn the AIDS dead, a point Riggs reiterates in his letter to Tubman by conjoining his own immediate world of mass loss with a past calamity where the dishonored had to mount an insurgent mourning for survival: "Dear Harriet. . . . Don't you see the chains, my Harriet, sweet Moses, the chains not so much of steel and the law, but more insidious: the invisible chains, linked over centuries, of silence and shame? In this latest crisis, our new master is the virus; his overseer—silence; and his whip—shame."[4] Amid these catastrophes, Riggs insists, a person living with AIDS and an ex-slave can confront so much death, silence, and shame and still openly assert a fearless politics, turning their mourning into a cry for justice.

Mourning takes on a form commensurate with its occasioning, and in the early era of AIDS that form assumed an expression of compounding loss, blurring the line between the subject and the object of mourning, between the death-bound who are mourning and the dead who are mourned. Reckoning with reflexive and multiples losses, this form resists closure, insisting on repetition and extension to account for the mounting past and pending losses. The torrential and open-ended quality of so much of the material gathered in this book—from Melvin Dixon's and Paul Monette's poems to Thomas Glave's short story, from ACT UP political funerals to Assotto Saint's obituaries, from Keith Haring's drawings to Sudden Flowers' epistles—is a reflection of the immeasurable devastation wrought by this catastrophe, while it is also an echo of the screams, cries, keening, and other visceral expressions of grief, which are hard to contain in elaborately formalized strains of mourning. Furthermore, like its form, the political content of early AIDS mourning also speaks to its occasioning, as disprized mourners placed public grief at the center of art and protest, insisting that lives could be saved through the very speech acts triggered by death. Rather than seeing the disease as a marker of stigma, these mourners embody AIDS with a fierce agency, refusing to live in silence and shame and to let their dead go ungrieved.

In looking back at the early era of AIDS, I certainly don't mean to turn a blind eye to the suffering that this catastrophe continues to exact on people the world over. It would take another book to examine the present history of AIDS loss carefully, especially in the wake of protease inhibitors and the changing domestic and international discourse surrounding the disease, including the rise of gay liberalism in the United States and its attendant "post-AIDS" narrative. Tallying loss is always an incomplete endeavor, especially tallying the loss of a catastrophe that is still unfolding. No one book can account for all the death, devastation, violence, malfeasance, silence, stigma, and shame fueled by this pandemic. No one book can capture the extraordinary acts of resistance, resilience, courage, care, will, and imagination that adults and children alike have used to brave this crisis. Nor can a single book sum the grief of many thousands gone, nor should it try to do so. But I do hope this book provides one critical way of recasting the early era of AIDS and its poetics and politics of mourning, and I hope it reanimates the lives and legacies of the dead who were disprized in their own time and too often disavowed in our own.

Notes

PREFACE

1. "An edir is a 'burial society' to which members make monthly contributions and receive a payment to help cover funeral expenses in return. Nearly every modern Ethiopian is thought to be a member of at least one edir, either a neighbourhood association, one based at work, or operating along age or gender lines." "Ethiopia: 'Edirs' for the Living as Well as the Dead," *Nazret*, http://nazret.com/blog/index.php/2006/11/22/ethiopia_edirs_for_the_living_as_well_as.

INTRODUCTION. Looking for the Dead

1. For powerful accounts of Tim Bailey's political funeral, see the video by James Wentzy, *Political Funerals* (1995); David B. Feinberg, *Queer and Loathing: Rants and Raves of a Raging AIDS Clone* (New York: Viking, 1994); and Joy Episalla, interview by Sarah Schulman, ACT UP Oral History Project, interview no. 36, December 6, 2003, transcript, http://www.actu poralhistory.org/interviews/interviews_06.html#episalla. This particular lament, "You've Dropped the Dead," is transcribed from Wentzy's video recording of the funeral.

2. Quoted on the flyer distributed at the funeral. See "Tim Bailey Political Funeral," ACT UP / New York, http://www.actupny.org/divatv/netcasts/tim_bailey.html.

3. Ibid.

4. Ibid.

5. Feinberg, *Queer and Loathing*, 260.

6. Episalla, interview.

7. Wentzy, *Political Funerals*.

8. Ibid.

9. Ibid.

10. Melvin Dixon, *Love's Instruments* (Chicago: Tia Chucha Press, 1995), 71–72.

11. Essex Hemphill, *Ceremonies: Prose and Poetry* (San Francisco, CA: Cleis, 1992), 4–21.

12. Larry Kramer, "1,112 and Counting," in his *Reports from the Holocaust: The Story of an AIDS Activist* (New York: St. Martin's, 1994), 49–50.

13. Paul Monette, *Borrowed Time: An AIDS Memoir* (New York: Avon, 1988), 1.

14. Paul Monette, *Love Alone: Eighteen Elegies for Rog* (New York: St. Martin's, 1988), xii–xiii.

15. Marlon Riggs, *Black Is . . . Black Ain't: A Personal Journey Through Black Identity* (San Francisco: California Newsreel, 1995). For a recording of the entire performance of *Still/Here*, see *Still/Here* (Alive TV, 1996); and for a documentary on the making of the dance, see Bill Moyers, *Bill T. Jones: Still/Here* (Princeton, NJ: Films for the Humanities and Sciences, 1997).

16. Bill T. Jones, Arnie Zane, et al., *Body Against Body: The Dance and Other Collaborations of Bill T. Jones and Arnie Zane* (New York: Station Hill Press, 1989).

17. Moyers, *Bill T. Jones: Still/Here.*

18. David Román, *Acts of Intervention: Performance, Gay Culture, and AIDS* (Bloomington: Indiana University Press, 1998).

19. Douglas Crimp, "Mourning and Militancy," *October* 51 (1989): 9 (emphasis in original).

20. Simon Watney, "Political Funeral," *Village Voice*, October 20, 1992, 18 (emphasis in original).

21. Debra Levine, "How to Do Things with Dead Bodies," *e-misférica* 6.1 (March 22, 2012), http://hemi.nyu.edu/hemi/en/e-misferica-61/levine.

22. David Wojnarowicz, "Post Cards from America: X-Rays from Hell," in *Witnesses: Against Our Vanishing* (New York: Artists Space, 1989), 11, reprinted in David Wojnarowicz, *Close to the Knives: A Memoir of Disintegration* (New York: Vintage, 1991), 122.

23. David Mager, "Funeral at the White House," *PWA Coalition Newsline* 83 (December 1992): 19–21.

24. Watney, "Political Funeral," 18.

25. Ibid.

26. Gene Jarrett, "A Song to Pass On: An Interview with Thomas Glave," *Callaloo* 23.4 (2000): 1235.

27. Dixon, *Love's Instruments*, 76–77.

28. Charles Nero, "Fixing Ceremonies: An Introduction," in Hemphill, *Ceremonies*, xiii.

29. Judith Butler, *Precarious Life: The Powers of Mourning and Violence* (New York: Verso, 2004), xx–xxi.

30. Mark Lowe Fisher, "Bury Me Furiously," ACT UP / NY, http://www.actupny.org/diva/polfunsyn.html.

31. I am borrowing the phrase "life-sustaining properties" from Toni Morrison, who writes of Abraham Lincoln's Gettysburg Address: "When a President of the United States thought about the graveyard his country had become, and said, 'The world will little note nor long remember what we say here. But it will never forget what they did here,' his simple words are exhilarating in their life-sustaining properties because they refused to encapsulate the reality of 600,000 dead men in a cataclysmic race war." Morrison, *The Nobel Lecture in Literature* (New York: Knopf, 1993), 20.

32. Hemphill, *Ceremonies*, 6.

33. Sigmund Freud, *The Freud Reader* (New York: Norton, 1989), 584.

34. David Eng and David Kazanjian, eds., *Loss: The Politics of Mourning* (Berkeley: University of California Press, 2003). Many of the essays in this important collection identify the limitation of Freud's binary, namely his pathologizing of negative feelings like melancholy. See, in particular, the editors' introduction, "Mourning Remains," 1–28.

35. Dixon, *Love's Instruments*, 75.

36. Fred Moten, *In the Break: The Aesthetics of the Black Radical Tradition* (Minneapolis: University of Minnesota Press, 2003), 210.

37. Karla Holloway, *Passed On: African-American Mourning Stories: A Memorial Collection* (Durham, NC: Duke University Press, 2002), 6.

38. Abdul R. JanMohamed, *Death-Bound Subject: Richard Wright's Archaeology of Death* (Durham, NC: Duke University Press, 2005), 2.

39. Hortense Spillers, *Black, White, and in Color: Essays on American Literature and Culture* (Chicago: University of Chicago Press, 2003), 25.

40. Frederick Douglass, *My Bondage and My Freedom* (Mineola, NY: Dover, 1969), 98.

41. W. E. B. Du Bois, *The Souls of Black Folk* (New York: Vintage / Library of America, 1990), 180.

42. Ibid., 185.

43. Howard Thurman, *The Negro Spiritual Speaks of Life and Death* (Richmond, IN: Friends United Press, 1975), 13.

44. Ibid.

45. James Cone, *The Spirituals and the Blues: An Interpretation* (New York: Seabury, 1972), 75.

46. Moyers, *Bill T. Jones: Still/Here*.

47. Max Cavitch, *The American Elegy: The Poetry of Mourning from the Puritans to Whitman* (Minneapolis: University of Minnesota Press, 2007), 181.

48. Quoted from Horace Ové's 1969 film, *Baldwin's Nigger* (London: British Film Institute, 2004).

49. See Lawrence W. Levine, *Black Culture and Black Consciousness: Afro-American Folk Thought from Slavery to Freedom* (New York: Oxford University Press, 1977); Albert J. Raboteau, *Slave Religion: The "Invisible Institution" in the Antebellum South* (New York: Oxford University Press, 1978); and Cornel West, "The Spirituals as Lyric Poetry," in *The Cornel West Reader* (New York: Basic Civitas, 1999), 463–470.

50. Eng and Kazanjian, "Mourning Remains," in their *Loss*, ix.

51. José Esteban Muñoz, *Disidentifications: Queers of Color and the Performance of Politics* (Minneapolis: University of Minnesota Press, 1999), 74. For a study on the workings of nonnormative grief, like melancholia, in nineteenth-century American cultural production, see Dana Luciano, *Arranging Grief: Sacred Time and the Body in Nineteenth-Century America* (New York: New York University Press, 2007).

52. Lisa Duggan, "The New Homonormativity: The Sexual Politics of Neoliberalism," in *Materializing Democracy*, edited by Russ Castronovo and Dana D. Nelson (Durham, NC: Duke University Press, 2002), 175–194; David Eng, *The Feeling of Kinship: Queer Liberalism and the Racialization of Intimacy* (Durham, NC: Duke University Press, 2010); Jasbir Puar, *Terrorist Assemblages: Homonationalism in Queer Times* (Durham, NC: Duke University Press, 2007); David Eng, Judith Halberstam, and José Esteban Muñoz, eds., special issue of *Social Text* 23.3–4 (2005), particularly the editors' introduction, "What's Queer about Queer Studies Now?" 1–17; Sarah Schulman, "Israel and 'Pinkwashing,'" *New York Times*, November 22, 2011, A31.

53. David Román, "Not-About-AIDS," *GLQ: A Journal of Lesbian and Gay Studies* 6.1 (2000): 1–28.

54. Michel-Rolph Trouillot, *Silencing the Past: Power and the Production of History* (Boston: Beacon, 1995), 26 (emphases in original).

55. Heather Love, *Feeling Backward: Loss and the Politics of Queer History* (Cambridge, MA: Harvard University Press, 2007), 30.

56. Ann Cvetkovich, *An Archive of Feelings: Trauma, Sexuality, and Lesbian Public Cultures* (Durham, NC: Duke University Press, 2003), 161.

57. Sarah Schulman, "Through the Looking Glass," in *Loss Within Loss: Artists in the Age of AIDS*, edited by Edmund White (Madison: University of Wisconsin Press, 2001), 13.

58. Douglas Crimp, "AIDS: Cultural Analysis / Cultural Activism," in *AIDS: Cultural Analysis / Cultural Activism*, edited by Douglas Crimp (Cambridge, MA: MIT Press, 1988), 3.

59. Paula Treichler, "An Epidemic of Signification," in Crimp, *AIDS: Cultural Analysis / Cultural Activism*, 37.

60. Simon Watney, "The Spectacle of AIDS," in Crimp, *AIDS: Cultural Analysis / Cultural*

Activism, 71–86; Susan Sontag, *AIDS and Its Metaphors* (New York: Farrar, Straus and Giroux, 1989).

61. Gregory Tomso, "The Humanities and HIV/AIDS: Where Do We Go from Here?" *PMLA* 125.2 (2010): 443–453.

62. Quoted in Crimp, "AIDS: Cultural Analysis / Cultural Activism," 8.

63. Ibid.

64. Pat Buchanan, "AIDS Disease: It's Nature Striking Back," *New York Post*, May 24, 1983, 31; Pat Buchanan, "Hordes Paid to See This Chaos," *Washington Times*, October 17, 1990, G1.

65. Cathy Caruth and Thomas Keenan, "'The AIDS Crisis Is Not Over': A Conversation with Gregg Bordowitz, Douglas Crimp, and Laura Pinsky," in *Trauma: Explorations in Memory*, edited by Cathy Caruth (Baltimore, MD: Johns Hopkins University Press, 1995), 268.

66. David Román's *Acts of Intervention* remains an indispensable book on gay performance and theater during the first decade of AIDS, illuminating the powerful uses of performance as protest and protest as performance. From lesser-known works like Pomo Afro Homos' *Fierce Love* to classic AIDS dramas like Tony Kushner's *Angels in America*, Román's book offers a comprehensive study of the gay performances that defined this early period, and how they transformed both the ascendant AIDS discourse and the heteronormative underpinnings of American theater. Román, *Acts of Intervention: Performance, Gay Culture, and AIDS* (Bloomington: Indiana University Press, 1998).

Roger Hallas's *Reframing Bodies* is an insightful study of AIDS video and film. As Hallas rightly notes, what distinguishes early AIDS videos and films—from Gregg Bordowitz's *Fast Trip, Long Drop* to Derek Jarman's *Blue* to Marlon Riggs's *Non, Je Ne Regrette Rien (No Regret)*—is "their capacity to hold the complex interplay of political, psychological, and social imperatives in productive tension," as well as their ability to bear witness to a catastrophe not after but during the event, thus engendering a powerful cinematic idiom of testimony that "pushed viewers to relinquish their normal positions of narrative identification and voyeuristic mastery in favor of entering an intersubjective space in which spectatorship may constitute an ethical encounter with the other." Hallas, *Reframing Bodies: AIDS, Bearing Witness, and the Queer Moving Image* (Durham, NC: Duke University Press, 2009), 4, 20.

Also interested in the reader's response and responsibility in looking at AIDS texts, Ross Chambers's *Facing It* offers a thoughtful discussion of three AIDS diaries—two video diaries, Hervé Guibert's *La pudeur ou l'impudeur* and Tom Joslin's *Silverlake Life*, and a written diary, Eric Michaels's *Unbecoming*—all three composed while the artists faced their imminent deaths. Offering a clear exposition of how Roland Barthes's phrase "the death of the author" takes on literal import in the context of AIDS, Chambers's study illuminates furthermore how the reader is implicated in these works fashioned on the precipice of death: "An author must face, and assume, his own death as an author, so that the surviving text, bearing witness to that death, can in turn challenge its readers with the evidence *they* must face, while simultaneously [facing] the evidence of that death, the evidence of their own readerly responsibility for the continued bearing of witness, and the evidence of their own inadequacy fully to complete the author's interrupted task and thus to ensure the author a form of survival." Chambers, *Facing It: AIDS Diaries and the Death of the Author* (Ann Arbor: University of Michigan Press, 1998), 23 (emphasis in original).

Sarah Brophy's *Witnessing AIDS*, also a notable study, focuses on the workings of unresolved grief in AIDS testimonial writing and includes works by women authors, Amy Hoffman's *Hospital Time* and Jamaica Kincaid's *My Brother*, showing the overlapping grief among different constituencies of AIDS mourners. Brophy, *Witnessing AIDS: Writing, Testimony, and the Work of Mourning* (Toronto: University of Toronto Press, 2004).

67. For a study of AIDS in the social sciences also situated at the intersection of these two fields, see Cathy Cohen's indispensable book, *Boundaries of Blackness: AIDS and the Breakdown of Black Politics* (Chicago: University of Chicago Press, 1999). There are also essays in the humanities at this intersection, notably Phillip Brian Harper, "Eloquence and Epitaph: Black Nationalism and the Homophobic Impulse in Responses to the Death of Max Robinson," *Social Text* 28 (1991): 68–86; and Harper, "Gay Male Identities, Personal Privacy, and Relations of Public Exchange: Notes on Directions for Queer Critique," in his *Private Affairs: Critical Ventures in the Culture of Social Relations* (New York: New York University Press, 1999), 89–124. More recently Kathryn Bond Stockton has observed, "AIDS provides the most dramatic switchpoint between 'black' and 'queer' we might consider. . . . AIDS is the most intense and sorrowful place where the signs 'black' and 'queer' (or 'gay' or 'homosexual') consistently meet." Stockton, *Beautiful Bottom, Beautiful Shame: Where "Black" Meets "Queer"* (Durham, NC: Duke University Press, 2006), 179.

68. Sharon Holland, *Raising the Dead: Readings of Death and (Black) Subjectivity* (Durham, NC: Duke University Press, 2000), 180.

69. For an insightful discussion of how certain places are designated as a "queer unthought," see Rinaldo Walcott, "Outside in Black Studies: Reading from a Queer Place in the Diaspora," in *Black Queer Studies: A Critical Anthology*, edited by Patrick Johnson and Mae G. Henderson (Durham, NC: Duke University Press, 2005), 90–105.

70. Holland, *Raising the Dead*, 103–104.

71. Dixon, *Love's Instruments*, 78–79.

CHAPTER 1. Lyric Mourning

1. Melvin Dixon, *Love's Instruments* (Chicago: Tia Chucha Press, 1995), 74.

2. Ibid., 70.

3. Paul Monette, *Love Alone: Eighteen Elegies for Rog* (New York: St. Martin's, 1988), 20 (emphases in original).

4. Peter M. Sacks, *The English Elegy: Studies in the Genre from Spenser to Yeats* (Baltimore, MD: Johns Hopkins University Press, 1985), 1.

5. Max Cavitch, *The American Elegy: The Poetry of Mourning from the Puritans to Whitman* (Minneapolis: University of Minnesota Press, 2007), 1.

6. Sigmund Freud, *The Freud Reader* (New York: Norton, 1989), 584–589.

7. Sacks, *The English Elegy*, 16–17, 63, 76.

8. Jahan Ramazani, *Poetry of Mourning: The Modern Elegy from Hardy to Heaney* (Chicago: University of Chicago Press, 1994), xi, 4.

9. Melissa F. Zeiger, *Beyond Consolation: Death, Sexuality, and the Changing Shapes of Elegy* (Ithaca, NY: Cornell University Press, 1997), 108.

10. For an insightful essay on the lyric that also calls for new and more expansive approaches to studying the genre, see Jonathan Culler, "Lyric, History, and Genre," *New Literary History* 40.4 (2009): 879–899.

11. As other critics have found, reading spirituals trans-generically and trans-periodically can be a generative enterprise in thinking about lyric mourning. In *The American Elegy*, for instance, Cavitch considers the spirituals alongside antebellum African American elegies, elaborating their common preoccupation with "the doubled displacements of slavery and

death" (185). In *Poetry of Mourning*, Ramazani frames his discussion of Langston Hughes's blues poems partly by delineating how the blues and the spirituals—as two different modes of African American lyric mourning—approach consolation. And in "The Spirituals as Lyric Poetry," Cornel West takes a transnational approach and compares the spirituals with the poetry of Fyodor Tyutchev and Giacomo Leopardi, emphasizing how these works "add new existential darkness and historical substance to the lyrical genre in poetry." West, "The Spirituals as Lyric Poetry," in *The Cornel West Reader* (New York: Basic Civitas, 1999), 463. Building on these expansive approaches that read spirituals and elegies together, I consider here a class of death songs in the spirituals repertoire, focusing on their poetics of loss as one critical frame through which we can recast early AIDS elegies. That said, my focus is narrowly on loss and thus my reading of spirituals brackets the historical process by which this oral art was transcribed into writing. For an incisive discussion of the initial transcription of spirituals and the racialisms that defined that enterprise, see Ronald Radano, "Denoting Difference: The Writing of the Slave Spirituals," *Critical Inquiry* 22.3 (Spring 1996): 506–544.

12. Indeed, as he underlines in his classic essay, Du Bois calls the spirituals *sorrow* songs, but also identifies "hope" and "faith" as common denominators of the genre: "Through all the sorrow of the Sorrow Songs there breathes a hope—a faith in the ultimate justice of things." W. E. B. Du Bois, *The Souls of Black Folk* (New York: Vintage/Library of America, 1990), 188.

13. Lawrence Levine, *Black Culture and Black Consciousness: Afro-American Folk Thought from Slavery to Freedom* (New York: Oxford University Press, 1977), 54.

14. Ibid., 32–33. Again, Levine characterizes the sacred temporality of death: "Continually, the slaves sang of reaching out beyond the world that confined them. . . . Continually, they held out the possibility of imminent rebirth" (38–39).

15. In focusing primarily on the form of the spirituals, and deriving from that a conceptual perspective, I am heeding Saidiya Hartman's caution not to use the spirituals simply as a synecdoche for *the* slave character or condition. As she puts it, "My task is neither to unearth the definitive meaning of song or dance nor to read song as an expression of black character as was common among nineteenth-century ethnographers but to give full weight to the opacity of these texts wrought by toil, terror, and sorrow and composed under the whip and in fleeting moments of reprieve. Rather than consider black song as an index or mirror of the slave condition, this examination emphasizes the significance of opacity as precisely that which enables something in excess of the orchestrated amusements of the enslaved and which similarly troubles distinctions between joy and sorrow and toil and leisure." Hartman, *Scenes of Subjection: Terror, Slavery, and Self-Making in Nineteenth-Century America* (New York: Oxford University Press, 1997), 35–36.

16. Howard Thurman, *The Negro Spiritual Speaks of Life and Death* (Richmond, IN: Friends United Press, 1975), 61.

17. Ibid., 62.

18. Abdul R. JanMohamed, *Death-Bound Subject: Richard Wright's Archaeology of Death* (Durham, NC: Duke University Press, 2005), 2.

19. Paying formal attention to how spirituals enact death might help us temper studies of the spirituals that read loss mainly in religious terms. Ramazani, for instance, concludes that the spirituals "subdue loss with heaven's consolatory promise"; strictly following Hughes's binary division of the spirituals and the blues, Ramazani writes that the spirituals "tend to be poems of normative mourning, whereas the blues are typically melancholic, unredemptive and anti-consolatory like many modern elegies. Admittedly there are nonconsolatory spiri-

tuals and consolatory blues that would complicate this partitioning of genres, but Hughes is emphatic about the general difference" (Ramazani, *Poetry of Mourning*, 142–143). Cornel West makes a similar conclusion: "The spirituals not only reveal the underside of America—in all of its stark nakedness; they also disclose the night side of the human condition—in all of its terror and horror. But they do so through an unequivocal Christian lens. So we often leap to the religious consolation of the spirituals without lingering for long on sadness and melancholia" (West, "The Spirituals as Lyric Poetry," 464). My readings of the spirituals jar against these claims, and not simply because I am focusing on a set of spirituals decidedly about death. When I examine the formal properties of these lyrics, I see that they enact loss in ways that do not conform to these overarching claims.

20. Frederick Douglass, *My Bondage and My Freedom* (Mineola, NY: Dover, 1969), 98. This is a point that Douglass also reiterates in his first narrative, stressing in a single page that hearing the spirituals could impress on the listener "the horrible character of slavery," "the dehumanizing character of slavery," and "the soul-killing effects of slavery." Douglass, *Narrative of the Life of Frederick Douglass, an American Slave* (New York: Barnes and Noble Classics, 2003), 26. See also Paul Gilroy, *The Black Atlantic: Modernity and Double Consciousness* (Cambridge, MA: Harvard University Press, 1993), 63.

21. Richard Newman, *Go Down Moses: A Celebration of the African-American Spiritual* (New York: Clarkson Potter, 1998), 101.

22. Orlando Patterson, *Slavery and Social Death* (Cambridge, MA: Harvard University Press, 1985). Characterizing this particular song, Newman writes: "This spiritual speaks directly to the separation by sale of a mother and child in a slave family. The reference to Georgia conjures up the dreaded large plantations of the Deep South, where men, women, and children were literally worked to death. Indeed, as the soil gave out in Virginia, some owners bred slave children for the market just as they did animals. When emancipation came with the Civil War, the roads were crowded with thousands of people seeking separated husbands, wives, children, brothers, sisters, and parents" (Newman, *Go Down Moses*, 101). Recalling songs like this one, Levine also notes that slaves "sang especially of the enforced separations that continually threatened them and haunted their songs" (Levine, *Black Culture and Black Consciousness*, 14).

23. Cavitch, *The American Elegy*, 207.

24. Jonathan Culler, "Apostrophe," in his *The Pursuit of Signs* (Ithaca, NY: Cornell University Press, 1981), 141.

25. This apostrophe recalls another one cited by James Baldwin in his seldom read but extraordinary essay "Of the Sorrow Songs: The Cross of Redemption": "It is hard to be black, and therefore officially, and lethally, despised. It is harder than that to despise so many of the people who think of themselves as white, before whose blindness you present the obligatory historical grin. And it is harder than that, out of this devastation—Ezekiel's valley: 'Oh, Lord, can these bones live?'—to trust life, and to live a life, to love, and be loved. It is out of this, and much more than this, that black American music springs. This music begins on the auction block." Baldwin, *The Cross of Redemption: Uncollected Writings*, edited by Randall Kennan (New York: Pantheon, 2010), 124.

26. For insightful discussions on the politics of death more broadly in slavery, particularly the politics of suicide, see Achille Mbembe, "Necropolitics," *Public Culture* 15.1 (2003): 11–40; Cavitch, *The American Elegy*, 209–225; Gilroy, *The Black Atlantic*, 58–71; Marcus Rediker, *The Slave Ship: A Human History* (New York: Penguin, 2007), 14–40.

27. For a comparative reading of Monette's poems alongside the works of three other

poets (Timothy Liu, Thom Gunn, and Mark Doty), see Deborah Landau, "'How to Love. What to Do.': The Poetics and Politics of AIDS," *American Literature* 68.1 (March 1996): 193–225. On Monette's poetry alone, see Joseph Cady, "Immersive and Counterimmersive Writing About Aids: The Achievement of Paul Monette's *Love Alone*," in *Writing AIDS: Gay Literature, Language, and Analysis*, edited by Timothy F. Murphy and Suzanne Poirier (New York: Columbia University Press, 1993), 244–264.

28. Monette, *Love Alone*, xii.

29. Ibid.

30. Philip Gambone, *Something Inside: Conversations with Gay Fiction Writers* (Madison: University of Wisconsin Press, 1999), 63.

31. Monette, *Love Alone*, 3. With only thirty lines, "Here" is the shortest poem in the collection; most of the others are double this length.

32. Paul Monette, *Borrowed Time: An AIDS Memoir* (New York: Avon, 1988), 37.

33. Monette, *Love Alone*, xii–xiii.

34. Ibid., 34.

35. Ibid., 36.

36. We may think of apostrophe here as an instrument of "worrying the line," to borrow from another form of lyric mourning, the blues. As Cheryl Wall explains, "For blues musicians, 'worrying the line' is the technique of breaking up a phrase by changing pitch, adding a shout, or repeating words in order to emphasize, clarify, or subvert a moment in a song." Wall, *Worrying the Line: Black Women Writers, Lineage, and Literary Tradition* (Chapel Hill: University of North Carolina Press, 2005), back cover. The "oh" in the last line of Monette's poem is precisely the sound of sorrow that breaks down the barrier between here (the space of the living) and there (the space of the dead). For an insightful discussion of worrying the line in blues poetry, see Theodore R. Hudson, "Technical Aspects of the Poetry of Langston Hughes," *Black World* 22.11 (1973): 24–45.

37. Monette, *Love Alone*, xi.

38. Ibid., xii–xiii.

39. Ibid., xi.

40. It's worth noting Monette's choice of Owen as a forebear. As a gay poet, Owen's poems for the World War I dead resonate with a mournful eroticism because he views the dead, in a sense, as lovers or potential lovers. I thank Jeremy Braddock for this insight.

41. Wilfred Owen, C. Day Lewis, and Edmund Blunden, *The Collected Poems of Wilfred Owen* (London: Chatto and Windus, 1963), 12.

42. John M. Clum, "'And Once I Had It All': AIDS Narratives and Memories of an American Dream," in *Writing AIDS: Gay Literature, Language, and Analysis*, edited by Timothy Murphy and Suzanne Poirier (New York: Columbia University Press, 1993), 207.

43. Ibid., 201.

44. Ibid., 210.

45. Dixon, *Love's Instruments*, 73.

46. Ibid.

47. Karla Holloway, *Passed On: African-American Mourning Stories: A Memorial Collection* (Durham, NC: Duke University Press, 2002), 55.

48. Quoted from Horace Ové's 1969 film, *Baldwin's Nigger* (London: British Film Institute, 2004).

49. Dixon, *Love's Instruments*, 62, 53, 68.

50. Newman, *Go Down Moses*, 115.

51. Ibid.

52. The epigraph to Toni Morrison, *Beloved* (New York: Knopf, 1987) (emphasis added).

53. Ibid., 59–60.

54. This is a point that Dixon reiterates in another poem, "Blood Positive": "We did nothing but worship our kind. / When you love as we did you will know / there is no life but this / and history will not be kind" (*Love's Instruments*, 58).

55. Melvin Dixon and Jerome de Romanet, "A Conversation with Melvin Dixon," *Callaloo* 23.1 (Winter 2000): 95. Dixon adds, "[Translation] is not only a re-creation; you are making an intellectual. . . . you are interpreting this work, trying to extrapolate its meaning; then you recast it. So the more I worked, the more I realized what a task of critical interpretation translation can be: you are investing a lot, not so much in your ability to render the work, but in your ability to understand what the work is about, and to imagine another life for that work, that will communicate to people who do not speak that work's original language" (ibid.).

56. "Translation," *New Oxford American Dictionary* (2011).

57. Dixon, *Love's Instruments*, 74 (emphasis added).

58. Ibid., 78–79.

59. Ibid., 72.

60. Jamaica Kincaid, *My Brother* (New York: Farrar, Straus and Giroux, 1997), 90, 107–108.

61. Ibid., 92.

62. Marie Howe, "What the Living Do," in her *What the Living Do* (New York: Norton, 1998), 89–90.

63. Sacks, *The English Elegy*, 23.

64. I am borrowing the phrase "middle passage epistemology" from Michelle Wright who, in an important work in progress, offers a critique of studies in contemporary American academic discourse that "interpellate any and all forms of black identities across a vast and diverse diaspora." Her critique is important in that it forces us to think through the workings of race and/or blackness in ways that aren't immediately freighted. So, here, I think about how a particular poetics of loss, like the spirituals, can be deployed as a critical heuristic in contexts that are not exclusively black. This should not be read as an easy conflation of contexts or collapsing of racial difference, but rather as a way of underscoring how other experiences besides race, especially something as grave as pending death, bear on a particular work, and how that experience can become the basis of one's identity.

65. Carl Phillips, *Coin of the Realm: Essays on the Life and Art of Poetry* (Saint Paul, MN: Graywolf, 2004), 165.

66. Ibid.

67. Cavitch, *The American Elegy*, 32.

68. Zeiger, *Beyond Consolation*, 20.

69. Monette, *Love's Instruments*, xii.

70. Ibid., xi.

71. Douglas Crimp, "Mourning and Militancy," *October* 51 (Winter 1989): 9 (emphasis in original).

72. Zeiger, *Beyond Consolation*, 107.

CHAPTER 2. Archiving the Dead

1. Dick Williams, "PBS Fare Tonight Shatters Bounds of Taste, Morality," *Atlanta Constitution*, July 16, 1991, 17.

2. Don Kowet, "'Tongues': Documentary for All Reasons," *Washington Times*, July 16, 1991, E4.

3. Riggs adds: "*Tongues Untied* was motivated by a singular imperative: to shatter America's brutalizing silence around matters of sexual and racial difference. Yet despite a concerted smear and censorship campaign, perhaps even because of it, this work achieved its aim. The 55-minute video documents a nationwide community of voices—some quietly poetic, some undeniably raw and angry—which together challenge society's most deeply entrenched myths about what it means to be black, gay, a man, and above all, human." Marlon Riggs, "Tongues Re-tied?" in *Resolutions: Contemporary Video Practices*, edited by Michael Renov and Erika Suderburg (Minneapolis: University of Minnesota Press, 1996), 188.

4. Robert Reid-Pharr, "In Memoriam," *Callaloo* 17.2 (1994): n.p.

5. Marlon Riggs, *Tongues Untied* (Santa Monica, CA: Strand Releasing, 1996).

6. Janice Hume, *Obituaries in American Culture* (Jackson: University Press of Mississippi, 2000); Bridget Fowler, *The Obituary as Collective Memory* (New York: Routledge, 2007); Judith Butler, "Violence, Mourning, and Politics," in her *Precarious Life: The Powers of Mourning and Violence* (New York: Verso, 2004), 19–49.

7. "Alvin Ailey, a Leading Figure in Modern Dance, Dies at 58," *New York Times*, December 2, 1989, 1.

8. Ibid., 14.

9. Butler, *Precarious Life*, 34.

10. "Paul Jacobs, Harpsichordist and Pianist of Philharmonic," *New York Times*, September 26, 1983, B14.

11. "Paul Jacobs Dies," *New York Native*, October 24–November 6, 1983, 7.

12. ACT UP New York Records, Manuscripts and Archives Division, New York Public Library, folders labeled "Actions, Demonstrations, and Zaps" and "Target Bush: 30 Days of Action, Kennebunkport, Maine, to the White House."

13. Ibid.

14. In Marlon Riggs, *Non, Je Ne Regrette Rien (No Regret)* (Frameline, 2009).

15. Assotto Saint, *Spells of a Voodoo Doll* (New York : Masquerade, 1996), 277, 323.

16. Riggs, "Tongues Re-tied?" 188.

17. Saint, *Spells of a Voodoo Doll*, 252.

18. Ibid., 128.

19. Quoted from the summary description of the Assotto Saint Papers archived at the Schomburg Center for Research in Black Culture, New York Public Library.

20. Assotto Saint Papers, box 3, folder 3. Notice published in *New York Times*, December 23, 1990.

21. Assotto Saint Papers, box 3, folder 3. Notice published in *New York Times*, May 13, 1991.

22. Assotto Saint, "David Warren Frechette," *PWA Coalition Newsline* 68 (August 1991): 55.

23. Ibid. (emphasis added).

24. Ibid.

25. Ibid.

26. Assotto Saint Papers, box 4, folder 3.

27. Ibid.

28. Ibid.

29. Saint, *Spells of a Voodoo Doll* (which includes *Wishing for Wings*), 119, 123, 127.

30. Ibid., 123

31. Ibid., 123–124.

32. Ibid., 123.

33. Marlon Ross pointed this out while reading a draft of the manuscript. His comment was so right and rightly put that I quote it here at length rather than paraphrasing it.

34. Although Saint and Holmgren are engaged in an embrace and not a kiss, one could certainly use Phillip Brian Harper's insights on the same-sex kiss to read the same-sex bodily intimacy that Saint illustrates in the embrace between him and his lover. Harper delineates the political character of the same-sex kiss: "What *is* different, though, about the same-sex kiss versus its counterpart in the heterosexual narrative is that the former potentially functions to reveal a secret not only about the character of the *relationship* between the persons who kiss but also about those persons themselves. In other words, owing precisely to the culturally predominant presumption that everyone is heterosexual unless proven otherwise, the same-sex kiss speaks to *identify* in a much more highly charged way than does a kiss between a woman and a man. . . . Given this potential of the same-sex kiss to bespeak a homosexual identity for the persons who engage in it—and the threat to social status that such an identity generally constitutes—it is not surprising that extensive cultural safeguards have been constructed to short-circuit that potential in the contexts where such a kiss is likely to occur. The extreme scarcity of such contexts itself attests to the degree of social danger that is generally identified in the same-sex kiss." Harper, *Private Affairs: Critical Ventures in the Culture of Social Relations* (New York: New York University Press, 1999), 22.

35. Thomas Glave, "The Final Inning," in his *Whose Song? and Other Stories* (San Francisco, CA: City Lights, 2000), 151–182. Glave received the O. Henry Prize in 1997 for "The Final Inning." I consider Glave's "The Final Inning" and Susan Sontag's "The Way We Live Now" (1986) to be the two most remarkable works of fiction on AIDS.

36. Ibid., 151.

37. Gene Jarrett, "A Song to Pass On: An Interview with Thomas Glave," *Callaloo* 23.4 (2000): 1237.

38. Glave, "The Final Inning," 166.

39. Ibid., 159, 163.

40. Ibid., 161.

41. Ibid., 178.

42. Ibid., 167.

43. Ibid., 160, 156, 157, 156.

44. Ibid., 168.

45. Robert O'Meally et al., *Seeing Jazz: Artists and Writers on Jazz* (San Francisco, CA: Chronicle Books in association with Smithsonian Institution Traveling Exhibition Service, 1997), 43.

46. Jarrett, *A Song to Pass On*, 1235.

47. "Donald Woods, 34, AIDS Film Executive," *New York Times*, June 29, 1992, http://www.nytimes.com/1992/06/29/obituaries/donald-w-woods-34-aids-film-executive.html.

48. Jarrett, *A Song to Pass On*, 1235.

49. Assotto Saint Papers, box 5, folder 8.

50. Robert Pogue Harrison, *The Dominion of the Dead* (Chicago: University of Chicago Press, 2003), xi.

51. Ibid., x–xi.

CHAPTER 3. Visions of Loss

1. Walter Benjamin, "Theses on the Philosophy of History," in his *Illuminations: Essays and Reflections* (New York: Schocken, 1969), 253–264.

2. Toni Morrison, *Playing in the Dark: Whiteness and the Literary Imagination* (New York: Vintage, 1992), 8.

3. David Sheff, "Keith Haring: An Intimate Conversation," *Rolling Stone*, August 10, 1989, 64.

4. Robert Farris Thompson, "Requiem for the Degas of the B-Boys," *Artforum*, May 1990, 135. The curator and art historian Bruce Kurtz also underlines this point: Haring and his work "embodied the possibility that the social class distinctions between fine art (upper class), popular art (middle class) and folk art (lower class) could be broken down; that the inequities of the races inherent in the class structure of visual imagery could be overturned; and that a young person making images in the visual language of youth could make art of consequence. This democratic equalization seemed to be [the] preposterously fresh possibility of a naïve art world outsider." Kurtz, "The Radiant Child (Keith Haring)," in *Keith Haring, Andy Warhol, and Walt Disney*, edited by Bruce D. Kurtz (Munich: Prestel, 1992), 150.

5. On the reception and politics of graffiti, see Joe Austin, *Taking the Train: How Graffiti Art Became an Urban Crisis in New York City* (New York: Columbia University Press, 2001).

6. Edward Ranzal, "Ronan Backs Lindsay Anti-Graffiti Plan, Including Cleanup Duty," *New York Times*, August 29, 1972, 66.

7. Morrison, *Playing in the Dark*, 8.

8. Nathan Glaser, "On Subway Graffiti in New York," *Public Interest* 54 (Winter 1979): 4.

9. Suzi Gablik, "Reports from New York: The Graffiti Question," *Art in America*, October 1982, 33.

10. Ibid. Another artist, Michael Craig-Martin, is quoted as saying: "Painting in the subways is a way of intimidating people. It's a part of a general sense of being intimidated in New York" (ibid.).

11. Ibid., 35.

12. Ibid.

13. Barry Blinderman, "Close Encounters with the Third Mind," in *Keith Haring: Future Primeval*, edited by Barry Blinderman (Normal: University Galleries, Illinois State University, 1990), 18. For books that pay particular attention to Haring's subway work, see Emma Politi, ed., *Keith Haring: Subway Drawings and New York Street Art* (Rome: Galleria Giulia, 1997); Keith Haring, *Keith Haring, 1988: A One-Man Exhibition in Los Angeles of Paintings, Drawings and Prints* (Los Angeles: M. Lawrence Limited Editions in association with M. Kohn Gallery, 1988); and Klaus Littmann, ed., *Keith Haring, Editions on Paper 1982–1990: The Complete Printed Works* (Stuttgart, Germany: Cantz, 1993).

14. For books on graffiti, see Henry Chalfant and Martha Cooper, *Subway Art* (New York: Holt, Rinehart and Winston, 1984); Ivor Miller, *Aerosol Kingdom: Subway Painters of New York City* (Jackson.: University of Mississippi Press, 2002); James Murray and Karla Murray, *Broken Windows* (Corte Madera, CA: Gingko, 2002). Also see the feature film

Wild Style (Charlie Ahearn, dir., 1983) and the documentary *Style Wars* (Tony Silver, dir., 1983).

15. Blinderman, "Close Encounters with the Third Mind," 19.

16. Gablik writes: "more than once [Haring] has been arrested for defacing property, although most of the police have by now come to recognize his special talent, and are aware of his reputation in the art world" ("Reports from New York," 35). To argue that the police left Haring alone simply because they recognized his "special talent" is to be blind to the machinations of race. Haring is seen as an exception precisely because the logic of graffiti as personified menace falters when the artist is white.

17. Robert Pincus-Witten, "Keith 'R' Us," in *Keith Haring*, edited by Elizabeth Sussman (New York: Whitney Museum of American Art, 1997), 257.

18. John Gruen, *Keith Haring: The Authorized Biography* (New York: Fireside, 1991), 44 (emphasis in original).

19. Ibid., 65.

20. Haring's identification with urban black life and graffiti should not be conflated with other white hipsters who embraced graffiti early on—like Norman Mailer, whose 1974 book, *The Faith of Graffiti*, champions graffiti but does so using the same essentializing, objectifying, and exoticizing language of blackness that informed his essay "The White Negro," in his *The White Negro* (San Francisco, CA: City Lights, 1957).

21. Gruen, *Keith Haring*, 74.

22. Thompson, "Requiem for the Degas of the B-Boys," 136.

23. Lawrence Alloway, "The Long Front of Culture," in *Modern Dreams: The Rise and Fall and Rise of Pop*, edited by Brian Wallis et al. (Cambridge, MA: MIT Press, 1988), 31.

24. Dick Hebdige, "In Poor Taste: Notes on Pop," in Wallis et al., *Modern Dreams*, 79–80.

25. Ibid., 81.

26. Thompson, in his introduction to Haring's posthumously published journals, uses the term in passing to refer to Haring's work: "Haring ensconced his visual thinking in a tough-minded vernacular, so that all could share and understand, and see their minds reflected, in the ideal Keatsian sense"; and "The text [the journal], in short, is a mirror of an extraordinary life: creativity, thought, and the vernacular, jousting in the crucible of contemporary time." Robert Farris Thompson, "Introduction," in Haring, *Keith Haring Journals* (New York: Viking, 1996), xiv, xii. Elizabeth Sussman writes: "Ultimately, Keith Haring's achievement was to have plumbed our American vernacular to its farthest limits." Sussman, "Songs of Innocence at the Nuclear Pyre," in her *Keith Haring*, 24.

27. Gruen, *Keith Haring*, 90.

28. See Tricia Rose, *Black Noise: Rap Music and Black Culture in Contemporary America* (Hanover, NH: University Press of New England, 1994); Nelson George, *Hip Hop America* (New York: Viking, 1999); Imani Perry, *Prophets of the Hood: Politics and Poetics in Hip Hop* (Durham, NC: Duke University Press, 2004); Mark Anthony Neal and Murray Forman, eds., *That's the Joint!: The Hip Hop Studies Reader* (New York: Routledge, 2004).

29. Grandmaster Caz, "South Bronx Subway Rap," *Wild Style (Original Soundtrack)* (recorded 1982, released 1994, Rhino Records).

30. Grandmaster Flash and the Furious Five, "The Message," *The Message* (Sugar Hill Records, 1982).

31. Michael Ralph, "'Flirt[ing] with Death' but 'Still Alive,'" *Cultural Dynamics* 18.1

(2006): 62. Ralph adds: "The idea, then, that rappers' preoccupations with death spring from the scarce possibilities present in their communities is confirmed by available sociological evidence. Whether their obsessions with fatality are fully justifiable requires further investigation. That they are engaged in a war of survival nevertheless seems to be a belief that persists among inhabitants of these communities and social scientists who study them. For many rappers, the perceived outcome is so bleak, they start to believe they face an inescapable existential predicament—a crisis they were born into and one in which they will die" (68).

32. Haring, *Keith Haring Journals*, 122 (emphasis in original).

33. Sheff, "Keith Haring: An Intimate Conversation," 102.

34. Haring, *Keith Haring Journals*, 124–125.

35. For a critical look at Haring's whiteness, see Arnaldo Cruz-Malavé, *Queer Latino Testimonio, Keith Haring, and Juanito Xtravaganza: Hard Tails* (New York: Palgrave, 2007). This book also includes a remarkable ethnography of Haring's lover, Juan Rivera.

36. Philip Shenon, "Family of Victim Levels Charges of Deceit in Autopsy Conclusion," *New York Times*, January 28, 1985, http://www.nytimes.com/1985/01/28/nyregion/family-of -victim-levels-charges-of-deceit-in-autopsy-conclusion.html.

37. Haring was an artist who experienced, firsthand, the art boom of Lower Manhattan—a boom that ended up introducing what some would see as an intrusive commercial dimension to the art world. The dollar signs in many of Haring's drawings certainly speak to this surge in the American capitalistic impulse in general during this era. Haring would end up making a powerful statement on the capitalist resurgence and enterprise by turning this commercialism upside down. When Haring in 1986 opened his Pop Shop—which sold Haringesque T-shirts, Swatch watches, buttons with his signature crawling baby, and so on—many critics decried that the artist had "sold out" to the world of money making. But what these critics seemed to overlook was the irony of the Pop Shop—the extent to which the store itself functioned as an interactive work of art that not only *parodied* American mass consumption, but also actively *took part* in it.

38. Gruen, *Keith Haring*, 15 (emphasis in original).

39. Ibid., 16.

40. Frank Kermode, *The Sense of an Ending: Studies in the Theory of Fiction* (New York: Oxford University Press, 2000), 8. See particularly the first chapter, "The End," 3–31.

41. Frank Kermode, "Millennium and Apocalypse," in *The Apocalypse and the Shape of Things to Come*, edited by Frances Carey (Toronto: University of Toronto Press, 1999), 20.

42. Benjamin, *Illuminations*, 257–258.

43. Quoted in David Galloway, "The Marriage of Heaven and Hell," in *Keith Haring: Heaven and Hell*, edited by Gotz Adriani (Karlsruhe, Germany: Hatje Cantz in association with Museum for Neue Kunst, 2001), 53.

44. Sedat Pakay, dir., *James Baldwin: From Another Place* (Hudson Film Works, 2007).

45. I am borrowing here Paul de Man's definition of rhetoric in his "Semiology and Rhetoric," in *The Norton Anthology of Theory and Criticism*, edited by Vincent Leitch (New York: Norton, 2001), 1520.

46. Keith Haring, *Eight Ball* (Kyoto: Kyoto Shoin, 1989), preface, n.p.

47. Gruen, *Keith Haring*, 44. Perhaps the essential use of the line in Haring's work echoes the "tick-tock" of the clock that Kermode identifies as an elemental form of a plot: "The clock's *tick-tock* I take to be a model of what we call a plot, an organization that humanizes time by giving it form; and the interval between *tock* and *tick* represent[s] purely successive,

disorganized time of the sort that we need to humanize.... *Tick* is a humble genesis, *tock* a feeble apocalypse." Kermode, *The Sense of an Ending*, 45 (emphasis in original).

48. Douglas Crimp and Adam Rolston, *AIDS Demo Graphics* (Seattle: Bay Press, 1990), 30–31.

CHAPTER 4. Epistles to the Dead

1. See *Policy on HIV/AIDS of the Federal Democratic Republic of Ethiopia* (1998) published by the Ethiopian Ministry of Health (available at Institute of Ethiopian Studies Archives). The first conference on AIDS in Ethiopia took place in November 1999 and was organized by Eleni Gebre Amlak of African AIDS Initiative International, who was instrumental in bringing together a cross section of people—from governmental, nongovernmental, academic, health, civic, religious, and social service organizations—and launching a public discussion of HIV/AIDS in Ethiopia. African AIDS Initiative International was also one of the first NGOs to provide HIV testing and counseling services in the country, and the first to build a center at Addis Ababa University's Sidist Kilo campus, where university students could receive testing and counseling.

2. On the stigma surrounding AIDS in Ethiopia, see Zena Berhanu, "Care and Support and People Living with HIV and AIDS: An Assessment at Four Selected Sites in Addis Ababa," master's thesis, Graduate School of Social Work, Addis Ababa University, 2005 (available at Institute of Ethiopian Studies Archives).

3. For more information on Mekdim Ethiopia, Dawn of Hope, and other organizations that provide care and empowerment for people living with HIV/AIDS, see http://plwha.etharc org/home and http://www.fhi360.org/countries/ethiopia. The second website includes a 2002 report by Family Health International entitled *Addis Ababa HIV Care and Support Service Assessment*, which provides information on the early HIV/AIDS support services in Addis Ababa.

4. Sudden Flowers is in the process of publishing a catalog of the collective's work entitled *May the Finest in the World Always Accompany You!* (London: Fishbar, forthcoming). To narrate the formation of the collective and to reference their works, I draw heavily from this manuscript. Eric Gottesman's website also provides choice examples of the collaborative work of the collective: http://www.ericgottesman.net.

5. The Hart Fellowship that Gottesman received was a joint grant from Duke's Center for Documentary Studies and the Terry Sanford Public Policy Institute, which also partnered him with a nongovernmental organization, Save the Children Ethiopia.

6. Since 1999 Gottesman has been an active member of the arts community in Addis Ababa and has produced a significant body of work on Ethiopia, both in collaboration with Sudden Flowers and in individual works that focus particularly on Ethiopia's Derg communist regime. For instance, his incisive visual essay "The Preservation of Terror" focuses on studio portraits made during the early days of the Derg, when the photo studio was the only site where photography was not officially prohibited. Gottesman, "The Preservation of Terror," *Callaloo* 33.1 (2010): 155–164. Currently, Gottesman is in the process of translating Baalu Girma's novel *Oromaye* from Amharic into English and adapting it for the screen. Many critics consider *Oromaye* to be one of the most important novels written during the Derg, a work for which Girma was assassinated (or, in Derg parlance, "disappeared"). Yawoinshet Masresha and Gottesman have already translated into English and published a portion of the novel: "An Excerpt of *Oromaye*: Prologue," *Hayden's Ferry Review* 50 (Spring–Summer 2012): 270–281.

7. Eric Gottesman, *If I Could See Your Face, I Would Not Need Food (Ka Fitfitu Feetu)* (project statement), http://www.ericgottesman.net/newsite/ificouldseeyourface.html.

8. Sudden Flowers, *May the Finest in the World Always Accompany You!* (manuscript draft).

9. Ibid.

10. I asked Gottesman a set of questions via email, including one about his age when he arrived in Ethiopia and if his relative youth helped him to identify with the plight of other young people. This quote is an excerpt from his answer dated June 7, 2013.

11. Toni Morrison, *The Nobel Lecture in Literature* (New York: Knopf, 1993), 23.

12. Eric Gottesman, "We Cheat Each Other: *The Nobel Lecture in Literature*, a Portrait of Salam (project statement)," http://www.ericgottesman.net/newsite/wecheateachother.html.

13. Salamawit Alemu, in Sudden Flowers, *May the Finest in the World Always Accompany You!* (manuscript draft).

14. Rut Alemu, ibid.

15. Amsale Shiferaw, ibid.

16. Bereket Muluneh, ibid.

17. Heywot Umer, ibid.

18. Salamawit Alemu, ibid.

19. Rut Alemu, ibid.

20. Amsale Shiferaw, ibid.

21. Rut Alemu, ibid.

22. Hana Muluneh, ibid.

23. Asrat Tessema, ibid.

24. Bereket Muluneh, ibid.

25. Asrat Tessema, ibid.

26. Heywot Umer, ibid.

27. Amsale Shiferaw, ibid.

28. Gottesman, email, June 7, 2013.

29. Robert Pogue Harrison, *The Dominion of the Dead* (Chicago: University of Chicago Press, 2003), xi.

30. Gottesman, *If I Could See Your Face.*

31. Ibid.

32. Ibid.

33. Ibid.

34. Berhanu, "Care and Support and People Living with HIV and AIDS," 53.

35. Gottesman, *If I Could See Your Face.*

36. Eric Gottesman, "I Am a Medium," in Sudden Flowers, *May the Finest in the World Always Accompany You!* (manuscript draft).

37. Eric Gottesman, "*Abul Thona Baraka*: A Traveling Coffee Ceremony (project statement)," http://www.ericgottesman.net/newsite/abulthonabaraka.html.

38. Eric Gottesman, "Yabat Ida Le Lij (project statement)," http://www.ericgottesman.net/newsite/yabatidalelij.html.

39. "Ethiopia: 'Edirs' for the Living as Well as the Dead," *Nazret*, http://nazret.com/blog/index.php/2006/11/22/ethiopia_edirs_for_the_living_as_well_as.

40. On the political uses of suicide, see Achille Mbembe, "Necropolitics," *Public Culture* 15.1 (2003): 11–40. Mbembe writes: "I have put forward the notion of necropolitics and necropower to account for the various ways in which, in our contemporary world, weapons are deployed in the interest of maximum destruction of persons and the creation of *death-worlds*, new and unique forms of social existence in which vast populations are subjected to condi-

tions of life conferring upon them the status of the *living dead*. The essay has also outlined some of the repressed topographies of cruelty (the plantation and the colony in particular) and has suggested that under conditions of necropower, the lines between resistance and suicide, sacrifice and redemption, martyrdom and freedom are blurred" (40, emphases in original).

41. *Yabat Ida Le Lij* explores the stories and pathos of these children with the same intensity as their epistles, although the film and the letters do differ in style and substance. However much drawn from the children's real experiences, the film is a fictional story, whereas the epistles are autobiographical. The film is a collaborative enterprise and amplifies the children's collective grief, while the epistles are individual meditations, intimate missives to the dead. Each form has its own defining ability to portray these children's experiences of loss. The film is able to evoke the physical and performative characteristics of mourning, and the letters show grief's inward and intimate workings. Also, each genre figures the dead differently—the film represents Alemu's death definitively with his corpse, while the letters embody the dead parents tentatively as "separated" addressees. Nevertheless, in both forms, the children insist on materializing their parents and reestablishing the familial attachments that have been severed in real life.

42. Gottesman, *If I Could See Your Face*.

43. Uzodinma Iweala, *Our Kind of People: A Continent's Challenge, a Country's Hope* (New York: HarperCollins, 2012), 143.

44. Morrison, *The Nobel Lecture in Literature*, 27.

45. "Put outdoors," a key phrase from Toni Morrison's *The Bluest Eye*, seems apt here: "There is a difference between being put *out* and being put out*doors*. If you are put out, you go somewhere else; if you are outdoors, there is no place to go. The distinction was subtle but final. Outdoors was the end of something, an irrevocable, physical fact, defining and complementing our metaphysical condition. Being a minority in both caste and class, we moved about anyway on the hem of life, struggling to consolidate our weakness and hang on, or to creep singly up into the major folds of the garment. Our peripheral existence, however, was something we had learned to deal with—probably because it was abstract. But the concreteness of being outdoors was another matter—like the difference between the concept of death and being, in fact, dead. Dead doesn't change, and outdoors is here to stay." Morrison, *The Bluest Eye* (New York: Plume, 1994), 17–18.

46. Philippe Ariès, *Centuries of Childhood: A Social History of Family Life* (New York: Knopf, 1963); Anne Higonnet, *Pictures of Innocence: The History and Crisis of Ideal Childhood* (New York: Thames and Hudson, 1998); James Kincaid, *Child-Loving: The Erotic Child and Victorian Culture* (New York: Routledge, 1992); James Kincaid, *Erotic Innocence: The Culture of Child Molesting* (Durham, NC: Duke University Press, 1998); Kathryn Bond Stockton, *The Queer Child; or, Growing Sideways in the Twentieth Century* (Durham, NC: Duke University Press, 2009).

47. This idea of children as a tabula rasa is from John Locke's oft-quoted formulation in *An Essay Concerning Human Understanding* (New York: Meridian, 1964).

48. Lee Edelman, *No Future: Queer Theory and the Death Drive* (Durham, NC: Duke University Press, 2004), 2.

49. Ibid., 13 (emphasis in original). Adds Edelman: "On every side, our enjoyment of liberty is eclipsed by the lengthening shadow of a Child whose freedom to develop undisturbed by encounters, or even by the threat of potential encounters, with an 'otherness' of which its parents, its church, or the state do not approve, uncompromised by any possible access to

what is painted as alien desire, terroristically holds us all in check and determines that political discourse conform to the logic of a narrative wherein history unfolds as the future envisioned for a Child who must never grow up" (21).

50. Ibid., 21.

51. Higonnet, *Pictures of Innocence*, 119.

52. Robin Bernstein, *Racial Innocence: Performing American Childhood from Slavery to Civil Rights* (New York: New York University Press, 2011).

53. Stockton, *The Queer Child*, 31.

54. José Esteban Muñoz, *Cruising Utopia* (New York: New York University Press, 2011), 95. Muñoz also says: "In the same way all queers are not the stealth-universal-white-gay-man invoked in queer antirelational formulations, all children are not the privileged white babies to whom contemporary society caters. Again, there is for me a lot to like in this critique of antireproductive futurism, but in Edelman's theory it is enacted by the active disavowal of a crisis in afrofuturism. Theories of queer temporality that fail to factor in the relational relevance of race or class merely reproduce a crypto-universal white gay subject that is weirdly atemporal —which is to say a subject whose time is a restricted and restricting hollowed-out present free of the need for the challenge of imagining a futurity that exists beyond the self or the here and now" (94).

55. Morrison, *The Bluest Eye*, 205–206.

56. James Baldwin et al., *Perspectives: Angles on African Art* (New York: Center for African Art, 1987), 127.

CONCLUSION. Tallying Loss

1. Marlon Riggs, "Letters to the Dead," in *Sojourner: Black Gay Voices in the Age of AIDS*, edited by B. Michael Hunter (New York: Other Countries Press, 1993).

2. Ibid., 20.

3. Ibid., 21.

4. Ibid., 23.

Index

Library of Congress Cataloging-in-Publication Data
Woubshet, Dagmawi, author.
The calendar of loss : race, sexuality, and mourning in the early era of AIDS
/ by Dagmawi Woubshet.
pages cm. — (The *Callaloo* African Diaspora series)
Includes bibliographical references and index.
ISBN 978-1-4214-1655-7 (hardcover : acid-free paper) — ISBN
978-1-4214-1656-4 (electronic) — ISBN 1-4214-1655-7 (hardcover :
acid-free paper) — ISBN 1-4214-1656-5 (electronic)   1. AIDS
(Disease) in mass media.   2. AIDS (Disease) in
literature.   3. Loss (Psychology)   4. Elegiac poetry—History and
criticism.   5. Bereavement—Psychological aspects—Cross-cultural
studies.   I. Title.
P96.A39W68 2015
809′.933548—dc23   2014027394